Canadian Living

THE COMPLETE
CHICKEN
COOKBOOK

BY THE CANADIAN LIVING TEST KITCHEN

JUNIPER
PUBLISHING
A Quebecor Media Corporation

FROM OUR KITCHEN

Chicken dinners are always big, big winners.

In the Canadian Living Test Kitchen, we love creating delicious recipes for chicken. You'd think we would have run out of ideas after 40 years, but chicken is such a versatile ingredient that it just never gets boring. We consider it a delightful—and tasty—challenge to keep coming up with fresh and inspiring ways to prepare it. Chicken fits seamlessly into every global cuisine and every occasion. Plus, it's well within just about everyone's "tastebud comfort zone"—the mild flavour of chicken is universally pleasing. It's a hit in households across the country, the continent and the world.

When you hear the word "chicken," any number of taste memories might jump to mind, whether it's tucking into a warm, comforting chicken pot pie at your grandparents' house, carving a classic Sunday roast served with velvety gravy, snatching up pieces of crispy-skinned fried chicken at a summer picnic or digging into a saucy stir-fry on a busy Wednesday night.

In this cookbook, we've gathered together all of those chicken classics—and then some. We don't want you to ever run out of interesting ways to cook one of your favourite ingredients, so within these pages you'll find enough recipes to introduce a different chicken dish every week for three years straight and still have plenty to spare. That's what I call a winning strategy.

Eat well!

ANNABELLE WAUGH
FOOD DIRECTOR

THE CANADIAN LIVING TEST KITCHEN
Clockwise from top left: Annabelle Waugh, Irene Fong, Amanda Barnier, Leah Kuhne, Gilean Watts and Jennifer Bartoli.

Our Tested-Till-Perfect guarantee means we've tested every recipe, using the same grocery store ingredients and household appliances as you do, until we're sure you'll get perfect results at home.

CANADIAN LIVING
TESTED TILL PERFECT
EST. 1975
TEST KITCHEN

**CHICKEN CURRY
IN A HURRY**
(PAGE 55)

**EASY CHICKEN CORDON BLEU
WITH ROASTED SWEET POTATO SALAD**
(PAGE 71)

**MIDDLE EASTERN
COUSCOUS BOWL**
(PAGE 195)

CONTENTS

CHAPTER 1

CHICKEN
HOW-TO

CHOOSING CHICKEN

Whether you're on the hunt for a whole bird or smaller cuts, such as wings, look for plump, well-shaped chicken with smooth skin, firm flesh and a fresh, neutral smell.

Types of Whole Chickens

CORNISH HEN

Very young chicken; typically weighs about 675 g. Cornish hens are usually sold frozen.

BROILER

Also known as fryer; usually weighs less than 1.8 kg and often closer to 1.35 kg. Broilers are the most popular size sold in supermarkets and restaurants. Most chicken pieces come from broilers, because they are all-purpose and suitable for roasting, braising, frying and grilling.

ROASTER

Older and more flavourful than a broiler; typically weighs more than 1.8 kg. Roasters are (obviously) ideal for roasting but can also be poached.

CAPON

Neutered rooster; usually weighs between 1.8 and 4.5 kg. Capons have a high ratio of white meat to dark and are ideal for roasting and stuffing.

GROUND CHICKEN: WATCH THE FAT

The fat content of ground chicken varies. It is often made from thigh meat, but some packages contain all-white breast meat at a premium price. Check labels and look for terms such as "lean" or "extra-lean" if you want to limit your fat intake.

CHILL OUT

Chickens are cooled two different ways during processing. There is no difference in nutritional value, cooking times or flavour between the two types; there is, however, a difference in texture.

Air-chilled: Blasts of cold air are used to chill the chicken. The flesh tends to be a creamy colour; an extra layer of skin is left on, so it appears drier and often yellowish. Less liquid is released during cooking, so air-chilled chicken browns well. It is more expensive than water-chilled chicken, but the Test Kitchen prefers it.

Water-chilled: Cold water is used to chill the chicken. The skin tends to be moist and white. The meat absorbs some of the water, making it more difficult to brown.

THE WORDS ON BIRDS

You see so many claims on product labels, and packaged chicken is no exception. So what do all those terms mean?

Free-range: Chickens are allowed access to the outside for part of the day. This is not a legally regulated term, so different farms have different standards.

Free-run: Chickens aren't raised with access to the outdoors, but their movement inside the barn is not restricted. In Canada, all chickens raised for meat are free-run.

Organic: National standards for organic chicken are under review, but each province has its own regulations around this term. In general, "organic" means chickens have been raised on certified organic feed that doesn't contain animal byproducts, and without the use of antibiotics.

Certified organic: Farmers who raise certified organic chicken must go through a strict certification process. All feed must be approved by a certification body.

Pastured: Chickens are kept outdoors in a movable enclosure with shelter from the elements and predators. Chickens may get some of their diet from the forage they find. Raising chickens outdoors is seasonal in Canada— cold winter weather is definitely not hospitable to the birds.

PARMESAN ROSEMARY CHICKEN WINGS
(page 158)

How to Thaw Frozen Chicken

Never thaw chicken at room temperature; use one of these three food-safe methods instead.
And remember: Never refreeze thawed chicken.

LOCATION	PREPARATION	TIME	WHAT NEXT?
Refrigerator	Wrapped, on rimmed baking sheet to catch drips	5 hours per every 450 g	Refrigerate and cook within 2 days
Large bowl or sinkful of cold water	In sealed package, changing water every hour	1 hour per every 450 g	Refrigerate and cook within 2 days
Microwave oven, on defrost	Loosely covered; turning, separating and rotating pieces several times	5 minutes per every 450 g	Cook immediately

HOW TO...

Cut Up a Whole Chicken

Some recipes ask you to cut up a raw whole chicken. That may make you want to just buy a box of chicken pieces, but trust us—it's easier than it sounds. Sharp kitchen shears are your best friend for this job.

1. Place chicken, breast side down, on a cutting board. Using kitchen shears, trim off and discard any visible fat around the cavity and neck.

2. Starting at body cavity, cut as closely as possible along both sides of the backbone. Cut off wing tips. Reserve backbone and wing tips to make stock.

3. Turn chicken over; open slightly. Cut in half lengthwise through the middle of the breastbone.

4. Lift one leg at a time away from body and cut along contour through skin and meat to separate leg from body.

5. Bend back thigh and drumstick until joint pops. Cut through skin and meat at joint.

6. Cut each breast in half, leaving wing attached to one half.

7. Trim off excess skin and fat from chicken pieces; remove and discard any bone shards.

 Learn how to cut up a whole chicken at canadianliving.com/chicken

Skin Chicken Pieces

To remove the skin from breasts, thighs or legs, grip skin at one end of the piece. Using a paper towel to prevent your fingers from slipping, pull firmly on the skin to remove it. For legs, you may need to cut around the end of the drumstick to complete the operation.

Bone a Chicken Breast

1. To make 450 g boneless skinless chicken breasts, start with three medium bone-in skin-on breasts.

2. If breast halves are attached, cut apart at breastbone using kitchen shears, sturdy kitchen scissors or a chef's knife.

3. Place breast, bone side down, on cutting board. Using your favourite sharp-tipped, thin-bladed sturdy knife (such as a paring, utility, chef's or boning knife), make a shallow cut along the ridge of the breastbone between the meat and the bone.

4. Holding the knife flat against the bone and using short strokes, cut between the meat and the bone to within about ¼ inch (5 mm) of other edge, lifting meat away with fingers.

5. Open breast out flat; cut meat neatly away from edge of bone. Remove any wishbone. Discard bones or save for stock.

Trim and Separate Whole Wings

Everyone loves wings, and you can make absolutely fabulous ones that are way better than pub grub. Whole wings take a bit of prep but are cheaper.

1. Start by cutting off the tip—this little bit at the end tends to dry out and burn before the rest of the wing is cooked. Lay wing flat on a cutting board; using a sharp chef's knife, cut off the tip neatly through the joint. (Save the tips for stock.)

2. Using kitchen shears or a sharp knife, trim away any visible fat and excess skin at the joint.

3. Lay the trimmed wing flat on cutting board. Using kitchen shears or a knife, cut into two sections through the centre joint.

Carve a Roast Chicken

Get everything ready before you begin: Make sure the serving platter is well warmed and the gravy or sauce that goes alongside is piping hot.

LARGE ROASTING CHICKEN

1. Place chicken, breast side up, on a cutting board. Point legs to the right if you are right-handed; to the left if you are left-handed. Remove skewers or string.

2. Gently pull one leg away from the body while cutting through the joint that holds the leg to the body. Place leg, meaty side up, on cutting board and cut through the joint to separate the drumstick from the thigh. Repeat with opposite leg. Arrange legs on heated platter and cover to keep warm.

3. Gently pull one wing away from the body while cutting through the joint that holds the wing to the body. Repeat with opposite wing and add to platter.

4. Insert a long-pronged fork into the ridge at the top of the breast to steady the bird. With a sharp carving knife, cut slices parallel to side of chicken. Start about halfway up side to divide the succulent skin equally. Overlap slices attractively on platter. Repeat on opposite side.

SMALL CHICKEN

1. Place chicken on a cutting board and steady with a long-pronged fork.

2. Using kitchen shears or sharp carving knife, cut chicken into quarters (two breast portions and two leg portions). For more than four portions, cut each leg at the joint to make drumstick and thigh pieces, and through each breast to make four portions of white meat.

Is It Done?

Watching for doneness cues or the correct internal temperature is a must when cooking chicken. This ensures harmful bacteria are eliminated all the way through.

UNSTUFFED WHOLE CHICKEN	Roast until instant-read thermometer inserted in thickest part of thigh reads 185°F (85°C). The guideline is 20 to 30 minutes per every 450 g in a 325°F (160°C) oven.*
STUFFED WHOLE CHICKEN	Roast until instant-read thermometer inserted in centre of stuffing reads 165°F (74°C). The guideline is 25 to 35 minutes per every 450 g in a 325°F (160°C) oven.*
WHOLE LEGS, THIGHS, DRUMSTICKS & WINGS	Cook until juices run clear when chicken is pierced. If the juices are cloudy or pink-tinged, the meat isn't ready.
BREASTS (WHOLE, IN PIECES OR IN KABOBS)	Cook until no longer pink inside and juices run clear when chicken is pierced.
GROUND CHICKEN (IN BURGERS, MEAT LOAVES, ETC.)	Cook until instant-read thermometer inserted in centre (or sideways for patties) reads 165°F (74°C).

* Some of the recipes in this book are cooked at a higher temperature than 325°F (160°C). See the recipe methods for timing at higher temperatures. The doneness cues will remain the same.

**LEEK-AND-CHEESE
CHICKEN BREASTS**
(PAGE 18)

CHAPTER 2

BREASTS, CUTLETS & TENDERS

SPINACH-STUFFED CHICKEN
WITH LATE-SUMMER VEGETABLES

MAKES 4 SERVINGS

Butterflying chicken breasts isn't hard (see tip, below), but it's an extra step.
If you're in a rush, ask your butcher to do it so you can get dinner on the table even faster.
Serve the finished chicken and veggies with crusty bread.

3 tbsp	olive oil
2	shallots, finely chopped
3	cloves garlic, minced
225 g	fresh spinach, trimmed
115 g	soft goat cheese
1 tbsp	grated lemon zest
1 tsp	pepper
4	boneless skinless chicken breasts (about 600 g)
¾ tsp	salt
3 tbsp	all-purpose flour
2 cups	fresh corn kernels (about 2 cobs)
1	zucchini, halved lengthwise and thickly sliced crosswise
half	red onion, coarsely chopped
2 tbsp	chopped fresh oregano

In large skillet, heat 2 tsp of the oil over medium-high heat; cook shallots until translucent, about 3 minutes. Add two-thirds of the garlic; cook for 1 minute. Add spinach and cook, tossing, until wilted, about 3 minutes.

In bowl, stir together spinach mixture, goat cheese, lemon zest and ½ tsp of the pepper.

Place one chicken breast on cutting board. Holding knife blade parallel to board and starting at thickest long side, slice horizontally almost all the way through breast; open. Repeat with remaining chicken.

Spread one-quarter of the filling evenly over half of each breast. Starting at filling side, roll up and secure tightly with toothpicks. Sprinkle with remaining pepper and half of the salt. Roll each breast in flour, shaking off excess.

In skillet, heat 2 tbsp of the remaining oil over medium-high heat. Cook chicken, turning occasionally, until golden all over, about 6 minutes. Transfer to rimmed baking sheet; bake in 400°F (200°C) oven until chicken is no longer pink inside, about 12 minutes.

Meanwhile, in skillet, heat remaining oil over high heat; cook corn, zucchini, red onion and remaining salt, stirring occasionally, until lightly browned, about 5 minutes. Add oregano and remaining garlic; cook until fragrant, about 1 minute.

Remove toothpicks from chicken; slice crosswise. Serve alongside vegetables.

PER SERVING: about 463 cal, 41 g pro, 20 g total fat (6 g sat. fat), 34 g carb, 6 g fibre, 90 mg chol, 663 mg sodium, 1,071 mg potassium. % RDI: 15% calcium, 33% iron, 73% vit A, 27% vit C, 67% folate.

TIP FROM THE TEST KITCHEN
The technique of cutting a chicken breast (or other thick piece of meat) in half horizontally almost but not all the way through and opening it up is called butterflying. Keep the knife steady as you cut, and try to make sure both halves are the same thickness.

LEEK-AND-CHEESE CHICKEN BREASTS

MAKES 2 SERVINGS

Chicken breasts stuffed with leeks, Gruyère cheese and sun-dried tomatoes are savoury with just a hint of sweetness. They're a wonderful dinner for two when served with Quick Rice Pilaf (below) and steamed green beans.

4 tsp	extra-virgin olive oil
⅔ cup	thinly sliced leeks (white and light green parts only)
½ tsp	dried thyme
¼ cup	dry white wine
⅓ cup	shredded Gruyère cheese
1 tbsp	chopped fresh parsley
1 tbsp	chopped drained oil-packed sun-dried tomatoes
2	boneless skin-on chicken breasts (about 300 g)
pinch	each salt and pepper

In large ovenproof skillet, heat half of the oil over medium heat; cook leeks and thyme, stirring occasionally, until softened, about 3 minutes. Stir in wine and bring to boil; cook, stirring, until no liquid remains, about 2 minutes. Transfer to bowl. Mix in Gruyère, parsley and sun-dried tomatoes. Set aside.

Place one chicken breast on cutting board. Holding knife blade parallel to board and starting at thickest long side, slice horizontally almost all the way through breast; open. Repeat with remaining chicken.

Spread half of the filling evenly over half of each breast. Fold over uncovered half; secure edge with toothpicks. Brush with remaining oil; sprinkle with salt and pepper. In same skillet, brown chicken over medium-high heat. Transfer to 425°F (220°C) oven; bake until chicken is no longer pink inside, about 15 minutes. Remove toothpicks before serving.

PER SERVING (WITHOUT SKIN): about 404 cal, 36 g pro, 26 g total fat (8 g sat. fat), 4 g carb, 1 g fibre, 117 mg chol, 148 mg sodium. % RDI: 20% calcium, 12% iron, 11% vit A, 12% vit C, 9% folate.

Quick Rice Pilaf

In saucepan, melt 2 tsp butter over medium heat; cook ¼ cup each diced carrot and onion until softened, about 4 minutes. Stir in ⅔ cup basmati rice, rinsed. Add ⅔ cup each chicken broth and water; bring to boil. Reduce heat, cover and simmer until rice is tender and no liquid remains, about 20 minutes.

MAKES 2 SERVINGS

SAGE BUTTER CHICKEN

MAKES 4 SERVINGS

This is a weeknight-friendly version of classic chicken kiev. Serve it with steamed potatoes or bread so you don't miss a drop of the decadent buttery filling.

Sandwich chicken between plastic wrap; using meat mallet or heavy-bottomed saucepan, pound to even thickness. Holding knife blade parallel to work surface, cut 2-inch (5 cm) wide pocket in each breast; stuff sage, butter and pepper into pockets.

Pour flour into shallow dish. In separate shallow dish, beat egg with 1 tbsp water. In third dish, spread bread crumbs. Press chicken into flour, turning to coat. Dip into egg mixture, letting excess drip back into dish. Dredge in bread crumbs, turning to coat all over.

Place in cast-iron skillet or 9-inch (2.5 L) square cake pan. Bake in 350°F (180°C) oven, turning once and basting with the melted butter that leaks out, until chicken is no longer pink inside, about 45 minutes. Transfer to plates; pour butter over top.

4	boneless skinless chicken breasts (about 600 g)
¼ cup	shredded fresh sage
¼ cup	cold butter, cut in 4 cubes
¼ tsp	pepper
¼ cup	all-purpose flour
1	egg
¼ cup	dried bread crumbs

PER SERVING: about 326 cal, 34 g pro, 15 g total fat (8 g sat. fat), 11 g carb, 1 g fibre, 155 mg chol, 218 mg sodium, 429 mg potassium. % RDI: 4% calcium, 10% iron, 13% vit A, 2% vit C, 15% folate.

CAESAR SALAD CHICKEN BREASTS

MAKES 4 SERVINGS

Garlic-kissed croutons and crispy bacon don't just make good salad toppers—they are also an awesome chicken stuffing.

STUFFED CHICKEN BREASTS: In skillet, cook bacon over medium heat, turning occasionally, until crisp, about 8 minutes. Drain and let cool on paper towel–lined plate. Crumble bacon and croutons into bowl. Stir in ¼ cup of the Parmesan, parsley, oil and garlic.

Place one chicken breast on cutting board. Holding knife blade parallel to board and starting at thickest long side, slice horizontally almost all the way through breast; open. Repeat with remaining chicken.

Leaving ½-inch (1 cm) border uncovered, spread one-quarter of the stuffing evenly over one side of each breast. Sprinkle some of the flour over each bottom border; close breast, pressing edge to seal. *(Make-ahead: Cover and refrigerate for up to 24 hours; add 5 minutes to roasting time.)* Place, skin side up, on foil-lined rimmed baking sheet.

CAESAR VINAIGRETTE: Whisk together oil, lemon juice, mustard, salt and pepper; set half aside for dressing.

ASSEMBLY: Brush remaining vinaigrette over chicken. Roast in 400°F (200°C) oven until chicken is golden and no longer pink inside, 15 to 20 minutes. Broil, watching carefully to avoid scorching, until deep golden brown, about 2 minutes.

Divide lettuce among four plates; drizzle with reserved vinaigrette. Top with chicken; sprinkle with remaining Parmesan.

PER SERVING (WITHOUT SKIN): about 476 cal, 36 g pro, 34 g total fat (8 g sat. fat), 7 g carb, 1 g fibre, 102 mg chol, 613 mg sodium. % RDI: 14% calcium, 12% iron, 19% vit A, 28% vit C, 40% folate.

STUFFED CHICKEN BREASTS:

6	strips bacon
½ cup	Caesar or garlic croutons
⅓ cup	grated Parmesan cheese
2 tbsp	chopped fresh parsley
2 tbsp	extra-virgin olive oil
2	cloves garlic, minced
4	boneless skin-on chicken breasts (about 600 g)
1 tsp	all-purpose flour

CAESAR VINAIGRETTE:

¼ cup	extra-virgin olive oil
4 tsp	lemon juice
2 tsp	Dijon mustard
¼ tsp	each salt and pepper
4 cups	torn romaine lettuce

TIP FROM THE TEST KITCHEN
Roasting chicken breasts with the skin adds flavour and keeps the meat moist and juicy during cooking. Eat the skin or not, as desired; it adds about seven grams of fat per breast.

HERBED CHEESE–STUFFED CHICKEN

MAKES 4 SERVINGS

You can stuff the breasts using a spoon, but a disposable piping bag makes prep—and cleanup—easier. For a sharper flavour, add 2 tbsp grated Parmesan cheese to the stuffing, or use black pepper cream cheese instead of the garlic-and-fine-herb.

75 g	garlic-and-fine-herb fresh soft cheese (such as Boursin)
¼ cup	fresh bread crumbs or panko bread crumbs
2 tbsp	drained oil-packed sun-dried tomatoes, thinly sliced
5	fresh basil leaves, chopped
4	boneless skinless chicken breasts (about 675 g), filets removed (see tip, below)
pinch	each salt and pepper
1 tsp	olive oil

Stir together garlic-and-fine-herb cheese, bread crumbs, sun-dried tomatoes and basil.

Holding paring knife horizontally, insert into thick end of each chicken breast and wiggle back and forth to form pocket. Using disposable piping bag or small spoon, stuff each pocket with one-quarter of the cheese mixture. Sprinkle chicken with salt and pepper.

In ovenproof skillet, heat oil over medium-high heat; brown chicken on both sides, about 6 minutes. Transfer to 400°F (200°C) oven; bake until chicken is no longer pink inside, about 8 minutes.

PER SERVING: about 256 cal, 34 g pro, 12 g total fat (6 g sat. fat), 3 g carb, trace fibre, 99 mg chol, 209 mg sodium, 454 mg potassium. % RDI: 2% calcium, 5% iron, 7% vit A, 7% vit C, 4% folate.

TIP FROM THE TEST KITCHEN

Chicken breast filets are the small, tender pieces of meat partially attached to the underside of the breast. They are delicious, but here it's easier to trim them off so you have a flat piece of meat to work with. You can use the reserved filets to make Parmesan Chicken Fingers (page 82) or Crispy Almond Chicken (page 83).

MUSHROOM-STUFFED CHICKEN
WITH ROASTED POTATOES AND LEMON BROCCOLI

MAKES 4 SERVINGS

A hearty mushroom filling adds a bit of style to boneless skinless chicken breasts. To avoid overcooking the broccoli, drain while it's still a touch underdone— it will keep cooking as it stands.

ROASTED POTATOES: Toss together potatoes, oil, salt and pepper; spread on foil-lined rimmed baking sheet. Bake in 425°F (220°C) oven, stirring once, until golden, about 25 minutes. Keep warm.

STUFFED CHICKEN: While potatoes are roasting, in skillet, heat 1 tsp of the oil over medium-high heat; sauté mushrooms and garlic for 2 minutes. Add red pepper and half each of the salt and pepper; sauté until mushrooms are browned and no liquid remains, about 3 minutes. Add green onions and lemon juice; sauté until green onions are softened, about 1 minute. Remove from heat; stir in Parmesan.

Place one chicken breast on cutting board. Holding knife blade parallel to board and starting at thickest long side, slice horizontally almost all the way through breast; open and place on separate foil-lined rimmed baking sheet. Repeat with remaining chicken.

Mound one-quarter of the mushroom mixture in centre of each breast; close and secure with toothpicks. Brush with remaining oil; sprinkle with remaining salt and pepper.

Bake in 425°F (220°C) oven until chicken is no longer pink inside, about 15 minutes. Broil until golden, about 2 minutes. Let rest for 5 minutes. Discard toothpicks; slice crosswise. Sprinkle with basil.

LEMON BROCCOLI: While chicken is resting, in saucepan of boiling salted water, cook broccoli until tender-crisp, about 2 minutes. Drain and transfer to bowl; toss with butter, lemon zest, salt and pepper. Serve with chicken and potatoes.

PER SERVING: about 415 cal, 35 g pro, 11 g total fat (4 g sat. fat), 45 g carb, 7 g fibre, 78 mg chol, 496 mg sodium, 1,689 mg potassium. % RDI: 14% calcium, 24% iron, 26% vit A, 128% vit C, 41% folate.

ROASTED POTATOES:

900 g	yellow-fleshed potatoes, cut in 1-inch (2.5 cm) chunks
2 tsp	olive oil
pinch	each salt and pepper

STUFFED CHICKEN:

1½ tsp	olive oil
half	pkg (227 g pkg) cremini mushrooms, thinly sliced
2	cloves garlic, minced
half	sweet red pepper, finely diced
¼ tsp	each salt and pepper
2	green onions, thinly sliced
2 tsp	lemon juice
¼ cup	grated Parmesan cheese
450 g	boneless skinless chicken breasts
3 tbsp	chopped fresh basil

LEMON BROCCOLI:

225 g	broccoli florets (about 4 cups)
1 tbsp	butter
1 tsp	grated lemon zest
pinch	each salt and pepper

GRILLED CHICKEN
WITH NAPA CABBAGE SLAW

MAKES 4 SERVINGS

This crunchy summer salad makes a great light dinner. Any leftovers will keep well for lunch the next day—simply scoop out the seeds after halving the cucumber to prevent the salad from becoming watery.

GRILLED CHICKEN:

450 g	boneless skinless chicken breasts
pinch	each salt and pepper

SOY VINAIGRETTE:

2 tbsp	vegetable oil
4 tsp	unseasoned rice vinegar
1 tbsp	sodium-reduced soy sauce
2 tsp	sesame oil
pinch	salt

NAPA CABBAGE SLAW:

4 cups	lightly packed shredded napa cabbage
1	carrot, grated or julienned
1	sweet red pepper, thinly sliced
1	rib celery, thinly sliced diagonally
half	English cucumber, halved lengthwise and thinly sliced diagonally
2	green onions, thinly sliced
⅓ cup	sliced almonds, toasted

GRILLED CHICKEN: Sprinkle chicken with salt and pepper. Place on greased grill over medium-high heat; close lid and grill, turning once, until no longer pink inside, 12 to 15 minutes. Let rest for 5 minutes before slicing.

SOY VINAIGRETTE: While chicken is resting, in large bowl, whisk together vegetable oil, vinegar, soy sauce, sesame oil and salt.

NAPA CABBAGE SLAW: Add cabbage, carrot, red pepper, celery, cucumber and green onions to vinaigrette; toss to coat. Top with chicken; sprinkle with almonds.

PER SERVING: about 293 cal, 30 g pro, 15 g total fat (2 g sat. fat), 11 g carb, 3 g fibre, 67 mg chol, 242 mg sodium, 786 mg potassium. % RDI: 10% calcium, 11% iron, 40% vit A, 123% vit C, 39% folate.

VARIATION
Grilled Chicken With Creamy Tahini Slaw

Replace soy vinaigrette with 2 tbsp olive oil, 4 tsp lemon juice, 1 tbsp tahini, 1 tbsp Balkan-style plain yogurt and ¼ tsp each salt and pepper.

LEEK AND GORGONZOLA CHICKEN BREASTS

MAKES 4 SERVINGS

Gorgonzola is especially good, but you can use another creamy blue-veined cheese, such as Borgonzola or Cambozola, to stuff this chicken. It has such a rich taste, all you need is Mixed Greens Salad (opposite) to enjoy alongside.

LEEK FILLING:

1 tbsp	butter
2 cups	thinly sliced leeks (white and light green parts only)
pinch	salt
¼ cup	dry sherry or chicken broth
⅓ cup	crumbled Gorgonzola cheese

STUFFED CHICKEN:

4	boneless skin-on chicken breasts (about 600 g)
1 tsp	all-purpose flour
4 tsp	extra-virgin olive oil
½ tsp	chopped fresh thyme (or pinch dried)
pinch	each salt and pepper

LEEK FILLING: In skillet, melt butter over medium-low heat; cook leeks and salt, stirring often, until softened, about 8 minutes. Add sherry; cook over medium-high heat just until evaporated, about 2 minutes. Scrape into bowl and let cool. Stir in Gorgonzola.

STUFFED CHICKEN: Place one chicken breast on cutting board. Holding knife blade parallel to board and starting at thickest long side, slice horizontally almost all the way through breast; open. Repeat with remaining chicken.

Leaving ½-inch (1 cm) border uncovered, spread one-quarter of the filling evenly over half of each breast. Sprinkle some of the flour over each bottom border; close breast, pressing edge to seal. *(Make-ahead: Cover and refrigerate for up to 24 hours; add 5 minutes to roasting time.)*

Place chicken, skin side up, on foil-lined rimmed baking sheet. Stir together oil, thyme, salt and pepper; brush over chicken.

Roast in 400°F (200°C) oven until golden and no longer pink inside, 15 to 20 minutes. Broil, watching carefully to avoid scorching, until skin is crisp and deep golden brown, about 2 minutes.

PER SERVING (WITHOUT SKIN): about 301 cal, 30 g pro, 17 g total fat (6 g sat. fat), 4 g carb, 1 g fibre, 107 mg chol, 285 mg sodium. % RDI: 8% calcium, 6% iron, 9% vit A, 2% vit C, 8% folate.

GRILLED CHICKEN BREASTS
WITH CHIMICHURRI VERDE

MAKES 3 SERVINGS

Basting poultry with an oil mixture is a great way to keep it moist during grilling. The herbal, garlicky chimichurri sauce is an Argentine favourite that has become popular all over the world. Serve with Mixed Greens Salad (below).

CHIMICHURRI VERDE: In food processor, finely chop together parsley, oregano, garlic, jalapeño pepper, salt and pepper. Add oil, 2 tbsp water and vinegar; pulse until combined. Set aside.

GRILLED CHICKEN BREASTS: In large glass bowl, combine 3 tbsp each of the lime juice and oil; add parsley, oregano, garlic, bay leaves, salt, pepper and thyme. Add chicken, turning to coat. Cover and refrigerate for 4 hours.

Stir remaining lime juice with remaining oil. Place chicken on greased grill over medium-high heat; close lid and grill, turning once and basting occasionally with oil mixture, until no longer pink inside, 12 to 14 minutes.

PER SERVING: about 469 cal, 35 g pro, 34 g total fat (5 g sat. fat), 5 g carb, 2 g fibre, 88 mg chol, 439 mg sodium, 601 mg potassium. % RDI: 7% calcium, 22% iron, 20% vit A, 53% vit C, 20% folate.

Mixed Greens Salad

In large bowl, whisk together 2 tbsp extra-virgin olive oil, 2 tsp lemon juice, ¼ tsp liquid honey, and pinch each salt and pepper. Add 6 cups packed mixed baby greens; toss to coat.

MAKES 4 SERVINGS

CHIMICHURRI VERDE:

1 cup	packed fresh parsley leaves
2 tbsp	packed fresh oregano leaves
2	cloves garlic
half	jalapeño pepper, seeded
¼ tsp	each salt and pepper
¼ cup	extra-virgin olive oil
1 tbsp	red wine vinegar

GRILLED CHICKEN BREASTS:

¼ cup	lime juice
¼ cup	extra-virgin olive oil
2 tbsp	each minced fresh parsley and oregano
3	cloves garlic, minced
3	bay leaves, torn
¼ tsp	each salt and coarsely ground pepper
¼ tsp	dried thyme
3	boneless skinless chicken breasts (about 450 g)

MOROCCAN CHICKEN
WITH GRILLED VEGETABLES
MAKES 4 SERVINGS

A blend of ginger, garlic and aromatic spices in the marinade makes for a flavourful main dish. The meat tastes even better the longer it marinates, so refrigerate it overnight if you can. Stuff leftovers in a pita for a quick lunch.

MOROCCAN CHICKEN: In bowl, stir together yogurt, tahini, lemon juice, garlic, ginger, coriander, cumin, cinnamon, salt and pepper. Add chicken; turn to coat. Cover and refrigerate for 2 hours. *(Make-ahead: Refrigerate for up to 24 hours.)*

Place chicken on greased grill over medium-high heat; close lid and grill, turning occasionally, until no longer pink inside, about 8 minutes. Let stand for 3 minutes before slicing.

GRILLED VEGETABLES: While chicken is marinating, in bowl, stir together lemon juice, oil, garlic, ginger, salt, pepper and cinnamon.

Place onion, zucchini, mushrooms and red pepper on greased grill over medium-high heat; close lid and grill, basting frequently with lemon mixture, until tender, about 7 minutes. Cut mushrooms in half. Place on platter along with remaining grilled vegetables; sprinkle with cilantro. Serve with chicken.

PER SERVING: about 288 cal, 31 g pro, 13 g total fat (3 g sat. fat), 14 g carb, 4 g fibre, 74 mg chol, 229 mg sodium, 946 mg potassium. % RDI: 8% calcium, 13% iron, 14% vit A, 92% vit C, 17% folate.

TIP FROM THE TEST KITCHEN
Removing the gills from portobello mushrooms is simple. Just use a teaspoon to scrape them out and discard them.

MOROCCAN CHICKEN:

⅓ cup	Greek yogurt
1 tbsp	tahini
1 tbsp	lemon juice
2	cloves garlic, minced
2 tsp	minced fresh ginger
1 tsp	ground coriander
½ tsp	ground cumin
¼ tsp	cinnamon
pinch	each salt and pepper
450 g	boneless skinless chicken breasts

GRILLED VEGETABLES:

2 tbsp	lemon juice
2 tbsp	olive oil
1	clove garlic, minced
1 tsp	minced fresh ginger
¼ tsp	each salt and pepper
pinch	cinnamon
1	small red onion, cut in ½-inch (1 cm) thick rounds
1	zucchini, cut lengthwise in ½-inch (1 cm) thick slices
2	portobello mushrooms, stems and gills removed (see tip, left)
1	sweet red pepper, quartered
2 tbsp	chopped fresh cilantro

CHIPOTLE LIME CHICKEN BREASTS

MAKES 4 SERVINGS

Chipotle peppers—those famous dried smoked jalapeño peppers you can easily find canned in tasty adobo sauce—add a distinctive smokiness to this dish.

2	canned chipotle peppers, minced (see tip, below)
¼ cup	butter, softened
2 tbsp	chopped fresh cilantro or parsley
1 tsp	grated lime zest
1 tsp	lime juice
½ tsp	ground cumin
¼ tsp	each salt and pepper
4	boneless skin-on chicken breasts (about 600 g)
1 tbsp	vegetable oil

Stir together chipotle peppers, butter, cilantro, lime zest, lime juice, cumin, salt and pepper. With fingers, loosen chicken skin along curved side of each breast to form pocket; spread chipotle mixture under skin. *(Make-ahead: Cover and refrigerate for up to 24 hours; add 5 minutes to roasting time.)*

Place chicken, skin side up, on foil-lined rimmed baking sheet; brush with oil. Roast in 400°F (200°C) oven until golden and no longer pink inside, 15 to 20 minutes. Broil, watching carefully to avoid scorching, until deep golden brown, about 2 minutes.

PER SERVING (WITHOUT SKIN): about 301 cal, 28 g pro, 20 g total fat (9 g sat. fat), 1 g carb, trace fibre, 123 mg chol, 483 mg sodium. % RDI: 1% calcium, 7% iron, 15% vit A, 3% vit C, 3% folate.

TIP FROM THE TEST KITCHEN
When you're working with hot peppers, wear rubber gloves and be careful not to let your hands come into contact with your face. That chili oil burns!

THAI RED CURRY ROAST CHICKEN BREASTS

MAKES 4 SERVINGS

Serve this colourful chicken with fragrant jasmine rice and sautéed baby bok choy for an exotic-tasting but dead-simple weeknight dinner.

Stir together red pepper, basil, garlic, oil, curry paste, brown sugar and salt. With fingers, loosen chicken skin along curved side of each breast to form pocket; spread curry mixture under skin. *(Make-ahead: Cover and refrigerate for up to 24 hours; add 5 minutes to roasting time.)*

Place chicken, skin side up, on foil-lined rimmed baking sheet. Roast in 400°F (200°C) oven until golden and no longer pink inside, 15 to 20 minutes. Broil, watching carefully to avoid scorching, until deep golden brown, about 2 minutes.

PER SERVING (WITHOUT SKIN): about 215 cal, 28 g pro, 10 g total fat (2 g sat. fat), 2 g carb, trace fibre, 87 mg chol, 275 mg sodium. % RDI: 1% calcium, 4% iron, 4% vit A, 13% vit C, 3% folate.

2 tbsp	finely chopped sweet red pepper
2 tbsp	chopped fresh basil, cilantro or parsley
1	clove garlic, minced
1 tbsp	peanut or vegetable oil
2 tsp	Thai red curry paste (see tip, below)
1 tsp	packed brown sugar
¼ tsp	salt
4	boneless skin-on chicken breasts (about 600 g)

TIP FROM THE TEST KITCHEN

Thai red curry paste is on the spicy side, so substitute mild Indian curry paste if you prefer.

GRILLED CHICKEN AND BALSAMIC RADICCHIO

MAKES 4 SERVINGS

Looking for an alternative to traditional grilled vegetables?
Try radicchio. Once grilled, the bitter leaves take on a lovely smoky
flavour and tenderness. Serve with a sliced warm baguette.

2 tbsp	liquid honey
1 tbsp	grainy mustard
¼ tsp	each salt and pepper
450 g	boneless skinless chicken breasts
2	heads radicchio
2 tbsp	balsamic vinegar
2 tbsp	extra-virgin olive oil
⅓ cup	crumbled soft goat cheese
1 tbsp	chopped fresh chives

Stir together honey, mustard and a pinch each of the salt and pepper; set aside.

Place chicken on greased grill over medium heat; close lid and grill, turning once, until browned, about 8 minutes. Brush with half of the honey mixture. Close lid and grill, turning and brushing frequently with honey mixture, until no longer pink inside, about 7 minutes. Transfer to cutting board and cover loosely with foil; let stand for 5 minutes before slicing.

Meanwhile, keeping root end intact, cut each radicchio into four wedges. Whisk together vinegar, oil and remaining salt and pepper; drizzle over radicchio wedges.

Add to grill; grill, covered and turning once, until lightly browned, 3 to 4 minutes. Transfer to platter; top with goat cheese and chives. Serve with sliced chicken.

PER SERVING: about 303 cal, 31 g pro, 13 g total fat (4 g sat. fat), 15 g carb, 1 g fibre, 76 mg chol, 349 mg sodium, 606 mg potassium. % RDI: 5% calcium, 11% iron, 7% vit A, 10% vit C, 20% folate.

GINGER SHIITAKE CHICKEN BREASTS

MAKES 4 SERVINGS

A mixture of earthy fresh shiitake mushrooms, bright ginger and nutty sesame oil is tucked under the skin of these easy, weeknight-friendly roasted chicken breasts. Serve with Garlic Bok Choy (below).

4 tsp	vegetable oil
1 tsp	sesame oil
175 g	shiitake mushroom caps, thinly sliced
¼ cup	chopped green onions (green parts only)
1 tsp	grated fresh ginger
1 tbsp	soy sauce
1 tsp	unseasoned rice vinegar or lemon juice
4	boneless skin-on chicken breasts (about 600 g)
¼ tsp	each salt and pepper

In skillet, heat 1 tsp of the vegetable oil and sesame oil over medium heat; cook mushrooms, stirring occasionally, until slightly softened, about 5 minutes.

Add green onions and ginger; cook for 2 minutes. Stir in soy sauce and vinegar; scrape into bowl and let cool.

With fingers, loosen chicken skin along curved side of each breast to form pocket; spread mushroom mixture under skin. *(Make-ahead: Cover and refrigerate for up to 24 hours; add 5 minutes to roasting time.)*

Place chicken, skin side up, on foil-lined rimmed baking sheet. Brush with remaining oil; sprinkle with salt and pepper. Roast in 400°F (200°C) oven until golden and no longer pink inside, 15 to 20 minutes. Broil, watching carefully to avoid scorching, until deep golden brown, about 2 minutes.

PER SERVING (WITHOUT SKIN): about 231 cal, 29 g pro, 11 g total fat (2 g sat. fat), 3 g carb, 1 g fibre, 87 mg chol, 472 mg sodium. % RDI: 1% calcium, 9% iron, 3% vit A, 2% vit C, 8% folate.

Garlic Bok Choy

Trim bases off 4 heads baby bok choy; cut each in half lengthwise. In large skillet, heat 1 tbsp vegetable oil over medium heat; cook 2 cloves garlic, minced, until fragrant, about 30 seconds. Add bok choy and 3 tbsp water; cover and steam until tender-crisp, about 5 minutes.
MAKES 4 SERVINGS

LEMON-THYME CHICKEN BREASTS
WITH BRIE
MAKES 4 SERVINGS

All it takes is the residual heat from the meat to melt the cheese to soft, creamy perfection and slightly wilt the greens. Be sure to have some crusty bread on hand as a quick side.

Whisk together oil, parsley, thyme, lemon zest, lemon juice, salt and pepper; brush over chicken. *(Make-ahead: Cover and refrigerate for up to 24 hours; add 5 minutes to roasting time.)*

Place chicken, skin side up, on foil-lined rimmed baking sheet. Roast in 400°F (200°C) oven until golden and no longer pink inside, 15 to 20 minutes. Broil, watching carefully to avoid scorching, until deep golden brown, about 2 minutes. Let stand for 2 minutes.

Meanwhile, divide spinach among four plates; top each with chicken breast. Cut Brie into quarters; place one-quarter on each breast.

PER SERVING (WITHOUT SKIN): about 332 cal, 35 g pro, 20 g total fat (7 g sat. fat), 2 g carb, 2 g fibre, 115 mg chol, 427 mg sodium. % RDI: 10% calcium, 16% iron, 45% vit A, 30% vit C, 60% folate.

2 tbsp	extra-virgin olive oil
2 tsp	chopped fresh parsley
1 tsp	chopped fresh thyme (or ¼ tsp dried)
1 tsp	grated lemon zest
1 tsp	lemon juice
¼ tsp	each salt and pepper
4	boneless skin-on chicken breasts (about 600 g)
4 cups	baby spinach or arugula (see tip, below)
125 g	Brie or Camembert cheese, at room temperature

TIP FROM THE TEST KITCHEN
Baby spinach and arugula are tasty, and they save time because they don't need to have their tender stems trimmed off. They are excellent to keep on hand for when you want to eat healthy greens without spending a lot of time prepping them.

BARBECUED CHICKEN PIZZA

MAKES 6 SLICES

This family-favourite pizza offers a delicious combination of grilled chicken
and cheese. We like Monterey Jack with the sweet barbecue sauce, but Cheddar,
mozzarella or a combination of all three cheeses would be tasty, too.

Brush chicken with 1 tsp of the oil; sprinkle with salt and pepper. Place on
greased grill over medium-high heat; close lid and grill, turning once, until no
longer pink inside, about 12 minutes. Let cool enough to handle; thinly slice.
In bowl, toss chicken with barbecue sauce; set aside.

On lightly floured surface, roll out dough to 16- x 12-inch (40 x 30 cm)
rectangle; transfer to lightly floured pizza peel or inverted baking sheet.

Brush dough with remaining oil. Place, oiled side down, directly on greased
grill over medium heat. Grill, uncovered and watching carefully to avoid
charring, until bubbles form on top and grill-marked underneath, 3 to
6 minutes.

Slide pizza peel, two wide spatulas or inverted baking sheet under crust.
Flip crust; close lid and grill just until set, about 1 minute. Transfer to lightly
floured pizza peel or inverted baking sheet. Reduce heat to medium-low.

Spread pizza sauce over crust; top with half of the Monterey Jack. Sprinkle
with red pepper, green onions and chicken mixture. Top with remaining
Monterey Jack. Slide back onto greased grill. Close lid and grill until Monterey
Jack is melted and bubbly, and underside is browned, 3 to 8 minutes.

PER SLICE: about 337 cal, 19 g pro, 15 g total fat (5 g sat. fat), 40 g carb,
7 g fibre, 35 mg chol, 700 mg sodium, 185 mg potassium. % RDI: 20% calcium,
17% iron, 9% vit A, 31% vit C, 5% folate.

1	boneless skinless chicken breast (about 150 g)
1 tbsp	vegetable oil
pinch	each salt and pepper
2 tbsp	prepared barbecue sauce
450 g	whole wheat pizza dough
½ cup	Tomato Pizza Sauce (below)
1¼ cups	shredded Monterey Jack cheese
⅓ cup	diced sweet red pepper
⅓ cup	sliced green onions

Tomato Pizza Sauce

Reserving juice, drain, seed and chop 1 can (796 mL) plum tomatoes; set aside. In saucepan, heat
2 tbsp extra-virgin olive oil over medium heat. Add ½ cup finely chopped onion; 2 cloves garlic,
minced; and ½ tsp dried oregano. Cook, stirring occasionally, until onion is translucent, about
4 minutes. Add tomatoes and reserved juice, ½ tsp red wine vinegar, ¼ tsp each salt and pepper, and
pinch granulated sugar. Simmer until thickened, 15 to 20 minutes. Let cool slightly. Transfer to food
processor; blend until smooth. *(Make-ahead: Freeze in ½-cup airtight containers for up to 2 months.)*
MAKES 2 CUPS

GRILLED BUFFALO CHICKEN

MAKES 4 SERVINGS

A hot, buttery sauce delivers all the sticky satisfaction of Buffalo wings, but using whole chicken breasts means there's no need for wet wipes. A simple slaw laced with blue cheese dressing (below) is the ultimate accompaniment.

⅓ cup	cayenne pepper sauce, such as Frank's RedHot Original
2 tbsp	butter
1 tsp	Worcestershire sauce
½ tsp	onion powder
4	boneless skinless chicken breasts (about 600 g)
pinch	salt

In small saucepan, bring cayenne pepper sauce, butter, Worcestershire sauce and onion powder to boil. Remove from heat; let cool to room temperature.

Toss chicken with ¼ cup of the sauce; let stand for 10 minutes. Sprinkle with salt.

Place chicken on greased grill over medium-high heat; close lid and grill, turning once, for 6 minutes. Brush with remaining sauce; close lid and grill, turning once, until no longer pink inside, about 4 minutes.

PER SERVING: about 221 cal, 34 g pro, 8 g total fat (4 g sat. fat), 1 g carb, trace fibre, 104 mg chol, 838 mg sodium, 434 mg potassium. % RDI: 1% calcium, 5% iron, 9% vit A, 2% folate.

Coleslaw With Blue Cheese Dressing

In large bowl, whisk together ¼ cup light mayonnaise, 2 tbsp sour cream, 4 tsp white wine vinegar, 1 tsp granulated sugar, and ¼ tsp each salt and pepper; stir in ¼ cup crumbled blue cheese. Add 4 cups shredded cabbage, 1 cup thinly sliced celery and 1 cup grated carrot; toss to coat. Refrigerate for 20 minutes before serving.

MAKES 4 SERVINGS

CILANTRO PESTO CHICKEN SALAD

MAKES 4 SERVINGS

This salad can be a one-dish wonder, but it's also tasty with simple boiled potatoes on the side. You might want to make a double batch of the cilantro pesto—it would also be very tasty tossed with pasta another night.

CILANTRO PESTO: In food processor, pulse cilantro, garlic and pine nuts until finely chopped. Add Parmesan, oil, salt and pepper; pulse to combine. With motor running, drizzle in warm water until smooth. Set aside.

CHICKEN SALAD: Cut chicken meat from bones; discard skin and bones. Sprinkle chicken with salt and pepper. In ovenproof skillet, heat 1 tbsp of the oil over medium-high heat; brown chicken, turning once, about 6 minutes.

Stir together 1 tbsp each of the pesto and remaining oil; brush over chicken. Roast in 350°F (180°C) oven until no longer pink inside, about 10 minutes. Let rest for 5 minutes before slicing.

In large bowl, toss together lettuce, tomato, lemon juice and remaining oil and pesto; divide among four plates. Top with chicken.

PER SERVING: about 425 cal, 32 g pro, 31 g total fat (6 g sat. fat), 4 g carb, 2 g fibre, 99 mg chol, 411 mg sodium. % RDI: 6% calcium, 11% iron, 34% vit A, 28% vit C, 36% folate.

CILANTRO PESTO:

½ cup	lightly packed fresh cilantro or parsley leaves
1	small clove garlic
2 tbsp	pine nuts, lightly toasted
2 tbsp	grated Parmesan cheese
1 tbsp	extra-virgin olive oil
¼ tsp	each salt and pepper
2 tbsp	warm water

CHICKEN SALAD:

4	bone-in skin-on chicken breasts (see tip, left), about 900 g
¼ tsp	each salt and pepper
¼ cup	extra-virgin olive oil
4 cups	chopped romaine lettuce
½ cup	coarsely chopped tomato
2 tbsp	lemon juice

TIP FROM THE TEST KITCHEN

Using bone-in chicken breasts is more economical than buying them pre-boned at the market. Our handy step-by-step boning tutorial (see page 12) will make you a pro if you aren't already.

TAIWANESE CRISPY FRIED CHICKEN
WITH BASIL

MAKES 4 SERVINGS

A fried coating of sweet potato starch gives this chicken its uniquely chewy yet crispy texture. The dish is bursting with flavour, so all it needs is steamed rice on the side.

2	boneless skinless chicken breasts (about 375 g)
4 tsp	soy sauce
2 tsp	Chinese rice wine, sake or dry sherry
1½ tsp	granulated sugar
1½ tsp	grated fresh ginger
1 tsp	five-spice powder
¼ tsp	cinnamon
½ cup	sweet potato starch (see tip, below)
	vegetable oil for deep-frying (about 3 cups)
1 cup	loosely packed fresh Thai or regular basil leaves
¼ tsp	sea salt
pinch	pepper

Cut chicken into 2- x 1-inch (5 x 2.5 cm) pieces. Toss together chicken, soy sauce, wine, sugar, ginger, five-spice powder and cinnamon; let stand for 10 minutes or for up to 30 minutes.

One piece at a time, press chicken into starch to coat; let stand for 10 minutes.

In wok or large deep skillet, heat oil over medium heat just until surface shimmers (or deep-fryer thermometer reads 275 to 300°F/135 to 149°C). Add chicken, separating pieces to prevent sticking; fry until light golden, about 3 minutes. Increase heat to high; fry until deep golden brown and crisp, 2 to 3 minutes.

Add basil; fry until crispy, 40 to 60 seconds. Using slotted spoon, scoop out chicken and basil; drain well on paper towel–lined plate. Transfer to serving dish. Sprinkle with salt and pepper.

PER SERVING: about 260 cal, 20 g pro, 15 g total fat (1 g sat. fat), 10 g carb, 1 g fibre, 49 mg chol, 445 mg sodium, 318 mg potassium. % RDI: 3% calcium, 9% iron, 5% vit A, 3% vit C, 4% folate.

TIP FROM THE TEST KITCHEN

Sweet potato starch is a specialty product in Taiwanese and Fujian cooking. It is available in fine and coarse grinds; coarse is best for frying. Buy it at a Chinese or Korean grocer. No other starch produces the same texture, but if it's unavailable, you can use cornstarch instead.

OVEN-FRIED BUTTERMILK CHICKEN

MAKES 4 SERVINGS

Bone-in chicken stays extra juicy when baked. By removing the skin, you reduce the amount of fat in this lightened-up dish. An oil spritzer will evenly distribute a small amount of oil and make the simple panko breading wonderfully crisp.

1 tsp	minced fresh thyme
½ tsp	garlic powder
½ tsp	sweet paprika
½ tsp	dry mustard
½ tsp	salt
¼ tsp	pepper
1½ cups	buttermilk (see tip, below)
4	bone-in skin-on chicken breasts (about 900 g total), skin removed
1½ cups	panko bread crumbs
	olive oil for spraying

Stir together thyme, garlic powder, paprika, mustard, salt and pepper; set aside.

In large bowl, whisk buttermilk with half of the thyme mixture; add chicken and turn to coat. Cover and refrigerate for 8 hours. *(Make-ahead: Refrigerate for up to 24 hours.)*

In shallow dish, combine panko with remaining thyme mixture. Remove chicken from marinade, discarding marinade; press chicken into panko mixture, turning to coat all over.

Place chicken on greased rimmed baking sheet; spray with oil. Bake in 375°F (190°C) oven until no longer pink inside, about 30 minutes. Let stand for 5 minutes before serving.

PER SERVING: about 253 cal, 38 g pro, 5 g total fat (2 g sat. fat), 11 g carb, trace fibre, 93 mg chol, 372 mg sodium, 540 mg potassium. % RDI: 7% calcium, 9% iron, 3% vit A, 3% vit C, 3% folate.

TIP FROM THE TEST KITCHEN
Most recipes don't use up a whole carton of buttermilk, leaving you with leftovers. Use it up in muffins, quick breads, pancakes and creamy salad dressings.

STRAWBERRY-BASIL CHICKEN
WITH GRILLED BROCCOLI

MAKES 4 SERVINGS

Grilling broccoli may seem unorthodox, but it makes for a crispy texture that's totally addictive. The fresh basil and spicy sriracha balance out the sweetness of the strawberries and create the perfect tension between flavours.

In saucepan, heat 1 tbsp of the oil over medium heat; cook shallot and ginger until fragrant, about 1 minute. Stir in sugar, lemon juice, ¼ tsp each of the salt and pepper, and chili sauce; cook, stirring, until sugar is dissolved, about 1 minute. Stir in strawberries; cook, stirring, until strawberries begin to soften, about 1 minute. Remove from heat; stir in basil.

Using immersion blender or food processor, purée strawberry mixture until smooth. Strain through fine-mesh sieve, pressing lightly on solids and reserving ¼ cup of the sauce in separate bowl for garnish; set aside. Discard pulp.

Toss together chicken, remaining strawberry sauce, 1 tsp of the remaining oil and a pinch each of the remaining salt and pepper. Place chicken on greased grill over medium heat; close lid and grill, turning once, until no longer pink inside, about 10 minutes. Transfer chicken to plate; keep warm. Discard marinade.

Meanwhile, in large pot of boiling salted water, cook broccoli until tender-crisp, about 2 minutes. Drain and chill in cold water; drain again. Toss with vinegar and remaining oil, salt and pepper. Arrange broccoli on greased grill; close lid and grill until lightly charred, about 6 minutes. Serve with chicken and reserved strawberry sauce.

2 tbsp	olive oil
1	shallot, minced
¼ tsp	minced fresh ginger
1 tbsp	granulated sugar
2 tsp	lemon juice
½ tsp	each salt and pepper
¼ tsp	Asian chili sauce (such as sriracha), see tip, below
3 cups	strawberries, hulled and diced
2 tbsp	chopped fresh basil
4	boneless skinless chicken breasts (about 675 g total)
1	head broccoli, cut in large florets
1 tbsp	balsamic vinegar

PER SERVING: about 320 cal, 42 g pro, 9 g total fat (2 g sat. fat), 18 g carb, 5 g fibre, 98 mg chol, 375 mg sodium, 954 mg potassium. % RDI: 6% calcium, 14% iron, 19% vit A, 178% vit C, 62% folate.

TIP FROM THE TEST KITCHEN
Chili sauces are popular in many different Asian cuisines. Here, sriracha or chili garlic sauce work well. You can also use a chili paste, such as sambal oelek, but it is a little spicier and offers more concentrated hot pepper flavour.

PECAN-CRUSTED CHICKEN FINGERS

MAKES 6 SERVINGS

Serve these nutty chicken fingers with honey or plum sauce for dipping. The combination of buttery pecans and crispy panko creates a wonderful coating that kids and adults will adore.

Sandwich chicken between plastic wrap; using meat mallet or heavy-bottomed saucepan, pound chicken to ½-inch (1 cm) thickness. Diagonally cut each breast lengthwise into four strips.

In shallow dish, whisk together flour, 1 tsp of the chili powder, salt and pepper. In bowl, beat eggs. Combine pecans, panko and remaining chili powder in separate shallow dish.

One at a time, dip chicken strips into flour, shaking off excess; dip into eggs, letting excess drip back into bowl. Dredge in pecan mixture to lightly coat, pressing to adhere.

Bake on parchment paper–lined rimmed baking sheet in 425°F (220°C) oven until golden and no longer pink inside, about 25 minutes.

PER SERVING: about 349 cal, 31 g pro, 22 g total fat (3 g sat. fat), 8 g carb, 3 g fibre, 125 mg chol, 186 mg sodium, 464 mg potassium. % RDI: 3% calcium, 12% iron, 4% vit A, 3% vit C, 11% folate.

675 g	boneless skinless chicken breasts
⅓ cup	all-purpose flour
2 tsp	chili powder
½ tsp	each salt and pepper
2	eggs
1½ cups	finely chopped pecans (see tip, below)
½ cup	panko bread crumbs

TIP FROM THE TEST KITCHEN
Whole pecans stay fresh longer than prechopped nuts and have better flavour. Store them in the freezer for up to six months, and use only what you need at one time.

PAN-FRIED CURRY CHICKEN
WITH RAISIN RICE
MAKES 4 SERVINGS

A dusting of curry powder pairs nicely with a dollop of herbed yogurt sauce.
The flavourful brown rice side dish also goes well with grilled steak or fish.

RAISIN RICE:

¾ cup	sliced almonds
1 tbsp	butter
2	shallots, chopped
¼ tsp	salt
1 cup	whole grain parboiled brown rice
2 cups	sodium-reduced chicken broth
½ cup	golden raisins
⅓ cup	chopped fresh cilantro

CURRY CHICKEN:

1 tsp	curry powder
½ tsp	ground coriander
¼ tsp	salt
pinch	pepper
450 g	boneless skinless chicken breasts
1 tbsp	canola oil

YOGURT SAUCE:

1 cup	plain Greek yogurt
¼ cup	chopped fresh cilantro
3 tbsp	lemon juice
¼ tsp	pepper
pinch	salt

RAISIN RICE: Spread almonds on rimmed baking sheet; toast on bottom rack in 350°F (180°C) oven until golden, about 5 minutes.

Meanwhile, in small saucepan, melt butter over medium heat; cook shallots and salt, stirring often, until translucent, about 2 minutes.

Stir in rice to coat; add broth and bring to boil. Reduce heat, cover and simmer until rice is tender and no liquid remains, about 20 minutes. Let stand, covered, for 10 minutes; fluff with fork. Stir in raisins and cilantro; sprinkle with almonds.

CURRY CHICKEN: While rice is cooking, mix together curry powder, coriander, salt and pepper; sprinkle all over chicken. In large ovenproof skillet, heat oil over medium heat; brown chicken, turning once, about 8 minutes.

Transfer skillet to 350°F (180°C) oven. Bake until no longer pink inside, 6 to 8 minutes. Transfer chicken to cutting board and cover loosely with foil; let rest for 5 minutes before slicing across the grain.

YOGURT SAUCE: Mix together yogurt, cilantro, lemon juice, pepper and salt; serve with chicken and rice.

PER SERVING: about 630 cal, 41 g pro, 25 g total fat (7 g sat. fat), 63 g carb, 5 g fibre, 98 mg chol, 735 mg sodium, 1,037 mg potassium. % RDI: 21% calcium, 17% iron, 6% vit A, 12% vit C, 10% folate.

SPICE-RUBBED CHICKEN
WITH TABBOULEH SALAD
MAKES 4 SERVINGS

Tabbouleh is so fresh and light—just the perfect accompaniment to simple spiced chicken. You can easily scale up the recipe to feed a larger group of people.

TABBOULEH SALAD: In heatproof bowl, pour boiling water over bulgur; cover and let stand until tender, about 15 minutes. Drain, squeezing out as much water as possible; return to bowl. Stir in parsley, green onion, lemon juice, oil, salt and pepper.

SPICE-RUBBED CHICKEN: While bulgur is standing, in separate bowl, stir together oil, garlic, mint, coriander, salt, cloves and cinnamon; brush over chicken. Let stand for 10 minutes.

Place chicken on greased grill over medium-high heat; close lid and grill, turning once, until no longer pink inside, about 10 minutes. Serve with tabbouleh salad.

PER SERVING: about 458 cal, 38 g pro, 16 g total fat (3 g sat. fat), 43 g carb, 7 g fibre, 79 mg chol, 522 mg sodium, 642 mg potassium. % RDI: 5% calcium, 28% iron, 14% vit A, 42% vit C, 31% folate.

TABBOULEH SALAD:

3 cups	boiling water
1½ cups	bulgur (see tip, below)
1 cup	chopped fresh parsley
1	green onion, minced
¼ cup	lemon juice
2 tbsp	extra-virgin olive oil
¼ tsp	each salt and pepper

SPICE-RUBBED CHICKEN:

2 tbsp	extra-virgin olive oil
2	cloves garlic, minced
1 tsp	dried mint or parsley
½ tsp	each ground coriander and salt
pinch	each ground cloves and cinnamon
4	boneless skinless chicken breasts (about 600 g)

TIP FROM THE TEST KITCHEN
Bulgur is ground to different textures—usually fine, medium and coarse. Medium bulgur is the all-purpose grind that's the star of tabbouleh and other salads, pilafs, soups and patties. Medium bulgur is easy to find in most supermarkets; look for all textures in Middle Eastern grocery stores.

BARBECUE CHICKEN BURRITOS

MAKES 4 SERVINGS

These saucy knife-and-fork burritos are a twist on the traditional Mexican-style wrap. Use your favourite prepared barbecue sauce to boost the flavour with minimal effort.

2 tbsp	vegetable oil
375 g	boneless skinless chicken breasts, cubed
1	onion, diced
1	sweet orange pepper, diced
1	Roma tomato, diced
half	pkg (227 g pkg) cremini or button mushrooms, halved and sliced
⅓ cup	prepared barbecue sauce
4	large (10-inch/25 cm) whole wheat tortillas
¼ cup	shredded Monterey Jack cheese
¼ cup	shredded Cheddar cheese

In large nonstick skillet, heat 1 tbsp of the oil over medium-high heat; sauté chicken until golden, about 3 minutes. Using slotted spoon, transfer to plate.

Add remaining oil to pan; heat over medium heat. Cook onion, stirring occasionally, until tender, about 5 minutes. Stir in orange pepper, tomato and mushrooms; cook, stirring occasionally, until tender, about 10 minutes.

Return chicken and any accumulated juices to pan. Stir in barbecue sauce; cook, stirring, until coated and chicken is no longer pink inside, about 3 minutes.

Divide chicken mixture among tortillas; roll up. Place, seam side down, on parchment paper–lined rimmed baking sheet. Sprinkle each burrito with one-quarter each of the Monterey Jack and Cheddar. Bake in 425°F (220°C) oven until bubbly and golden, 5 to 7 minutes.

PER SERVING: about 459 cal, 32 g pro, 18 g total fat (5 g sat. fat), 42 g carb, 4 g fibre, 68 mg chol, 831 mg sodium, 547 mg potassium. % RDI: 13% calcium, 14% iron, 10% vit A, 85% vit C, 19% folate.

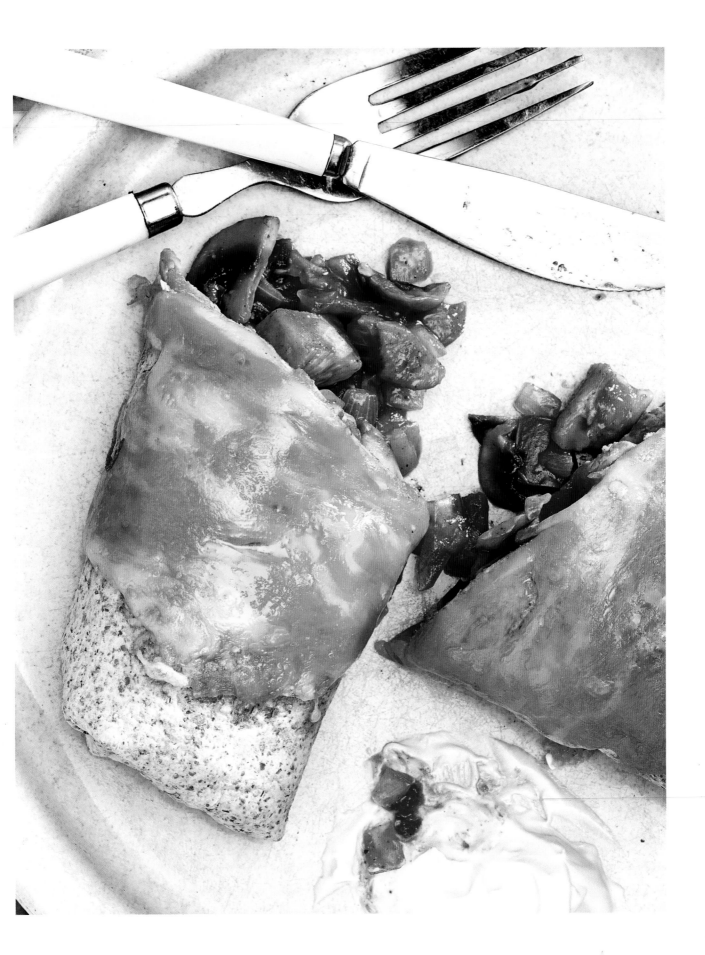

CHICKEN CRÊPES
WITH MOREL MUSHROOMS
MAKES 8 SERVINGS

Dried morel mushrooms are intense and smoky—perfect with mild chicken. To ensure light, thin crêpes, make the batter at least one hour before using to allow the flour to expand in the liquid. You can also use a blender to combine the ingredients.

CHIVE CRÊPES:

1⅓ cups	all-purpose flour
¼ tsp	salt
4	eggs
1½ cups	milk
¼ cup	butter, melted
¼ cup	chopped fresh chives

CHICKEN FILLING:

2½ cups	boiling water
1	pkg (14 g) dried morel mushrooms
2	bone-in skin-on chicken breasts
2 tbsp	butter
3	shallots, minced
¼ tsp	each salt and pepper
3 tbsp	all-purpose flour
¼ cup	whipping cream (35%)
3 tbsp	dry sherry or brandy

CHIVE CRÊPES: In bowl, whisk flour with salt. Whisk together eggs, milk and 2 tbsp of the butter; pour over flour mixture and whisk until smooth. Strain through fine-mesh sieve into clean bowl. Cover and refrigerate for 1 hour. *(Make-ahead: Refrigerate for up to 24 hours.)* Stir in chives.

Heat 8-inch (20 cm) crêpe pan or nonstick skillet over medium heat; brush with some of the remaining butter. Pour scant ¼ cup batter into centre of pan, swirling to coat; pour out excess. Cook, turning once, until golden, about 2 minutes. Transfer to plate; trim edge of crêpe even. Repeat with remaining batter and butter. *(Make-ahead: Layer between waxed paper and wrap in plastic wrap; refrigerate for up to 3 days or freeze in airtight container for up to 1 month.)*

CHICKEN FILLING: In bowl, pour boiling water over mushrooms; let stand until softened, about 20 minutes. Strain liquid into shallow saucepan or skillet. Remove mushroom stems; discard. Halve caps lengthwise; set aside.

Bring soaking liquid to simmer. Add chicken; cover and poach until no longer pink inside, about 20 minutes. Transfer chicken to plate; let cool.

Strain poaching liquid through cheesecloth-lined sieve to make 1½ cups. Discard skin and bones from chicken; shred chicken and set aside. *(Make-ahead: Refrigerate chicken and poaching liquid in separate airtight containers for up to 24 hours.)*

In small skillet, melt 1 tbsp of the butter over medium heat; cook mushrooms with one-third of the shallots for 3 minutes. Transfer to plate; set aside.

In saucepan, melt remaining butter over medium heat; cook remaining shallots, salt and pepper until softened, about 5 minutes. Sprinkle with flour; cook, whisking, for 1 minute.

Whisk in reserved poaching liquid; bring to boil. Reduce heat and simmer, whisking often, until smooth and thickened, about 5 minutes. Add cream and sherry. Stir in chicken and mushrooms; heat through. Spoon generous 2 tbsp of the filling onto half of each crêpe. Fold in half; fold in half again.

PER SERVING: about 321 cal, 15 g pro, 18 g total fat (9 g sat. fat), 23 g carb, 1 g fibre, 153 mg chol, 275 mg sodium, 253 mg potassium. % RDI: 8% calcium, 11% iron, 17% vit A, 2% vit C, 30% folate.

TOMATO AND CHEDDAR BAKED CHICKEN

MAKES 4 SERVINGS

A good tomato sauce needs time while cooking to develop flavour, so we use a jarred pasta sauce to speed things up. Serve with couscous to soak up all the yummy sauce, and Baby Kale Salad (below).

In large skillet, heat 1½ tsp of the oil over medium heat; cook onion and garlic, stirring occasionally, until fragrant and light golden, about 6 minutes.

Stir in zucchini and Italian herb seasoning; cook until zucchini is softened, about 4 minutes. Using slotted spoon, transfer to plate.

Sprinkle chicken with salt and pepper. Add remaining oil to skillet; heat over medium heat. Cook chicken until light golden, about 3 minutes per side.

Pour pasta sauce into greased 8-cup (2 L) casserole dish. Drain any liquid from zucchini mixture; stir mixture into sauce. Top with chicken. Bake in 400°F (200°C) oven until chicken is no longer pink inside, 10 to 12 minutes.

Sprinkle with Cheddar; broil until melted, about 2 minutes.

1 tbsp	olive oil
1	onion, chopped
2	cloves garlic, minced
2	zucchini, chopped
¼ tsp	Italian herb seasoning
450 g	boneless skinless chicken breasts, cut in 4 portions
pinch	each salt and pepper
1½ cups	pasta sauce
⅓ cup	shredded old Cheddar cheese

PER SERVING: about 303 cal, 31 g pro, 11 g total fat (4 g sat. fat), 19 g carb, 4 g fibre, 78 mg chol, 510 mg sodium, 886 mg potassium. % RDI: 10% calcium, 11% iron, 19% vit A, 13% vit C, 14% folate.

Baby Kale Salad

In large bowl, whisk together 2 tbsp extra-virgin olive oil, 2 tsp balsamic vinegar, 1 tsp each Dijon mustard and liquid honey, and pinch each salt and pepper. Add 6 cups packed baby kale; toss to coat.

MAKES 4 SERVINGS

CHICKEN AND SNOW PEA STIR-FRY

MAKES 4 SERVINGS

Why bother with takeout when you can whip up this stir-fry in about 20 minutes?
This one gets its unique flavour profile from smoked paprika, salty ham and a little bit
of earthy cumin. Steamed rice is a natural match.

In bowl, toss together chicken, 1 tbsp of the oil, garlic, paprika and cumin.

In wok or skillet, heat remaining oil over high heat; stir-fry cured ham for
10 seconds. Add chicken mixture; stir-fry until seared all over. Add snow peas;
stir-fry for 30 seconds.

Add broth, salt and sugar; stir-fry until snow peas are tender-crisp and
chicken is no longer pink inside, 2 to 3 minutes.

PER SERVING: about 216 cal, 25 g pro, 10 g total fat (2 g sat. fat), 7 g carb, 2 g fibre,
57 mg chol, 413 mg sodium, 493 mg potassium. % RDI: 4% calcium, 16% iron,
11% vit A, 65% vit C, 12% folate.

340 g	boneless skinless chicken breasts, thinly sliced
2 tbsp	extra-virgin olive oil
2	cloves garlic, thinly sliced
¾ tsp	smoked or sweet paprika
¼ tsp	ground cumin
55 g	cured ham (such as prosciutto or serrano), julienned
5 cups	snow peas (about 350 g), strings removed (see tip, left)
¼ cup	sodium-reduced chicken broth
¼ tsp	salt
pinch	granulated sugar

TIP FROM THE TEST KITCHEN
Snow peas and sugar snap peas both have
unpleasantly chewy strings that run along the
edges of the pods. As you trim off the tops of the
pods, pull these strings off.

KUNG PAO CHICKEN

MAKES 4 SERVINGS

This dish has a fun, spicy kick to it, but you can add as much or as little of the chili garlic sauce as you like. Serve with hot cooked rice or egg noodles.

1 tbsp	vegetable oil
450 g	boneless skinless chicken breasts, sliced
1	onion, sliced
225 g	green beans, trimmed
2 tsp	grated fresh ginger
2	cloves garlic, minced
2 tbsp	oyster sauce
2 tsp	cornstarch
2 tsp	chili garlic sauce or sambal oelek (see tip, below)
1	sweet red pepper, thinly sliced
½ cup	roasted unsalted peanuts

In large nonstick skillet or wok, heat 1 tsp of the oil over medium-high heat; stir-fry chicken until lightly browned, about 5 minutes. Transfer to plate.

Add remaining oil to pan; stir-fry onion, green beans, ginger and garlic until fragrant, about 2 minutes. Add ⅓ cup water; cover and cook over medium heat until no liquid remains and beans are slightly softened, about 3 minutes.

Whisk together oyster sauce, cornstarch, chili garlic sauce and ¼ cup water; set aside.

Add red pepper to pan; stir-fry over medium-high heat until tender-crisp, about 3 minutes. Pour in oyster sauce mixture. Return chicken to pan; stir-fry until chicken is no longer pink inside, about 2 minutes. Sprinkle with peanuts.

PER SERVING: about 303 cal, 32 g pro, 14 g total fat (2 g sat. fat), 15 g carb, 3 g fibre, 66 mg chol, 342 mg sodium, 614 mg potassium. % RDI: 5% calcium, 9% iron, 15% vit A, 93% vit C, 22% folate.

TIP FROM THE TEST KITCHEN

Chili garlic sauce offers both the spiciness of hot peppers and the fragrant zip of garlic. Not so much a fan of garlic? Use sambal oelek instead; it is more of a pure pepper purée, so you won't have quite as big a hit of garlic.

CHICKEN CURRY IN A HURRY

MAKES 4 SERVINGS

Mild curry paste gives this quick Indian dish mass appeal, but go ahead and use medium
or hot pastes if you like your curry a little spicier. Serve over rice or with warm naan.

Cook basmati rice according to package directions.

While rice is cooking, in large nonstick skillet, heat 1 tsp of the oil over
medium-high heat; sauté chicken, salt and pepper until golden, about
4 minutes. Transfer to plate.

Add remaining oil to pan; heat over medium-high heat. Sauté garlic and
ginger until fragrant, about 30 seconds. Stir in onion and curry paste; sauté
until onion is softened, about 3 minutes. Stir in cauliflower, broth, soy sauce
and ½ cup water; bring to boil. Reduce heat and simmer, stirring occasionally,
until cauliflower is just tender, about 5 minutes.

Whisk flour with ¼ cup water; stir into curry mixture along with chicken and
any accumulated juices, red pepper and peas. Bring to boil; reduce heat to
medium and simmer, stirring occasionally, until thickened and red pepper is
softened, about 4 minutes. Serve over rice.

PER SERVING: about 456 cal, 35 g pro, 10 g total fat (1 g sat. fat), 55 g carb,
5 g fibre, 65 mg chol, 678 mg sodium, 664 mg potassium. % RDI: 6% calcium,
14% iron, 12% vit A, 162% vit C, 35% folate.

1 cup	basmati rice, rinsed (see tip, below)
4 tsp	vegetable oil
450 g	boneless skinless chicken breasts, cut in ¾-inch (2 cm) pieces
pinch	each salt and pepper
6	cloves garlic, minced
4 tsp	minced fresh ginger
1	onion, chopped
4 tsp	mild Indian curry paste
4 cups	cauliflower florets (¾-inch/2 cm pieces)
2 cups	sodium-reduced chicken broth
1 tbsp	sodium-reduced soy sauce
3 tbsp	all-purpose flour
1	sweet red pepper, cut in ¾-inch (2 cm) pieces
½ cup	frozen peas

TIP FROM THE TEST KITCHEN
Rinse basmati rice before cooking to remove
any excess rice starch that's gotten loose in
the package. This helps the finished rice grains
stay separate and fluffy.

SWEET-AND-SOUR PINEAPPLE CHICKEN

MAKES 4 SERVINGS

People love this retro Chinese-restaurant dish, and for good reason: It's sticky, sweet-tart and so delish. With the exception of the chicken and a few fresh veggies, most of the ingredients are convenient pantry staples.

450 g	boneless skinless chicken breasts, cut in 1-inch (2.5 cm) cubes
1	egg white
2 tbsp	each cornstarch and all-purpose flour
¼ tsp	salt
¼ tsp	white or black pepper
⅓ cup	vegetable oil
⅓ cup	sodium-reduced chicken broth
3 tbsp	ketchup
1 tbsp	dry sherry (optional)
1 tbsp	sodium-reduced soy sauce
1 tbsp	unseasoned rice vinegar
2 tsp	minced fresh ginger
1 tsp	granulated sugar
1	onion, cut in ¾-inch (2 cm) cubes
1	each sweet red and green pepper, cut in ¾-inch (2 cm) pieces
1 cup	drained canned pineapple chunks

In bowl, combine chicken, egg white, cornstarch, flour, salt and pepper; let stand for 10 minutes.

In wok or large skillet, heat oil over medium-high heat; working in batches and reserving cornstarch mixture in bowl, stir-fry chicken until golden, about 3 minutes. Transfer to plate.

Add broth, ⅓ cup water, ketchup, sherry (if using), soy sauce, vinegar, ginger and sugar to reserved cornstarch mixture; whisk to combine. Set aside.

Drain all but 1 tbsp of the oil from wok. Stir-fry onion, and red and green peppers until tender-crisp, about 3 minutes.

Add chicken, pineapple and broth mixture to wok; stir-fry until thickened and chicken is coated with sauce, 2 to 3 minutes.

PER SERVING: about 273 cal, 29 g pro, 7 g total fat (1 g sat. fat), 25 g carb, 2 g fibre, 66 mg chol, 548 mg sodium. % RDI: 3% calcium, 9% iron, 13% vit A, 125% vit C, 12% folate.

CHICKEN TIKKA MASALA

MAKES 4 TO 6 SERVINGS

Chicken tikka is yet another dish many people go out for, but you won't want to once you've tried this homemade version. And while it tastes decadent, this curry is also calorie-smart, thanks to the addition of lean chicken breast.

MARINADE:

2 tbsp	Balkan-style plain yogurt
half	green or red finger hot pepper, seeded and minced
2	cloves garlic, minced
2 tsp	sweet paprika
2 tsp	grated fresh ginger
1 tsp	vegetable oil

CHICKEN TIKKA MASALA:

565 g	boneless skinless chicken breasts, cubed
1 tbsp	vegetable oil
1	onion, thinly sliced
2	cloves garlic, minced
1 tbsp	minced fresh ginger
2 tsp	garam masala
1 tsp	each sweet paprika and ground cumin
¾ tsp	salt
¼ tsp	turmeric
4 cups	diced plum tomatoes (about 8)
2 tbsp	tomato paste
⅓ cup	whipping cream (35%)
¼ cup	chopped fresh cilantro
1 tsp	lemon juice

MARINADE: In bowl, whisk together yogurt, hot pepper, garlic, paprika, ginger and oil until combined.

CHICKEN TIKKA MASALA: Add chicken to marinade; toss to coat. Let stand for 20 minutes. *(Make-ahead: Cover and refrigerate for up to 1 hour.)*

Scrape chicken mixture onto foil-lined rimmed baking sheet. Broil, turning once, until edges are lightly charred, 8 to 10 minutes.

Meanwhile, in large saucepan, heat oil over medium heat; cook onion, stirring occasionally, until softened, about 4 minutes. Add garlic and ginger; cook, stirring, for 1 minute.

Add garam masala, paprika, cumin, salt and turmeric; cook, stirring, for 1 minute. Stir in tomatoes, 1 cup water and tomato paste; bring to boil. Reduce heat and simmer, stirring occasionally and breaking up tomatoes with spoon, for 10 minutes.

Add chicken mixture; simmer, stirring occasionally, until chicken is no longer pink inside, about 2 minutes. Stir in cream and cilantro; cook for 1 minute. Stir in lemon juice.

PER EACH OF 6 SERVINGS: about 226 cal, 24 g pro, 10 g total fat (4 g sat. fat), 11 g carb, 3 g fibre, 73 mg chol, 363 mg sodium, 728 mg potassium. % RDI: 5% calcium, 13% iron, 22% vit A, 33% vit C, 9% folate.

CREAMY CHICKEN AND GREEN BEAN TOSS
MAKES 4 SERVINGS

A few dollops of light sour cream are all you need to add richness to this one-dish meal. Israeli couscous adds really nice texture, but you can substitute orzo pasta if you have it in your pantry.

In saucepan, cook Israeli couscous according to package directions; drain and set aside.

In nonstick skillet, heat oil over medium heat; cook onion and garlic until onion is translucent, about 2 minutes.

Sprinkle chicken with sumac, salt and pepper. Add to skillet and cook, stirring occasionally, until chicken is light golden and no longer pink inside, about 8 minutes.

Meanwhile, in large saucepan of boiling water, cook green beans until tender-crisp, about 4 minutes.

Whisk together sour cream, 1 tbsp of the lemon juice and the mustard; add to skillet along with couscous and green beans, stirring until combined. Sprinkle with remaining lemon juice and tarragon.

1 cup	Israeli (pearl) couscous
2 tsp	olive oil
1	small onion, sliced
2	cloves garlic, minced
225 g	boneless skinless chicken breast, cut in ¾-inch (2 cm) chunks
1½ tsp	sumac (see tip, below)
pinch	each salt and pepper
225 g	green beans, trimmed
¼ cup	light sour cream
2 tbsp	lemon juice
2 tsp	grainy mustard
2 tbsp	chopped fresh tarragon

PER SERVING: about 279 cal, 20 g pro, 5 g total fat (1 g sat. fat), 39 g carb, 3 g fibre, 35 mg chol, 126 mg sodium, 391 mg potassium. % RDI: 7% calcium, 9% iron, 4% vit A, 13% vit C, 18% folate.

TIP FROM THE TEST KITCHEN
You'll find sumac—a fruity, sweet-tart Middle Eastern spice—in specialty stores and select grocery stores. If you can't find sumac, use smoked paprika instead.

SWEET AND SPICY CASHEW CHICKEN

MAKES 4 SERVINGS

Cashews add buttery richness to this fantastic stir-fry.
Make sure to choose unsalted nuts, because there is already a
reasonable amount of sodium in the dish.

Whisk together broth, oyster sauce, sugar, cornstarch and vinegar; set aside.

In wok, heat 1 tbsp of the oil over medium-high heat; stir-fry chicken, salt and
pepper until golden, about 4 minutes. Transfer to plate.

Add remaining oil to wok; stir-fry red peppers, onions and chili paste for
3 minutes. Return chicken and any accumulated juices to wok; stir-fry until
chicken is no longer pink inside, about 1 minute.

Add cornstarch mixture; stir-fry for 1 minute. Add cashews and green onions;
stir-fry for 1 minute.

PER SERVING: about 352 cal, 30 g pro, 17 g total fat (2 g sat. fat), 22 g carb,
3 g fibre, 66 mg chol, 675 mg sodium, 643 mg potassium. % RDI: 4% calcium,
15% iron, 23% vit A, 168% vit C, 15% folate.

½ cup	sodium-reduced chicken broth
3 tbsp	oyster sauce (see tip, below)
1 tbsp	granulated sugar
1 tbsp	cornstarch
1 tbsp	white vinegar
2 tbsp	vegetable oil
450 g	boneless skinless chicken breasts, cut in chunks
¼ tsp	each salt and pepper
2	sweet red peppers, chopped
2	onions, chopped
1 tsp	Thai chili paste or sambal oelek
½ cup	roasted unsalted cashews
3	green onions, chopped

TIP FROM THE TEST KITCHEN
Oyster sauce is one of the classic Chinese sauces
that makes a terrific base for stir-fries. Unopened,
a bottle will keep for up to a year in your pantry.
Once opened, it will keep, refrigerated, for three
to six months.

CHICKEN KATSU

MAKES 4 SERVINGS

Similar to a schnitzel or a breaded cutlet, this easy Japanese dish is so good when hot, and it's also amazing cold in a sandwich. If you want it to be part of a complete dinner, serve it with steamed rice and a salad.

KATSU SAUCE:

½ cup	ketchup
3 tbsp	Worcestershire sauce
2 tbsp	granulated sugar
2 tbsp	sodium-reduced soy sauce
2 tbsp	mirin (see tip, below)
2 tsp	minced garlic
2 tsp	grated fresh ginger
¼ tsp	dry mustard

CHICKEN KATSU:

4	boneless skinless chicken breasts (about 600 g)
2 tsp	sodium-reduced soy sauce
1	clove garlic, minced
½ tsp	salt
¼ tsp	pepper
½ cup	all-purpose flour
2	eggs
1¾ cups	panko bread crumbs
	vegetable oil for cooking
	lemon slices

KATSU SAUCE: In small saucepan, bring ketchup, Worcestershire sauce, sugar, soy sauce, mirin, garlic, ginger and mustard to boil. Reduce heat and simmer until reduced to ¾ cup, about 10 minutes. Let cool. *(Make-ahead: Refrigerate in airtight container for up to 1 week.)*

CHICKEN KATSU: While sauce is cooling, sandwich chicken between plastic wrap; using meat mallet or heavy-bottomed saucepan, pound to ¼-inch (5 mm) thickness. In large bowl, combine soy sauce, garlic and half each of the salt and pepper; add chicken and toss to coat.

In shallow dish, whisk flour with remaining salt and pepper. In separate shallow dish, whisk eggs with 2 tbsp water. Pour panko into third shallow dish. Dip chicken into flour mixture, shaking off excess. Dip into egg mixture, letting excess drip back into dish. Dredge in panko, turning and patting to coat evenly.

In deep skillet or shallow Dutch oven, heat 1 inch (2.5 cm) oil over medium-high heat; working in batches, cook chicken until no longer pink inside, about 6 minutes.

Cut chicken crosswise into ¾-inch (2 cm) wide strips. Place on platter; drizzle with katsu sauce. Serve with lemon slices.

PER SERVING: about 634 cal, 43 g pro, 21 g total fat (3 g sat. fat), 67 g carb, 3 g fibre, 170 mg chol, 1,587 mg sodium, 802 mg potassium. % RDI: 12% calcium, 36% iron, 7% vit A, 23% vit C, 48% folate.

TIP FROM THE TEST KITCHEN
If you can't find mirin (Japanese sweet rice wine), substitute 1 tbsp each boiling water and granulated sugar.

SESAME CHICKEN
WITH FENNEL AND ORANGE SALAD
MAKES 4 SERVINGS

The classic pairing of orange and fennel gets a new twist with the addition of crunchy red cabbage and a creamy dressing. Make sure to add the oranges at the last minute—they'll give the salad a brighter flavour if they sit in the dressing only briefly.

SESAME CHICKEN: Place one chicken breast on cutting board. Holding knife blade parallel to board and starting at thickest long side, slice horizontally to make two thin cutlets. Repeat with remaining chicken; sprinkle with pepper and salt.

Place chicken on greased grill over medium heat; close lid and grill, turning once, until no longer pink inside, about 8 minutes.

Meanwhile, stir together sesame seeds, honey and lime juice; brush all over chicken. Cook, turning once, until glazed, about 1 minute.

FENNEL AND ORANGE SALAD: In large bowl, whisk together mayonnaise, vinegar, mustard and garlic. Add fennel, red cabbage and cilantro; toss to coat. Scrape onto platter; top with orange and chicken.

PER SERVING: about 280 cal, 26 g pro, 12 g total fat (2 g sat. fat), 19 g carb, 4 g fibre, 66 mg chol, 275 mg sodium, 733 mg potassium. % RDI: 8% calcium, 11% iron, 4% vit A, 90% vit C, 17% folate.

SESAME CHICKEN:

400 g	boneless skinless chicken breasts
¼ tsp	pepper
pinch	salt
1 tbsp	sesame seeds, toasted
1 tbsp	liquid honey
2 tsp	lime juice

FENNEL AND ORANGE SALAD:

⅓ cup	light mayonnaise
1 tbsp	cider vinegar
1 tbsp	grainy mustard
1	clove garlic, grated or pressed
1	bulb fennel, cored and thinly sliced
3 cups	finely shredded red cabbage
½ cup	chopped fresh cilantro
1	orange, peeled and cut in sections

CREAMY TARRAGON CHICKEN MEDALLIONS
MAKES 4 SERVINGS

Tangy mustard and sweet honey give this dish lots of flavour.
Serve with a glass of white wine to complement the creamy chicken.

CHICKEN MEDALLIONS:

450 g	chicken cutlets
¼ tsp	pepper
pinch	salt
2 tsp	olive oil
¾ cup	white wine
½ cup	sodium-reduced chicken broth
¼ cup	whipping cream (35%)
2 tbsp	chopped fresh tarragon (or 2 tsp dried)
1 tbsp	grainy mustard

HONEY MUSTARD VEGGIES:

2 tbsp	olive oil
2	sweet potatoes, peeled and cut in ½-inch (1 cm) cubes
255 g	green beans, cut diagonally in 1-inch (2.5 cm) pieces
1 tbsp	liquid honey
1 tbsp	grainy mustard

CHICKEN MEDALLIONS: Sandwich chicken between plastic wrap; using meat mallet or heavy-bottomed saucepan, pound chicken to 1-inch (2.5 cm) thickness. Sprinkle with pepper and salt.

In skillet, heat oil over medium-high heat; brown chicken, turning once, 6 to 8 minutes. Add wine and broth; cover and cook until chicken is no longer pink inside, about 5 minutes. Transfer to plate; keep warm.

Boil pan juices until reduced to ½ cup. Whisk in cream, tarragon and mustard; cook until thick enough to coat back of spoon, about 2 minutes. Serve over chicken.

HONEY MUSTARD VEGGIES: While chicken is browning, in nonstick skillet, heat oil over medium-high heat; cook sweet potatoes, stirring occasionally, until tender-crisp, about 10 minutes.

Add green beans; cook for 2 minutes. Add ¼ cup water; cover and cook until potatoes are fork-tender, about 2 minutes. Drain; toss with honey and mustard. Serve with chicken.

PER SERVING: about 401 cal, 30 g pro, 17 g total fat (5 g sat. fat), 30 g carb, 5 g fibre, 12 mg chol, 277 mg sodium, 737 mg potassium. % RDI: 8% calcium, 15% iron, 188% vit A, 35% vit C, 14% folate.

SESAME-CRUSTED CHICKEN

MAKES 4 SERVINGS

Instead of the typical bread crumbs, a mixture of flour and sesame seeds creates a crispy coating on these simple chicken cutlets. Serve this quick and easy dinner with sautéed greens, such as spinach or kale.

⅓ cup	sesame seeds
4 tsp	all-purpose flour
½ tsp	each salt and cayenne pepper
¼ tsp	black pepper
4	boneless skinless chicken breasts (about 600 g)
1 tbsp	each butter and olive oil

In blender or food processor, blend together sesame seeds, flour, salt, cayenne pepper and black pepper until fine yet some whole seeds remain. Transfer to shallow dish.

Sandwich chicken between plastic wrap; using meat mallet or heavy-bottomed saucepan, pound chicken to ½-inch (1 cm) thickness. Press into sesame seed mixture, turning and patting to coat.

In large skillet, heat butter and oil over medium heat; cook chicken, turning once, until no longer pink inside, 12 to 14 minutes.

PER SERVING: about 247 cal, 32 g pro, 12 g total fat (3 g sat. fat), 2 g carb, 1 g fibre, 85 mg chol, 241 mg sodium, 414 mg potassium. % RDI: 1% calcium, 8% iron, 4% vit A, 2% vit C, 5% folate.

TIP FROM THE TEST KITCHEN
Pounding chicken can get a little messy. To keep the work surface and tools clean, place the chicken between two layers of plastic wrap before you pound it. Or, use waxed paper if you prefer; it can break, so pound a little more gently.

GRILLED CHICKEN MOZZARELLA

MAKES 8 SERVINGS

If you like Caprese salad, you'll love this chicken. Topped with fragrant fresh basil, juicy tomato and melty mozzarella, it's a tasty summertime treat on the barbecue.

Place one chicken breast on cutting board. Holding knife blade parallel to board and starting at thickest long side, slice horizontally to make two thin cutlets. Repeat with remaining chicken. If chicken is uneven, sandwich between plastic wrap; using meat mallet or heavy-bottomed saucepan, pound to even thickness.

In bowl, whisk together oil, garlic, lemon juice, oregano, salt and pepper; remove one-quarter and set aside. Add chicken to remaining oil mixture, turning to coat; let stand for 10 minutes.

Discarding marinade, place chicken and tomato on greased grill over medium-high heat; close lid and grill for 4 minutes. Turn chicken and tomato. Top chicken with mozzarella; cook until chicken is no longer pink inside and tomato is softened and slightly charred, about 2 minutes.

To serve, top each chicken breast with tomato; drizzle with reserved oil mixture. Top with basil leaf.

4	large boneless skinless chicken breasts (about 900 g)
3 tbsp	olive oil
2	cloves garlic, minced
1 tbsp	lemon juice
¾ tsp	dried oregano
½ tsp	each salt and pepper
8	thick slices tomato
8	slices mozzarella cheese (see tip, below)
8	fresh basil leaves

PER SERVING: about 221 cal, 31 g pro, 10 g total fat (4 g sat. fat), 2 g carb, trace fibre, 86 mg chol, 220 mg sodium, 402 mg potassium. % RDI: 12% calcium, 4% iron, 7% vit A, 7% vit C, 4% folate.

TIP FROM THE TEST KITCHEN

While snow white-balls of fresh mozzarella are the best choice for salads, here you should purchase one of the yellower balls of pizza-style mozzarella. It has a drier texture than fresh and will melt nicely over the chicken.

CHICKEN MILANESE
WITH CELERY ROOT PURÉE
MAKES 4 SERVINGS

This dish is low-fuss because you can bread and refrigerate the chicken up to eight hours ahead. If you can't find watercress, arugula makes an equally appealing salad topper for the meal.

CHICKEN MILANESE: Sprinkle chicken with salt and pepper. Place flour in shallow dish. In separate shallow dish, whisk egg with mustard. Place panko in third shallow dish. Dip chicken into flour, shaking off excess; dip into egg mixture, letting excess drip back into dish. Dredge in panko, turning and patting to coat. Place on waxed paper–lined rimmed baking sheet; refrigerate for 10 minutes. *(Make-ahead: Cover and refrigerate for up to 8 hours.)*

In large nonstick skillet, heat oil over medium heat; cook chicken, turning once, until no longer pink inside, 8 to 10 minutes.

CELERY ROOT PURÉE: While chicken is chilling, in large pot of boiling salted water, cook celery root, potato and garlic until tender, 12 to 15 minutes. Drain; return to pot. Dry over low heat, shaking pan often, for 1 minute. Transfer to food processor; add Gruyère, cream and salt. Purée until smooth.

WATERCRESS SALAD: In bowl, whisk oil with lemon juice; toss with watercress. Serve over chicken and celery root purée.

PER SERVING: about 492 cal, 36 g pro, 20 g total fat (5 g sat. fat), 42 g carb, 5 g fibre, 124 mg chol, 1,459 mg sodium, 1,088 mg potassium. % RDI: 20% calcium, 20% iron, 12% vit A, 47% vit C, 16% folate.

CHICKEN MILANESE:

450 g	chicken cutlets
½ tsp	each salt and pepper
¼ cup	all-purpose flour
1	egg
1 tbsp	grainy mustard
1 cup	panko bread crumbs
2 tbsp	vegetable oil

CELERY ROOT PURÉE:

1	celery root (about 675 g), peeled and cut in 1-inch (2.5 cm) chunks
1	russet potato (about 340 g), peeled and cut in 1-inch (2.5 cm) chunks
2	cloves garlic, smashed
⅓ cup	shredded Gruyère cheese
¼ cup	10% cream
¼ tsp	salt

WATERCRESS SALAD:

1½ tbsp	extra-virgin olive oil
1 tbsp	lemon juice
2 cups	lightly packed watercress leaves

TIP FROM THE TEST KITCHEN
We boil our pasta and potatoes (and some other vegetables, like celery root, above) in salted water to brighten their flavours. When we call for "salted water," use 2 tbsp salt and 5 quarts (20 cups) water for 450 g potatoes or pasta. When we call for "lightly salted water," reduce the salt to 1 tbsp. Of course, if you're worried about your sodium intake, you can reduce that amount even more, but the taste of the finished dish will change.

CRISPY ROASTED PISTACHIO CHICKEN

MAKES 4 SERVINGS

Pistachios and orange are a gorgeous combination, tucked under golden crispy chicken skin.
The same flavours go into a vinaigrette for accompanying peppery dandelion greens.

⅔ cup	shelled salted pistachios
1 tbsp	chopped fresh parsley
1 tbsp	chopped fresh thyme (or 1 tsp dried)
1½ tsp	grated orange zest
2 tbsp	orange juice
½ cup	extra-virgin olive oil
1	clove garlic, minced
½ tsp	pepper
pinch	salt
4	chicken breast supremes (see tip, below)
4 cups	torn dandelion greens or whole baby arugula
	orange slices

In food processor, pulse together pistachios, parsley, thyme and half each of the orange zest and orange juice to make coarse paste. With motor running, drizzle in half of the oil. Stir in garlic, pepper and salt. Scoop all but 2 tbsp into small bowl for stuffing. Place remaining paste in separate bowl for vinaigrette; whisk in remaining orange zest, orange juice and oil. Set aside.

Using fingers, loosen chicken skin along curved side of each breast to form pocket; spread stuffing under skin. *(Make-ahead: Place on plate; cover chicken and vinaigrette separately and refrigerate for up to 24 hours.)*

Place chicken, skin side up, on foil-lined rimmed baking sheet. Roast in 400°F (200°C) oven until golden and no longer pink inside, about 30 minutes. Broil, watching carefully to avoid scorching, until skin is crisp and deep golden brown, about 2 minutes.

Divide dandelion greens among plates; drizzle with vinaigrette. Top with chicken; garnish with orange slices.

PER SERVING (WITHOUT SKIN): about 571 cal, 33 g pro, 44 g total fat (7 g sat. fat), 14 g carb, 4 g fibre, 87 mg chol, 270 mg sodium. % RDI: 12% calcium, 23% iron, 81% vit A, 60% vit C, 18% folate.

TIP FROM THE TEST KITCHEN

Chicken breast supremes have the skin attached and are boneless except for the attached first wing bone, which adds more flavour. They are attractive on the plate, so they are often served in restaurants. Buy them in butcher shops, or use boneless skin-on chicken breasts.

EASY CHICKEN CORDON BLEU
WITH ROASTED SWEET POTATO SALAD

MAKES 4 SERVINGS

We've cut the prep and cooking time of this retro classic in half. Our secret?
Skip the stuffing step, while retaining all the same delicious flavours.

SWEET POTATO SALAD: Toss sweet potato with 1 tbsp of the oil; spread on lightly greased rimmed baking sheet. Roast in 400°F (200°C) oven, turning occasionally, until tender and golden, about 20 minutes.

In bowl, whisk together remaining oil, lime juice, honey, salt and pepper. Stir in sweet potato and spinach.

CHICKEN CORDON BLEU: While sweet potatoes are roasting, place one chicken breast on cutting board. Holding knife blade parallel to board and starting at thickest long side, slice horizontally to make two thin cutlets. Repeat with remaining chicken.

Sprinkle chicken with salt and pepper. Mix mustard with thyme; brush over tops of chicken. Wrap each cutlet with one slice of ham. Arrange, seam side down, on lightly greased rimmed baking sheet. Bake in 400°F (200°C) oven until chicken is no longer pink inside, about 18 minutes. Sprinkle with Swiss; bake until melted, about 1 minute. Serve with salad.

PER SERVING: about 466 cal, 35 g pro, 20 g total fat (5 g sat. fat), 38 g carb, 6 g fibre, 82 mg chol, 314 mg sodium, 1,293 mg potassium. % RDI: 19% calcium, 19% iron, 339% vit A, 68% vit C, 33% folate.

SWEET POTATO SALAD:

1	large sweet potato (about 640 g), cut in ½-inch (1 cm) cubes
¼ cup	extra-virgin olive oil
2 tbsp	lime juice
1 tsp	liquid honey
pinch	each salt and pepper
4 cups	baby spinach

CHICKEN CORDON BLEU:

2	boneless skinless chicken breasts (about 450 g total)
pinch	each salt and pepper
4 tsp	Dijon mustard
2 tsp	chopped fresh thyme
2	slices Black Forest ham, halved
½ cup	shredded Swiss cheese

CRISPY HERBED CHICKEN
WITH APPLE SLAW

MAKES 4 SERVINGS

If you love schnitzel, you're guaranteed to enjoy this tasty variation.
We skip the hassle of dipping the chicken into flour, then egg during the breading stage
and just brush it with flavourful herbed mustard before pressing it into the panko.

CRISPY HERBED CHICKEN:

2	boneless skinless chicken breasts (about 450 g total)
pinch	each salt and pepper
⅔ cup	panko bread crumbs
½ tsp	grated lemon zest
3 tbsp	minced fresh tarragon
4 tsp	Dijon mustard
1 tsp	lemon juice
2 tbsp	olive oil

APPLE SLAW:

3 tbsp	extra-virgin olive oil
1 tbsp	lemon juice
1 tsp	liquid honey
pinch	each salt and pepper
4 cups	coleslaw mix (see tip, below)
1	Empire apple, cut in ½-inch (1 cm) chunks

CRISPY HERBED CHICKEN: Place one chicken breast on cutting board. Holding knife blade parallel to board and starting at thickest long side, slice horizontally to make two thin cutlets. Repeat with remaining chicken. Sandwich chicken between plastic wrap; using meat mallet or heavy-bottomed saucepan, pound to ½-inch (1 cm) thickness. Sprinkle with salt and pepper.

In shallow dish, mix panko with lemon zest. Stir together tarragon, mustard and lemon juice; spread all over chicken. Press all sides of chicken firmly into panko mixture to adhere.

In nonstick skillet, heat oil over medium-high heat; working in batches, cook chicken, turning once, until golden, crispy and no longer pink inside, about 6 minutes.

APPLE SLAW: While chicken is cooking, in bowl, whisk together oil, lemon juice, honey, salt and pepper; stir in coleslaw mix and apple until coated. Serve with chicken.

PER SERVING: about 355 cal, 28 g pro, 19 g total fat (3 g sat. fat), 19 g carb, 3 g fibre, 65 mg chol, 155 mg sodium, 384 mg potassium. % RDI: 4% calcium, 9% iron, 11% vit A, 35% vit C, 14% folate.

TIP FROM THE TEST KITCHEN
Coleslaw mix is a lifesaver on busy nights. Here, it's the base for a simple slaw, but you can add it to stir-fries, as well as hearty soups and stews. Or, use up any leftovers as a garnish on tacos or a crunchy accent in wraps.

PAN-FRIED CHICKEN
WITH GLAZED HERBED CARROTS

MAKES 4 SERVINGS

Adding a little sugar to sliced carrots helps bring out their inherent sweetness. Tossed with almonds and herbs, they are perfect for dressing up simple pan-fried chicken. Serve with Baby Spinach Salad (below) or steamed green vegetables.

2 tsp	olive oil
1	shallot, finely chopped
2	cloves garlic, chopped
pinch	cinnamon
3	large carrots (about 250 g total), cut in ⅛-inch (3 mm) slices
¼ tsp	each salt and pepper
⅔ cup	sodium-reduced chicken broth
¼ cup	chopped fresh parsley
2 tbsp	chopped fresh tarragon
1 tbsp	packed brown sugar
1 tbsp	butter
1 tbsp	lemon juice
2	large boneless skinless chicken breasts (about 450 g total)
¼ cup	slivered almonds, toasted

In skillet, heat 1 tsp of the oil over medium heat; cook shallot, garlic and cinnamon until shallot is softened, about 2 minutes. Add carrots and a pinch each of the salt and pepper; cook until carrots start to soften, about 2 minutes. Add broth; cook until almost no liquid remains, about 10 minutes.

Add parsley, tarragon, brown sugar and butter; cook, stirring, until carrots are coated, about 2 minutes. Stir in lemon juice. Transfer to platter; keep warm.

Meanwhile, place one chicken breast on cutting board. Holding knife blade parallel to board and starting at thickest long side, slice horizontally to make two thin cutlets. Repeat with remaining chicken. Sprinkle both sides with remaining salt and pepper.

In large nonstick skillet, heat remaining oil over medium heat; cook chicken, turning once, until no longer pink inside, about 8 minutes.

Sprinkle almonds over carrots. Serve with chicken.

PER SERVING: about 254 cal, 29 g pro, 11 g total fat (3 g sat. fat), 11 g carb, 3 g fibre, 73 mg chol, 366 mg sodium, 567 mg potassium. % RDI: 5% calcium, 10% iron, 105% vit A, 15% vit C, 9% folate.

Baby Spinach Salad

In large bowl, whisk together 2 tbsp extra-virgin olive oil, 2 tsp cider vinegar, ½ tsp each Dijon mustard and liquid honey, and pinch each salt and pepper. Add 6 cups packed fresh baby spinach; toss to coat.
MAKES 4 SERVINGS

LIME-GRILLED CHICKEN BREASTS
WITH AVOCADO SALSA

MAKES 4 SERVINGS

Cutting and pounding chicken breasts into thin cutlets means they cook through in a wink on the barbecue. Lime juice helps keep them tender and juicy, and adds its bright, fresh flavour to the easy avocado and tomato salsa.

Place one chicken breast on cutting board. Holding knife blade parallel to board and starting at thickest long side, slice horizontally to make two thin cutlets. Repeat with remaining chicken. Sandwich chicken between plastic wrap; using meat mallet or heavy-bottomed saucepan, pound to even thickness.

In glass bowl, combine ¼ cup of the lime juice, 3 tbsp of the cilantro, 2 tbsp of the oil, garlic, ½ tsp of the salt and a pinch of the pepper. Add chicken, turning to coat. Cover and refrigerate for 30 minutes.

Meanwhile, combine tomatoes, red onion, jalapeños, vinegar and remaining lime juice, cilantro, oil, salt and pepper. Peel and cut avocado into large dice; gently toss with tomato mixture, without breaking up. Set aside.

Place chicken on greased grill over medium-high heat; close lid and grill until no longer pink inside, about 3 minutes per side. Serve topped with salsa and lime wedges.

PER SERVING: about 380 cal, 33 g pro, 23 g total fat (4 g sat. fat), 12 g carb, 5 g fibre, 79 mg chol, 655 mg sodium, 851 mg potassium. % RDI: 3% calcium, 9% iron, 8% vit A, 32% vit C, 31% folate.

4	boneless skinless chicken breasts (about 600 g)
⅓ cup	lime juice
¼ cup	fresh cilantro leaves, minced
¼ cup	extra-virgin olive oil
2	cloves garlic
1 tsp	salt
¼ tsp	pepper
2	tomatoes, chopped
half	red onion, finely chopped
2	jalapeño peppers, seeded and finely chopped
1 tbsp	red wine vinegar
1	ripe avocado (see tip, below)
	lime wedges

TIP FROM THE TEST KITCHEN
A perfectly ripe avocado should be firm but yield to your thumb when pressed gently. If you buy an avocado that's underripe, you can help speed nature along: Place it in a paper bag with an apple for a day or two. The ethylene gas the apple gives off will encourage the avocado to ripen. Once it's ready, transfer the avocado to the fridge, where it will keep for a couple of days at its peak ripeness.

CHICKEN PARMIGIANA
WITH SPAGHETTI
MAKES 4 SERVINGS

A super-quick tomato sauce made with bottled passata does double duty in this restaurant-style favourite, acting as a sauce for both the chicken and the pasta.

In saucepan, heat 1 tsp of the oil over medium heat; cook garlic, stirring, for 1 minute. Add carrots, onion and Italian herb seasoning; cook, stirring occasionally, until vegetables are softened, about 8 minutes.

Stir in strained tomatoes, red pepper and a pinch each of the salt and pepper; bring to boil. Reduce heat, partially cover and simmer until sauce is slightly thickened, about 5 minutes.

Meanwhile, place one chicken breast on cutting board. Holding knife blade parallel to board and starting at thickest long side, slice horizontally to make two thin cutlets. Repeat with remaining chicken. Sprinkle both sides with remaining salt and pepper.

In large nonstick skillet, heat remaining oil over medium-high heat; working in batches, cook chicken, turning once, until golden, about 6 minutes per batch. Transfer to foil-lined rimmed baking sheet.

Spoon 2 tbsp of the tomato sauce over each chicken cutlet, spreading evenly; sprinkle with Parmesan. Bake in 400°F (200°C) oven until Parmesan is melted and chicken is no longer pink inside, about 10 minutes.

While chicken is baking, in saucepan of boiling lightly salted water, cook pasta according to package instructions until al dente. Drain and toss with remaining tomato sauce to coat.

Stir in basil. Serve with chicken.

2 tsp	olive oil
2	cloves garlic, minced
2	carrots, finely diced
1	small onion, finely diced
1 tsp	Italian herb seasoning
1	bottle (660 mL) strained tomatoes (passata)
half	sweet red pepper, diced
¼ tsp	each salt and pepper
450 g	boneless skinless chicken breasts
½ cup	grated Parmesan cheese
350 g	spaghetti
3 tbsp	chopped fresh basil

PER SERVING: about 603 cal, 44 g pro, 10 g total fat (3 g sat. fat), 80 g carb, 4 g fibre, 76 mg chol, 1,027 mg sodium, 898 mg potassium. % RDI: 18% calcium, 48% iron, 71% vit A, 52% vit C, 100% folate.

ITALIAN-STYLE CHICKEN BREASTS

MAKES 4 SERVINGS

Simple, affordable and delicious: What more could you want from a weeknight dinner?
When paired with tasty grilled eggplant and a green salad, this is a light, satisfying meal.

4	boneless skinless chicken breasts (about 600 g)
3 tbsp	extra-virgin olive oil
2 tbsp	chopped fresh parsley
2 tbsp	lemon juice
½ tsp	Italian herb seasoning
3	cloves garlic, minced
½ tsp	salt
¼ tsp	pepper

Place one chicken breast on cutting board. Holding knife blade parallel to board and starting at thickest long side, slice horizontally to make two thin cutlets. Repeat with remaining chicken. Sandwich chicken between plastic wrap; using meat mallet or heavy-bottomed saucepan, pound to even thickness.

In bowl, whisk together oil, parsley, lemon juice, Italian herb seasoning, garlic, salt and pepper; add chicken, turning to coat. Cover and let stand for 15 minutes.

Place chicken on greased grill over medium-high heat; brush with remaining marinade. Close lid and grill, turning once, until no longer pink inside, 6 to 8 minutes.

PER SERVING: about 243 cal, 31 g pro, 12 g total fat (2 g sat. fat), 2 g carb, trace fibre, 79 mg chol, 359 mg sodium. % RDI: 1% calcium, 6% iron, 2% vit A, 7% vit C, 3% folate.

Grilled Eggplant

Cut 1 eggplant into ½-inch (1 cm) thick slices; sprinkle with ½ tsp salt. Let stand in colander until moisture seeps out, about 10 minutes. Pat dry with paper towel. Whisk together ¼ cup extra-virgin olive oil; 2 tsp balsamic vinegar; ½ tsp dried oregano; and pinch each salt and pepper. Brush half over eggplant. Place on greased grill over medium heat; close lid and grill, turning once and brushing with remaining oil mixture, until tender, about 10 minutes.
MAKES 4 SERVINGS

THE ULTIMATE CHICKEN POT PIE

MAKES 12 SERVINGS

This classic creamy casserole packs buttery herb-flecked
pastry and rich, savoury chicken in every delightful bite.

FILLING:

3 tbsp	unsalted butter
1.125 kg	boneless skinless chicken breasts or thighs, cubed
1	pkg (227 g) button mushrooms, quartered
10	shallots, halved lengthwise and thinly sliced crosswise (about 2 cups)
5	sprigs fresh thyme
1	bay leaf
½ cup	dry white wine
1	rutabaga (about 915 g), peeled and cut in ¾-inch (2 cm) chunks
375 g	mini red-skinned potatoes, quartered
2	carrots, cut in ½-inch (1 cm) chunks
1 tsp	salt
½ tsp	pepper
3 cups	sodium-reduced chicken broth
½ cup	all-purpose flour
¾ cup	frozen peas
¼ cup	chopped fresh parsley
¼ cup	whipping cream (35%)
1 tbsp	lemon juice

TOPPING:

	Flaky Butter Herb Pastry (opposite)
1	egg yolk

FILLING: In Dutch oven or heavy-bottomed saucepan, melt 2 tbsp of the butter over medium-high heat; working in batches, sauté chicken until browned, 4 to 5 minutes per batch. Transfer to bowl.

In same Dutch oven, melt remaining butter over medium heat; cook mushrooms, shallots, thyme and bay leaf, stirring occasionally, until softened and golden, about 6 minutes. Add wine; cook, stirring, until no liquid remains, about 2 minutes.

Stir in rutabaga, potatoes, carrots, salt and pepper; cook, stirring occasionally, for 5 minutes. Stir in broth, chicken and any juices; bring to boil. Reduce heat, cover and simmer until vegetables are tender-crisp, about 12 minutes.

Whisk flour with ½ cup water; stir into chicken mixture. Bring to boil; reduce heat and simmer, stirring occasionally, until liquid is thickened and vegetables are tender, 6 minutes. Stir in peas, parsley and cream; cook for 1 minute. Remove from heat; stir in lemon juice. Discard thyme and bay leaf.

Scrape mixture into 13- x 9-inch (3 L) baking dish; let cool for 30 minutes. *(Make-ahead: Refrigerate until cold; cover and refrigerate for up to 24 hours. Increase baking time by 15 to 20 minutes.)*

TOPPING: While filling is cooling, on floured work surface, roll out pastry to 15- x 11-inch (38 x 28 cm) rectangle (large enough to fit top of baking dish and leave 1-inch/2.5 cm overhang). Transfer to rimless baking sheet; refrigerate until firm, about 30 minutes.

Arrange pastry over top of baking dish, pulling taut over rim. Whisk egg yolk with 1 tsp water; brush over pastry. Using sharp knife, cut three or four steam vents in top. Bake on rimmed baking sheet in 425°F (220°C) oven until pastry is puffed and golden, about 35 minutes. Let cool for 20 minutes before serving.

PER SERVING: about 465 cal, 25 g pro, 26 g total fat (14 g sat. fat), 33 g carb, 4 g fibre, 149 mg chol, 661 mg sodium, 745 mg potassium. % RDI: 7% calcium, 25% iron, 60% vit A, 37% vit C, 33% folate.

Flaky Butter Herb Pastry

Cut 1 cup cold butter into cubes. In food processor, pulse 1⅔ cups all-purpose flour with ½ tsp salt. Add ¼ cup of the butter; pulse until combined. Add remaining butter; pulse until mixture forms pea-size pieces, about five times. Drizzle ⅓ cup ice water evenly over mixture (not through feed tube). Pulse six to eight times, until loose ragged dough forms (do not let mixture form ball). Transfer to floured 20-inch (50 cm) length of waxed paper; press dough into rectangle. Dust with flour; top with another 20-inch (50 cm) length of waxed paper. Roll out to 15- x 12-inch (38 x 30 cm) rectangle; remove top sheet of waxed paper. Sprinkle with 2 tbsp chopped fresh parsley.

Using bottom sheet of waxed paper to lift, fold one long edge over one-third of pastry; fold opposite long edge over top (pastry will form 15- x 4-inch/38 x 10 cm rectangle). Starting from one short end, roll up tightly into cylinder; flatten into 5-inch (12 cm) square. Wrap in plastic wrap; refrigerate until firm, about 1 hour. *(Make-ahead: Refrigerate for up to 5 days or freeze in airtight container for up to 2 weeks.)*

PARMESAN CHICKEN FINGERS

MAKES 4 SERVINGS

Baking is a healthier, safer alternative to frying chicken fingers in hot oil, which may spatter. Using panko ensures you'll have a super-crispy exterior, even without frying.

½ cup	all-purpose flour
2	eggs
1 cup	panko bread crumbs
½ cup	grated Parmesan cheese
450 g	chicken tenders (see tip, below)
¼ tsp	each salt and pepper

Pour flour into shallow dish. In bowl, beat eggs. In another shallow dish, stir panko with Parmesan.

Sprinkle chicken with salt and pepper. One at a time, dip chicken tenders into flour, shaking off excess; dip into eggs, letting excess drip back into bowl. Dredge in panko mixture, pressing to adhere.

Bake on parchment paper–lined rimmed baking sheet in 425°F (220°C) oven until light golden and no longer pink inside, about 20 minutes.

PER SERVING: about 221 cal, 32 g pro, 6 g total fat (3 g sat. fat), 8 g carb, trace fibre, 124 mg chol, 369 mg sodium, 362 mg potassium. % RDI: 10% calcium, 9% iron, 4% vit A, 2% vit C, 9% folate.

TIP FROM THE TEST KITCHEN
A chicken tender is the little filet that separates easily from the rest of the breast. You'll find packages of them in the poultry area of the meat counter. They are the perfect ready-to-use size for chicken fingers—no cutting required.

CRISPY ALMOND CHICKEN

MAKES 4 SERVINGS

Ground almonds give this dish a nice, crunchy texture with a little bit of nutty flavour. Serve with a simple salad or steamed veggies.

Pour flour into shallow dish. In bowl, beat eggs. In another shallow dish, stir almonds with Italian herb seasoning.

Sprinkle chicken with salt and pepper. One at a time, dip chicken tenders into flour, shaking off excess; dip into eggs, letting excess drip back into bowl. Dredge in almond mixture, pressing to adhere.

Arrange on parchment paper–lined rimmed baking sheet; drizzle with oil. Bake in 400°F (200°C) oven, turning once, until light golden and no longer pink inside, 15 to 18 minutes.

PER SERVING: about 272 cal, 31 g pro, 13 g total fat (2 g sat. fat), 8 g carb, 2 g fibre, 102 mg chol, 219 mg sodium, 458 mg potassium. % RDI: 5% calcium, 12% iron, 3% vit A, 2% vit C, 10% folate.

¼ cup	all-purpose flour
1	egg
¾ cup	ground almonds (see tip, below)
1 tsp	Italian herb seasoning
450 g	chicken tenders (see tip, opposite)
¼ tsp	salt and pepper
2 tsp	vegetable oil

TIP FROM THE TEST KITCHEN
You can buy ground almonds, but it's easy and economical to grind them yourself at home. Spoon blanched almonds into food processor and pulse them until they are finely ground but not pasty. If you go too fast or too far, you'll wind up with almond butter, so watch carefully as you pulse.

**ROAST CHICKEN
WITH CHORIZO**
(PAGE 140)

CHAPTER 3

THIGHS, DRUMSTICKS & LEGS

GRILLED ROSEMARY-MUSTARD CHICKEN

MAKES 4 SERVINGS

Combining Dijon and grainy mustards adds a rich, slightly spicy flavour and pleasant crunchy finish to the glaze. Serve with steamed rice and Green Beans Amandine (below).

1½ tsp	grainy mustard
1½ tsp	Dijon mustard
1½ tsp	lemon juice
1 tsp	liquid honey
¾ tsp	chopped fresh rosemary
450 g	boneless skinless chicken thighs
pinch	each salt and pepper

Whisk together grainy mustard, Dijon mustard, lemon juice, honey and rosemary; set aside.

Sprinkle chicken with salt and pepper. Place on greased grill over medium-high heat; close lid and grill, turning once, for 8 minutes. Brush with mustard mixture; cook, turning once, until juices run clear when chicken is pierced, about 2 minutes. Let stand for 5 minutes before serving.

PER SERVING: about 154 cal, 22 g pro, 6 g total fat (2 g sat. fat), 2 g carb, 0 g fibre, 94 mg chol, 146 mg sodium, 270 mg potassium. % RDI: 2% calcium, 9% iron, 2% vit A, 5% vit C, 3% folate.

Green Beans Amandine

Crush ⅔ cup sliced almonds. In dry skillet, toast almonds over medium-high heat just until golden, about 4 minutes. Remove and set aside. Add ¾ cup water, 2 tbsp butter and ¼ tsp salt to skillet; bring to boil. Add 450 g green beans, trimmed; reduce heat, cover and simmer until bright green, about 3 minutes. Uncover and simmer, turning beans often, until tender and no liquid remains, about 8 minutes. Toss with almonds.

MAKES 4 TO 6 SERVINGS

STICKY GLAZED GRILLED CHICKEN
WITH CUCUMBER SALAD

MAKES 4 SERVINGS

Sweet from the honey and tart from the lime juice, this glaze is so tasty on simple chicken thighs. Serve with cold cooked soba noodles or steamed brown rice.

CUCUMBER SALAD:

⅓ cup	unseasoned rice vinegar
2 tsp	liquid honey
1 tsp	sesame oil
¼ tsp	each hot pepper flakes and salt
1	English cucumber, thinly sliced diagonally
2	green onions, thinly sliced

GLAZED GRILLED CHICKEN:

¼ cup	liquid honey
2 tbsp	lime juice
2 tbsp	sodium-reduced tamari (see tip, below)
1 tbsp	sesame oil
2	cloves garlic, minced
2 tsp	grated fresh ginger
8	boneless skinless chicken thighs (about 675 g)
1 tbsp	sesame seeds, toasted

CUCUMBER SALAD: In large bowl, whisk together vinegar, honey, sesame oil, hot pepper flakes and salt. Add cucumber and toss until coated; set aside in refrigerator.

GLAZED GRILLED CHICKEN: In large bowl, whisk together honey, lime juice, tamari, sesame oil, garlic and ginger; remove 3 tbsp and set aside. Add chicken to bowl, turning to coat; let stand for 10 minutes.

Place chicken on greased grill over medium heat; close lid and grill, turning once and brushing with reserved marinade in final 2 minutes, until juices run clear when chicken is pierced, about 10 minutes.

Stir green onions into cucumber salad. Sprinkle sesame seeds over salad and chicken.

PER SERVING: about 313 cal, 27 g pro, 12 g total fat (3 g sat. fat), 24 g carb, 1 g fibre, 95 mg chol, 531 mg sodium, 438 mg potassium. % RDI: 4% calcium, 16% iron, 4% vit A, 8% vit C, 10% folate.

TIP FROM THE TEST KITCHEN
Tamari is similar to soy sauce but has a mellower flavour. It's also gluten-free in many cases, but always check the label to be sure. It comes in regular and sodium-reduced versions, like soy sauce.

CHICKEN PAPRIKASH
MAKES 4 SERVINGS

Traditionally, this Hungarian dish is simmered for quite a while—but this recipe uses boneless chicken thighs to cut down on time without sacrificing flavour so you can enjoy paprikash on weeknights.

In large nonstick skillet, heat 1 tbsp of the oil over medium-high heat; brown chicken, 4 to 5 minutes. Using slotted spoon, transfer chicken to plate.

Drain fat from pan; add remaining oil and heat over medium heat. Cook onion, garlic, mushrooms and paprika, stirring often, until onion is softened, 1 to 2 minutes.

Add flour and tomato paste; cook, stirring, for 1 minute. Gradually stir in broth and bring to boil; reduce heat and simmer until thickened, about 1 minute. Return chicken to pan; add lemon juice, salt and pepper.

Meanwhile, in saucepan of boiling salted water, cook noodles according to package directions. Drain noodles and serve topped with chicken mixture. Garnish with sour cream and parsley.

PER SERVING: about 676 cal, 40 g pro, 20 g total fat (4 g sat. fat), 84 g carb, 7 g fibre, 176 mg chol, 1,159 mg sodium, 873 mg potassium. % RDI: 13% calcium, 52% iron, 23% vit A, 17% vit C, 135% folate.

2 tbsp	olive oil
450 g	boneless skinless chicken thighs, quartered
1	onion, thinly sliced
3	cloves garlic, minced
2½ cups	sliced trimmed cremini mushrooms
2 tbsp	sweet paprika
3 tbsp	all-purpose flour
2 tbsp	tomato paste
2 cups	sodium-reduced chicken broth
1 tsp	lemon juice
½ tsp	salt
pinch	pepper
1	pkg (375 g) broad egg noodles
½ cup	5% sour cream
2 tbsp	chopped fresh parsley

PEPPER-BRAISED CHICKEN THIGHS

MAKES 4 TO 6 SERVINGS

A bit of chili powder and some balsamic vinegar give this chicken great flavour. And it's so easy—because you're using thighs plus a whole bunch of pantry staples, this dish is a relatively inexpensive option you can make again and again.

Sprinkle chicken with ¼ tsp each of the salt and pepper. In large shallow Dutch oven, heat oil over medium-high heat; working in batches, brown chicken, 4 to 5 minutes per batch. Using slotted spoon, transfer to plate.

Add onion, garlic and green peppers to pan; cook over medium heat, stirring occasionally, until softened, about 5 minutes.

Stir in chili powder, thyme and remaining salt and pepper. Add ¼ cup water and balsamic vinegar; cook, scraping up browned bits from bottom of pan, until almost no liquid remains, about 1 minute.

Add tomatoes, breaking up with spoon. Return chicken and any accumulated juices to pan, spooning sauce over top; bring to boil. Reduce heat, cover and simmer, stirring occasionally, until juices run clear when chicken is pierced, about 25 minutes.

Using slotted spoon, transfer chicken and peppers to serving plate; keep warm. Stir parsley into sauce and bring to boil; cook until thickened. Spoon over chicken.

12	boneless skinless chicken thighs (about 900 g)
½ tsp	each salt and pepper
2 tbsp	olive oil
1	onion, chopped
2	cloves garlic, minced
2	sweet green peppers, thinly sliced
1 tsp	chili powder
½ tsp	dried thyme
1 tbsp	balsamic vinegar
1	can (796 mL) whole tomatoes
¼ cup	chopped fresh parsley

PER EACH OF 6 SERVINGS: about 235 cal, 24 g pro, 11 g total fat (2 g sat. fat), 11 g carb, 2 g fibre, 95 mg chol, 466 mg sodium. % RDI: 6% calcium, 24% iron, 8% vit A, 88% vit C, 13% folate.

HONEY-LIME CHICKEN
WITH ROASTED SPICED CAULIFLOWER

MAKES 4 SERVINGS

Brush chicken thighs with the sweet-and-sour honey-lime glaze about two minutes before the end of cooking. Serve with Romaine Salad With Fresh Lemon Dressing (below) and lime wedges.

ROASTED CAULIFLOWER:

6 cups	small cauliflower florets (about 1 small head)
4 tsp	olive oil
1 tsp	ground cumin
1 tsp	ground coriander
¼ tsp	each salt and pepper

HONEY-LIME CHICKEN:

2 tbsp	liquid honey
2 tbsp	lime juice
1 tbsp	Dijon mustard
1	clove garlic, grated or pressed
pinch	smoked paprika
450 g	boneless skinless chicken thighs
pinch	each salt and pepper
1 tsp	olive oil
2 tbsp	chopped fresh parsley

ROASTED CAULIFLOWER: Toss together cauliflower, oil, cumin, coriander, salt and pepper. Arrange in single layer on parchment paper–lined rimmed baking sheet; bake in 425°F (220°C) oven for 15 minutes.

HONEY-LIME CHICKEN: While cauliflower is roasting, whisk together honey, lime juice, mustard, garlic and paprika; set aside. Sprinkle chicken with salt and pepper. In nonstick skillet, heat oil over medium heat; cook chicken, turning once, until golden all over, about 8 minutes. Brush half of the honey mixture over chicken; cook, turning once, until glossy and coated, about 2 minutes.

Move cauliflower to one side of baking sheet; add chicken, brushing with remaining glaze. Bake until cauliflower is tender and browned, and juices run clear when chicken is pierced, about 10 minutes.

TO FINISH: Sprinkle parsley over cauliflower; serve with chicken.

PER SERVING: about 269 cal, 25 g pro, 13 g total fat (2 g sat. fat), 16 g carb, 5 g fibre, 93 mg chol, 316 mg sodium, 513 mg potassium. % RDI: 5% calcium, 17% iron, 4% vit A, 118% vit C, 34% folate.

Romaine Salad With Fresh Lemon Dressing

In measuring cup, whisk together ⅓ cup extra-virgin olive oil; 3 tbsp lemon juice; 2 tbsp thinly sliced green onions; 1 clove garlic, minced; ¼ tsp each ground cumin and salt; and pinch granulated sugar. Set dressing aside. Cut half English cucumber in half lengthwise; thinly slice diagonally. Place in salad bowl; add 4 cups chopped hearts of romaine lettuce and 1 cup grated radishes. Drizzle dressing over top; toss to coat.
MAKES 4 SERVINGS

KOREAN-STYLE CHICKEN
WITH CUCUMBER PICKLES

MAKES 4 SERVINGS

Spicy pickles and kimchi are some of the hallmarks of Korean cuisine. Here, we've created a quick cucumber pickle that has the flavours of kimchi without the long pickling time.

CUCUMBER PICKLES: In bowl, toss cucumber with salt; let stand for 15 minutes. Drain well. Add vinegar, sugar, sesame oil, garlic and hot pepper flakes; toss to combine. Set aside.

KOREAN-STYLE CHICKEN: While cucumber is standing, trim any fat from chicken; cut chicken into bite-size pieces. In bowl, whisk together soy sauce, sesame oil, sugar, sesame seeds, ginger, pepper and garlic; add chicken and green onions. Let stand for 15 minutes, stirring occasionally.

Transfer chicken mixture to foil-lined rimmed baking sheet; broil, stirring occasionally, until juices run clear when chicken is pierced, green onions are slightly charred and almost no soy sauce mixture remains, about 10 minutes. Serve with cucumber pickles.

PER SERVING: about 251 cal, 27 g pro, 12 g total fat (3 g sat. fat), 10 g carb, 2 g fibre, 95 mg chol, 424 mg sodium. % RDI: 4% calcium, 14% iron, 7% vit A, 10% vit C, 11% folate.

CUCUMBER PICKLES:

1	English cucumber, thinly sliced
½ tsp	salt
1 tbsp	unseasoned rice vinegar
1 tsp	granulated sugar
1 tsp	sesame oil
2	cloves garlic, minced
½ tsp	hot pepper flakes

KOREAN-STYLE CHICKEN:

8	boneless skinless chicken thighs (about 675 g)
¼ cup	sodium-reduced soy sauce
2 tbsp	sesame oil
4 tsp	granulated sugar
2 tsp	sesame seeds
2 tsp	minced fresh ginger
½ tsp	pepper
4	cloves garlic, thinly sliced
4	green onions, cut in 2-inch (5 cm) lengths

MARMALADE-GLAZED CHICKEN THIGHS

MAKES 4 SERVINGS

Orange marmalade isn't just for toast—it also makes an amazing instant glaze on grilled chicken thighs. Whole Wheat Couscous With Parsley (below) adds a nice bit of fresh, herby flavour to the grilled meat.

2 tbsp	lemon juice
1 tbsp	extra-virgin olive oil
2 tsp	chopped fresh rosemary
1	clove garlic, minced
¼ tsp	each salt and pepper
8	boneless skinless chicken thighs (about 675 g)
2 tbsp	orange marmalade, melted

In bowl, whisk together lemon juice, oil, rosemary, garlic, salt and pepper; set aside.

Cut chicken thighs in half crosswise; add to marinade, tossing to coat. Let stand for 15 minutes. *(Make-ahead: Cover and refrigerate for up to 8 hours.)*

Thread chicken onto eight pairs of soaked wooden skewers. Place on greased grill over medium heat; brush with any remaining marinade. Close lid and grill, turning once, until juices run clear when chicken is pierced, 12 to 15 minutes.

Brush with marmalade; grill, turning, until glazed, about 1 minute.

PER SERVING: about 204 cal, 22 g pro, 9 g total fat (2 g sat. fat), 8 g carb, trace fibre, 95 mg chol, 248 mg sodium, 285 mg potassium. % RDI: 2% calcium, 9% iron, 2% vit A, 12% vit C, 5% folate.

Whole Wheat Couscous With Parsley

In heatproof bowl, pour 1½ cups boiling water over 1 cup whole wheat couscous; cover and let stand for 5 minutes. Fluff with fork. Whisk together 1 tbsp each lemon juice and extra-virgin olive oil, and ¼ tsp each salt and pepper. Stir into couscous; stir in ¼ cup finely chopped fresh parsley.
MAKES 4 SERVINGS

YOGURT-SPICED CHICKEN
WITH GRILLED TOMATO KABOBS

MAKES 4 SERVINGS

These kabobs are an easy dinner, especially if you assemble them a day ahead and marinate them overnight in the fridge. Add some chopped fresh cilantro for a brightly flavoured garnish, and serve with grilled naan or Greek-style pita bread.

¼ cup	2% plain yogurt
2 tbsp	lemon juice
1 tbsp	grated fresh ginger
1 tbsp	tomato paste
2	cloves garlic, grated
2 tsp	garam masala or Homemade Garam Masala (below)
½ tsp	salt
450 g	boneless skinless chicken thighs
1 tbsp	olive oil
2 cups	cherry tomatoes
half	red onion, cut in ¾-inch (2 cm) chunks

In shallow dish, combine yogurt, 1 tbsp of the lemon juice, ginger, tomato paste, garlic, 1½ tsp of the garam masala and ¼ tsp of the salt. Add chicken and toss to coat; let stand for 15 minutes. *(Make-ahead: Cover and refrigerate for up to 24 hours.)*

Meanwhile, combine oil and remaining lemon juice, garam masala and salt; set aside. Alternately thread tomatoes and onion onto metal skewers.

Place chicken on greased grill over medium-high heat; close lid and grill, turning halfway through, until juices run clear when chicken is pierced, about 4 minutes.

Meanwhile, add skewers; grill, turning four times and brushing with oil mixture, until onion is slightly softened and tomatoes are slightly charred, about 4 minutes. Serve with chicken.

PER SERVING: about 222 cal, 23 g pro, 10 g total fat (2 g sat. fat), 10 g carb, 2 g fibre, 81 mg chol, 383 mg sodium, 546 mg potassium. % RDI: 6% calcium, 14% iron, 9% vit A, 23% vit C, 10% folate.

Homemade Garam Masala

Lightly crush 2 tsp green cardamom pods; reserve seeds and discard pods. Break half cinnamon stick into pieces. In skillet over medium heat, toast cardamom seeds, cinnamon stick, 4 tsp each cumin seeds and coriander seeds, 2 tsp black peppercorns and 1½ tsp whole cloves, stirring, until slightly darkened and fragrant, 1 to 2 minutes. Let cool. Grind using a spice grinder, clean coffee grinder or a mortar and pestle. *(Make-ahead: Store in airtight container for up to 1 month.)*

MAKES ⅓ CUP

BASQUE-STYLE CHICKEN

MAKES 4 TO 6 SERVINGS

Red wine and smoky paprika give this chicken a sophisticated edge
without a lot of extra ingredients or work. It's great over buttered egg noodles
or simple steamed rice.

Sprinkle chicken with ¼ tsp each of the salt and pepper. In large shallow
Dutch oven, heat oil over medium-high heat; working in batches, brown
chicken, 4 to 5 minutes per batch. Transfer to plate.

Drain any fat from pan. Add onion, garlic and green peppers; cook over
medium heat, stirring occasionally, until softened, about 5 minutes. Stir in
paprika, thyme and remaining salt and pepper. Add wine; cook, scraping
up browned bits from bottom of pan, until almost no liquid remains, about
1 minute.

Add tomatoes, breaking up with spoon. Return chicken and any accumulated
juices to pan, spooning sauce over top; bring to boil. Reduce heat, cover and
simmer, stirring occasionally, until juices run clear when chicken is pierced,
about 25 minutes.

Using slotted spoon, transfer chicken and peppers to serving plate; keep
warm. Stir parsley into sauce and bring to boil; cook until thickened.
Spoon over chicken.

PER EACH OF 6 SERVINGS: about 235 cal, 24 g pro, 11 g total fat (2 g sat. fat),
11 g carb, 2 g fibre, 95 mg chol, 466 mg sodium. % RDI: 6% calcium, 24% iron,
8% vit A, 88% vit C, 13% folate.

12	boneless skinless chicken thighs (about 900 g)
½ tsp	each salt and pepper
2 tbsp	olive oil
1	onion, chopped
2	cloves garlic, minced
2	sweet green peppers, thinly sliced
1 tsp	smoked paprika
½ tsp	dried thyme
⅓ cup	dry red wine (see tip, below)
1	can (796 mL) whole tomatoes
¼ cup	chopped fresh parsley

TIP FROM THE TEST KITCHEN
Since this is a Spanish dish, why not use a dry
Spanish red wine? Save super-expensive Riojas for
drinking; for this recipe, look for a reasonably
priced, easy-to-drink wine made with the typical
Spanish grape varietals that go into red Riojas,
such as Tempranillo, Garnacha and Mazuelo.

MISO CHICKEN
WITH BROCCOLI SLAW
MAKES 2 SERVINGS

You know what saves time in the kitchen? Making a marinade that doubles as a salad dressing base. It's easy, tasty and dirties fewer dishes—all good things!

In large bowl, stir together miso, sesame oil and soy sauce until smooth; set aside 2 tsp for marinade.

Whisk olive oil and vinegar into remaining miso mixture. Add broccoli slaw and red pepper; toss to coat. Cover and refrigerate for 1 hour.

Meanwhile, stir reserved miso mixture with chicken to coat; let stand for 10 minutes.

Bake chicken on parchment paper–lined rimmed baking sheet in 400°F (200°C) oven until juices run clear when chicken is pierced, about 20 minutes.

Let chicken cool enough to handle. Slice chicken; serve with slaw.

PER SERVING: about 435 cal, 31 g pro, 25 g total fat (4 g sat. fat), 25 g carb, 9 g fibre, 82 mg chol, 573 mg sodium, 291 mg potassium. % RDI: 17% calcium, 33% iron, 84% vit A, 565% vit C, 124% folate.

2 tsp	miso paste
2 tsp	sesame oil
2 tsp	sodium-reduced soy sauce
2 tbsp	light-tasting olive oil
2 tbsp	unseasoned rice vinegar
3 cups	broccoli slaw (see tip, below)
half	sweet red pepper, thinly sliced
225 g	boneless skinless chicken thighs

TIP FROM THE TEST KITCHEN
Broccoli slaw is available in the produce section near the prewashed salad greens. It is the ultimate healthy shortcut and a tasty alternative to regular cabbage slaw. Even broccoli haters might have a new favourite!

CHICKEN PILAF
WITH SPINACH AND WALNUTS

MAKES 4 SERVINGS

Economical one-pot recipes like this one are essential to everyone's repertoire. Toasted walnuts and fragrant dill bring a pleasant crunch and a fresh edge to the Mediterranean-inspired pilaf.

½ cup	chopped walnuts (see tip, below)
450 g	boneless skinless chicken thighs, cubed
¾ tsp	salt
½ tsp	pepper
2 tbsp	olive oil
1	onion, diced
1	clove garlic, minced
1 cup	basmati or other long-grain white rice
½ tsp	ground cumin
¼ tsp	ground allspice
pinch	cinnamon
4 cups	loosely packed baby spinach, coarsely chopped
2 tbsp	chopped fresh dill

On rimmed baking sheet, toast walnuts in 350°F (180°C) oven until golden, about 8 minutes; set aside.

Sprinkle chicken with half each of the salt and pepper. In large saucepan, heat oil over medium-high heat; brown chicken, 4 to 5 minutes. Using slotted spoon, transfer to bowl.

In same saucepan, cook onion and garlic over medium heat until slightly softened, about 2 minutes. Stir in rice, cumin, allspice, cinnamon and remaining salt and pepper; cook, stirring, for 2 minutes. Return chicken and any accumulated juices to pan, stirring to coat.

Stir in 1¾ cups water; bring to boil. Reduce heat, cover and simmer until rice is tender and no liquid remains, about 20 minutes. Turn off heat; let stand on burner for 5 minutes.

Stir in spinach, dill and toasted walnuts.

PER SERVING: about 489 cal, 29 g pro, 23 g total fat (3 g sat. fat), 43 g carb, 3 g fibre, 94 mg chol, 553 mg sodium, 560 mg potassium. % RDI: 8% calcium, 24% iron, 32% vit A, 10% vit C, 33% folate.

TIP FROM THE TEST KITCHEN

Chopped walnuts sold in bags at the supermarket are often rancid. Buy the freshest whole California walnut halves you can find (preferably when they're on sale!), and freeze the nuts in a resealable freezer bag for up to six months. Simply scoop out and chop what you need for recipes.

HUNTER'S CHICKEN
WITH CREAMY POLENTA
MAKES 4 SERVINGS

This savoury, saucy stew is perfect for a cold winter's night.
Chicken thighs and beans are a great way to bump up the protein,
and polenta is a satisfying side dish.

HUNTER'S CHICKEN: In large nonstick skillet, heat 2 tsp of the oil over medium-high heat; working in batches, brown chicken, 4 to 5 minutes per batch. Using slotted spoon, transfer to plate.

Add remaining oil to pan; heat over medium heat. Cook onion, stirring occasionally, until softened, about 5 minutes. Add mushrooms and garlic; cook, stirring occasionally, for 3 minutes.

Stir in broth, strained tomatoes, beans, tomato paste, Italian herb seasoning, salt, and chicken and any accumulated juices; bring to boil. Reduce heat and simmer until thickened, about 15 minutes. Stir in parsley.

CREAMY POLENTA: While chicken is simmering, in large saucepan, bring 6 cups water to boil. Whisk in cornmeal, salt and pepper; simmer over medium-low heat, stirring often, until thick enough to mound on spoon, about 10 minutes. Stir in butter. Serve with chicken.

PER SERVING: about 708 cal, 46 g pro, 26 g total fat (10 g sat. fat), 72 g carb, 13 g fibre, 172 mg chol, 961 mg sodium, 1,104 mg potassium. % RDI: 9% calcium, 44% iron, 18% vit A, 23% vit C, 65% folate.

HUNTER'S CHICKEN:

1 tbsp	olive oil
8	boneless skinless chicken thighs (about 675 g), cut in 1-inch (2.5 cm) chunks
1	onion, chopped
225 g	button mushrooms, sliced
3	cloves garlic, minced
1 cup	sodium-reduced chicken broth
1 cup	bottled strained tomatoes (passata)
1	can (540 mL) white kidney beans, drained and rinsed
1 tbsp	tomato paste
2 tsp	Italian herb seasoning
pinch	salt
¼ cup	chopped fresh parsley

CREAMY POLENTA:

1⅔ cups	cornmeal
¼ tsp	each salt and pepper
¼ cup	butter, cubed

GINGER SOY CHICKEN SKEWERS

MAKES 4 SERVINGS

This simple take on yakitori—classic Japanese chicken kabobs—
is terrific with plain steamed rice and a green salad, such as
Mixed Greens With Ginger Vinaigrette (below).

¼ cup	sodium-reduced soy sauce
4 tsp	granulated sugar
4 tsp	sesame oil
3	cloves garlic, minced
2 tsp	minced fresh ginger
¼ tsp	hot pepper flakes
8	boneless skinless chicken thighs (about 675 g), quartered
1	onion
8	green onions (white and light green parts only), cut in 1½-inch (4 cm) pieces

In large bowl, whisk together ¼ cup water, soy sauce, sugar, sesame oil, garlic, ginger and hot pepper flakes until sugar is dissolved. Add chicken and toss to coat; let stand for 15 minutes, turning several times.

Cut onion into quarters; separate into pieces three layers thick. Reserving marinade, alternately thread chicken, onion and green onions onto four metal or soaked wooden skewers.

Place on greased grill over medium heat; close lid and grill, turning once and brushing with marinade halfway through, until juices run clear when chicken is pierced, 12 to 15 minutes.

PER SERVING: about 236 cal, 24 g pro, 11 g total fat (2 g sat. fat), 11 g carb, 1 g fibre, 95 mg chol, 636 mg sodium. % RDI: 4% calcium, 15% iron, 5% vit A, 13% vit C, 13% folate.

Mixed Greens With Ginger Vinaigrette

In salad bowl, whisk together 2 tbsp each seasoned rice vinegar and vegetable oil, 2 tsp grated fresh ginger, ½ tsp sesame oil and pinch salt. Add 4 cups mixed greens, ½ cup each thinly sliced cucumber and radish, and 2 tbsp thinly sliced green parts of green onion. Toss to coat.

MAKES 4 SERVINGS

SPANISH CHICKEN STEW

MAKES 10 SERVINGS

Red peppers, garlic and tomatoes are three hallmark ingredients in the cuisine of northern Spain. Using roasted red peppers from a jar saves prep time and adds a slight smoky overtone to this chunky stew.

1 tsp	vegetable oil
12	boneless skinless chicken thighs (about 900 g), cut in ¾-inch (2 cm) pieces
2 cups	sliced leeks (white and light green parts only), about 2 small
6	cloves garlic, thinly sliced
1 tbsp	tomato paste
¼ tsp	salt
1	jar (300 mL) roasted red peppers, drained and chopped
1	can (796 mL) stewed whole tomatoes
675 g	mini yellow-fleshed potatoes, scrubbed and halved
1 cup	frozen peas
2 tbsp	chopped fresh flatleaf parsley

In Dutch oven, heat oil over high heat; working in batches, brown chicken, 4 to 5 minutes per batch. Using slotted spoon, transfer chicken to plate.

Add leeks and garlic to pan; reduce heat to medium-high. Cook, stirring, until garlic is fragrant, about 1 minute. Return chicken to pan; cook, stirring frequently, until leeks begin to soften, about 4 minutes. Add tomato paste, salt and red peppers; cook, stirring, for 2 minutes. Stir in tomatoes, breaking up with spoon; bring to boil. Reduce heat and simmer for 10 minutes.

Meanwhile, in pot of boiling lightly salted water, cook potatoes just until tender, about 8 minutes. Drain and add to stew. Simmer until thickened, about 15 minutes.

Stir in peas and parsley; cook until peas are hot, about 2 minutes.

PER SERVING: about 218 cal, 21 g pro, 5 g total fat (1 g sat. fat), 23 g carb, 3 g fibre, 75 mg chol, 569 mg sodium, 708 mg potassium. % RDI: 6% calcium, 24% iron, 13% vit A, 95% vit C, 15% folate.

THAI COCONUT CHICKEN SIMMER
MAKES 4 SERVINGS

Fragrant with coconut, ginger and shallots, this Thai curry is
best served over jasmine rice or rice noodles. Garnish with fresh cilantro
or basil leaves and serve with braised bok choy.

Sprinkle chicken with salt and pepper. In large skillet, heat oil over medium-high heat; brown chicken, turning once, about 5 minutes. Using slotted spoon, transfer to plate.

Add shallots, ginger, curry paste and garlic to pan; cook over medium heat, stirring, for 2 minutes. Stir in coconut milk and chicken; bring to boil. Reduce heat and simmer, turning once, until juices run clear when chicken is pierced, about 15 minutes.

PER SERVING: about 374 cal, 24 g pro, 30 g total fat (20 g sat. fat), 6 g carb, 1 g fibre, 94 mg chol, 264 mg sodium, 506 mg potassium. % RDI: 4% calcium, 33% iron, 3% vit A, 15% vit C, 10% folate.

450 g	boneless skinless chicken thighs
pinch	each salt and pepper
1 tbsp	vegetable oil
2	shallots, thinly sliced
1 tbsp	minced fresh ginger
1 tbsp	Thai green curry paste
2	cloves garlic, minced
1	can (400 mL) coconut milk (see tip, below)

TIP FROM THE TEST KITCHEN
Choose full-fat coconut milk unless reduced-fat is specified in the ingredient list. It has a creamier consistency and more flavour, which is better in curries and soups.

CHICKEN TERIYAKI SKEWERS

MAKES 4 SERVINGS

This recipe makes more teriyaki sauce than you need; refrigerate the extra for another time. The chicken livers are succulent prepared this way, but you can swap in more chicken thighs for them if you aren't a fan.

QUICK TERIYAKI SAUCE: In saucepan, bring soy sauce, mirin, sugar, sake (if using), ginger and ¾ cup water to boil. Reduce heat and simmer until reduced to about 1 cup, about 10 minutes.

Whisk cold water with cornstarch; add to pan and cook, stirring, until thickened. Discard ginger. Let cool.

CHICKEN SKEWERS: While sauce is cooling, cut green onions into 1½-inch (4 cm) pieces. Alternately thread chicken thighs and half of the green onions onto four greased metal or soaked wooden skewers. Repeat with livers and remaining green onions.

Place skewers on greased grill over medium-high heat; close lid and grill, turning halfway through and brushing with half of the teriyaki sauce, until juices run clear when chicken is pierced, about 8 minutes for thighs and 4 minutes for livers. Brush with more teriyaki sauce if desired.

PER SERVING: about 178 cal, 22 g pro, 5 g total fat (2 g sat. fat), 8 g carb, 1 g fibre, 306 mg chol, 963 mg sodium, 268 mg potassium. % RDI: 3% calcium, 34% iron, 209% vit A, 15% vit C, 155% folate.

QUICK TERIYAKI SAUCE:

½ cup	soy sauce
⅓ cup	mirin
2 tbsp	granulated sugar
2 tbsp	sake (optional), see tip, below
2	slices fresh ginger
2 tbsp	cold water
1 tbsp	cornstarch

CHICKEN SKEWERS:

1	bunch green onions
225 g	boneless skinless chicken thighs, cut in bite-size pieces
250 g	chicken livers (or additional boneless skinless chicken thighs, cut in bite-size pieces)

TIP FROM THE TEST KITCHEN
The sake is authentic, but if you don't have any on hand, you can substitute dry sherry. The recipe is also delicious without any alcohol at all.

SLOW COOKER
THAI CHICKEN CURRY

MAKES 8 SERVINGS

Chicken, squash and all the exotic flavours of a restaurant-style Thai curry mingle in this scrumptious slow cooker main. Serve over steamed jasmine rice and garnish with lemon or lime wedges to squeeze over top.

900 g	boneless skinless chicken thighs, cut in 1-inch (2.5 cm) chunks
4 cups	cubed seeded peeled butternut squash (1½-inch/4 cm cubes)
1	can (400 mL) coconut milk (see tip, page 105)
2 tbsp	minced fresh ginger
2 tbsp	Thai red curry paste
2 tbsp	tomato paste
3	makrut lime leaves (optional), see tip, below
1 tbsp	packed brown sugar
1 tbsp	each fish sauce and sodium-reduced soy sauce
3	cloves garlic, minced
½ tsp	salt
2 tbsp	all-purpose flour
2	heads Shanghai bok choy (about 150 g), cut lengthwise in ½-inch (1 cm) thick wedges
2 tbsp	lime juice
⅓ cup	finely chopped peanuts

In slow cooker, combine chicken, squash, coconut milk, ginger, curry paste, tomato paste, lime leaves (if using), brown sugar, fish sauce, soy sauce, garlic and salt.

Cover and cook on low until chicken is fall-apart tender, 6 to 8 hours.

Whisk flour with 3 tbsp water until smooth; stir into slow cooker. Stir in bok choy; cover and cook on high until sauce is thickened and bok choy is tender, about 15 minutes. Discard lime leaves. Stir in lime juice; sprinkle with chopped peanuts.

PER SERVING: about 344 cal, 26 g pro, 21 g total fat (11 g sat. fat), 17 g carb, 3 g fibre, 94 mg chol, 512 mg sodium, 787 mg potassium. % RDI: 8% calcium, 29% iron, 98% vit A, 37% vit C, 22% folate.

TIP FROM THE TEST KITCHEN
Makrut lime leaves give traditional curries a lovely floral-citrus note, but they can be a little hard to find. Look for them in Asian supermarkets—fresh leaves are more fragrant, but dried ones can work in saucy dishes like this curry.

CHICKEN SQUASH CURRY

MAKES 4 SERVINGS

Curries often simmer for quite a while, but this speedy one is ready in about 30 minutes. The mix of sweet, hot, savoury and fresh flavours is surprisingly rich for a dish that takes so little time to cook.

In Dutch oven, heat half of the oil over medium-high heat; brown chicken, 4 to 5 minutes. Using slotted spoon, transfer to plate.

Add remaining oil to pan; heat over medium heat. Cook onion and hot peppers, stirring occasionally, until softened, about 5 minutes.

Add squash and curry paste; cook, stirring, until fragrant, about 1 minute.

Add tomatoes and bring to boil, scraping up browned bits from bottom of pan. Return chicken and any accumulated juices to pan. Reduce heat, cover and simmer until squash is tender, about 20 minutes. Sprinkle with cilantro.

PER SERVING: about 345 cal, 25 g pro, 19 g total fat (3 g sat. fat), 21 g carb, 4 g fibre, 94 mg chol, 673 mg sodium, 928 mg potassium. % RDI: 10% calcium, 27% iron, 96% vit A, 88% vit C, 17% folate.

2 tbsp	vegetable oil
450 g	boneless skinless chicken thighs, cubed
1	onion, chopped
2	green hot peppers, seeded and chopped
2 cups	cubed seeded peeled butternut squash (about 450 g)
3 tbsp	mild Indian curry paste
1	can (796 mL) diced tomatoes
¼ cup	chopped fresh cilantro

CHICKEN RATATOUILLE
WITH LEMONY BASIL POLENTA

MAKES 4 SERVINGS

This sodium-reduced, vegetable-packed dinner is full of flavour and comes together in just half an hour. Add a few fresh basil leaves for a pretty garnish.

CHICKEN RATATOUILLE:

450 g	boneless skinless chicken thighs, quartered
1 tsp	dried oregano
2 tbsp	olive oil
1	Asian eggplant, thinly sliced
half	onion, thinly sliced
1	zucchini, thinly sliced
1	sweet red pepper, chopped
3	cloves garlic, minced
1	can (398 mL) diced tomatoes
½ tsp	pepper
¼ tsp	hot pepper flakes
pinch	salt

LEMONY BASIL POLENTA:

1 tsp	olive oil
half	onion, diced
3	cloves garlic, minced
2 cups	no-salt-added chicken broth
¼ tsp	pepper
pinch	salt
¾ cup	cornmeal
1 tsp	grated lemon zest
1 tbsp	lemon juice
1 tbsp	unsalted butter
¼ cup	torn basil leaves

CHICKEN RATATOUILLE: Sprinkle chicken with half of the oregano. In Dutch oven or heavy-bottomed saucepan, heat 1 tsp of the oil over medium heat; brown chicken, about 5 minutes. Using slotted spoon, transfer to plate.

Add remaining oil to pan; cook eggplant and onion, stirring frequently, until beginning to soften, about 5 minutes. Stir in zucchini, red pepper and garlic; cook, stirring occasionally, until tender-crisp, about 4 minutes.

Stir in tomatoes, pepper, hot pepper flakes, salt and remaining oregano. Return chicken and any accumulated juices to pan; cook, stirring occasionally, until vegetables are tender and juices run clear when chicken is pierced, about 10 minutes.

LEMONY BASIL POLENTA: While eggplant and onions are softening, in separate saucepan, heat oil over medium heat; cook onion and garlic, stirring occasionally, until softened, about 5 minutes.

Add broth, ⅓ cup water, pepper and salt; bring to boil. Reduce heat to medium-low. Gradually whisk in cornmeal; cook, stirring often, until polenta is thick enough to mound on spoon, 5 to 10 minutes. Stir in lemon zest, lemon juice and butter. Fold in basil. Serve topped with ratatouille.

PER SERVING: about 405 cal, 27 g pro, 17 g total fat (5 g sat. fat), 36 g carb, 5 g fibre, 102 mg chol, 264 mg sodium, 819 mg potassium. % RDI: 7% calcium, 24% iron, 21% vit A, 122% vit C, 31% folate.

TIP FROM THE TEST KITCHEN

The colourful mix of vegetables makes this dish a good source of fibre and provides more than 100 percent of your daily vitamin C requirement.

LEMONGRASS CHICKEN BANH MI

MAKES 4 SERVINGS

Banh mi are Vietnamese subs stuffed with aromatic grilled meat, savoury condiments and crunchy pickles. The signature is the lovely crisp Vietnamese roll, which you can buy in many Asian supermarkets. If you can't find one, substitute a crusty sub roll.

LEMONGRASS CHICKEN:

1	stalk lemongrass, shredded
1	piece (1 inch/2.5 cm) fresh ginger, peeled and sliced
2	green onions, thickly sliced
2	cloves garlic
1 tbsp	each liquid honey and lime juice
2 tsp	each fish sauce, sodium-reduced soy sauce and vegetable oil
¼ tsp	pepper
450 g	boneless skinless chicken thighs

PICKLED ZUCCHINI AND CARROT:

1 tbsp	white vinegar
1 tsp	liquid honey
1	each zucchini and carrot

SPICY CORN AND TOMATO SALSA:

1 tsp	vegetable oil
1	small onion, diced
2	cloves garlic, minced
¾ cup	fresh or frozen corn kernels
1	Thai bird's-eye pepper, thinly sliced
1	tomato, seeded and diced
2 tbsp	lime juice
pinch	each salt and pepper

SPINACH AND GARLIC MAYO:

2½ cups	packed fresh spinach, trimmed
2 tbsp	light mayonnaise
1	clove garlic, chopped
4	crusty sub rolls
½ cup	fresh cilantro leaves

LEMONGRASS CHICKEN: In food processor or using immersion blender, purée lemongrass, ginger, green onions, garlic, honey, lime juice, fish sauce, soy sauce, oil, pepper and 3 tbsp water. In bowl, pour lemongrass mixture over chicken; toss to coat. Cover and refrigerate for 2 hours. *(Make-ahead: Refrigerate for up to 24 hours.)*

Place chicken on greased grill over medium-high heat; close lid and grill, turning once, until juices run clear when chicken is pierced, about 6 minutes. Transfer to cutting board and cover loosely with foil; let rest for 3 minutes before slicing.

PICKLED ZUCCHINI AND CARROT: While chicken is chilling, in bowl, whisk vinegar with honey. Halve zucchini and carrot lengthwise; thinly slice diagonally. Add to bowl; toss to coat. Cover and refrigerate for 2 hours. *(Make-ahead: Refrigerate for up to 2 days.)*

SPICY CORN AND TOMATO SALSA: While chicken and pickled vegetables are chilling, in skillet, heat oil over medium-high heat; cook onion and garlic, stirring, until onion is softened, about 3 minutes. Add corn and bird's-eye pepper; sauté until corn is softened and tender, about 3 minutes. Stir in tomato, lime juice, salt and pepper. Use warm or let cool to room temperature. *(Make-ahead: Refrigerate in airtight container for up to 24 hours.)*

SPINACH AND GARLIC MAYO: In pot of boiling water, wilt spinach, about 30 seconds. Drain and immerse in cold water; drain, squeeze dry and chop. In small bowl and using immersion blender, purée spinach, mayonnaise and garlic. *(Make-ahead: Refrigerate in airtight container for up to 2 days.)*

ASSEMBLY: Halve rolls lengthwise almost but not all the way through; remove all but ½ inch (1 cm) bread from top and bottom halves. Grill rolls, cut sides down, until warmed, about 1 minute.

Spread bottom halves of rolls with spinach mayo; top with lemongrass chicken, pickled zucchini mixture and salsa. Top with cilantro.

PER SERVING: about 634 cal, 36 g pro, 17 g total fat (3 g sat. fat), 85 g carb, 6 g fibre, 97 mg chol, 1,131 mg sodium, 936 mg potassium. % RDI: 17% calcium, 49% iron, 57% vit A, 40% vit C, 85% folate.

CHICKEN AND EGG DONBURI

MAKES 2 OR 3 SERVINGS

Served over steaming rice, this combination of chicken and softly set egg is the ultimate quick comfort food. It's a staple in Japanese cafés, but it's so easy to make at home.

In bowl, beat eggs with pepper; set aside. In glass measuring cup, whisk together ½ cup water, mirin, soy sauce and sugar; set aside.

In nonstick skillet, sprinkle onion evenly over pan; top with chicken, green onions, watercress (if using) and mushrooms. Pour soy sauce mixture over top; cover and simmer over medium heat until juices run clear when chicken is pierced, 3 to 5 minutes.

Pour eggs over chicken; cover and simmer on low heat until lightly set, about 30 seconds. Serve over rice.

PER EACH OF 3 SERVINGS: about 341 cal, 25 g pro, 9 g total fat (3 g sat. fat), 37 g carb, 2 g fibre, 250 mg chol, 534 mg sodium, 464 mg potassium. % RDI: 6% calcium, 14% iron, 9% vit A, 7% vit C, 21% folate.

3	eggs
pinch	pepper
2 tbsp	mirin (see tip, page 62)
4 tsp	soy sauce
2 tsp	granulated sugar
¾ cup	thinly sliced sweet onion
4	boneless skinless chicken thighs (about 325 g), cut in 1-inch (2.5 cm) chunks
2	green onions, cut in pieces
2 cups	lightly packed watercress leaves and stems (optional), see tip, left
1 cup	sliced cremini mushrooms
1½ cups	hot cooked rice

TIP FROM THE TEST KITCHEN
Watercress is in season in the spring, so it's easier to find then. If you want to make this dish year-round, try substituting baby spinach.

CHICKEN AND UDON STIR-FRY
WITH SHIITAKE MUSHROOMS AND SNOW PEAS
MAKES 4 SERVINGS

Japanese udon noodles are usually served in a mild-flavoured broth,
but here they star in a tasty stir-fry. Linguine makes a good substitute;
just cook it for two minutes less than the package directions suggest.

In wok or large skillet, heat vegetable oil over medium-high heat; stir-fry
chicken, garlic and ginger until chicken is lightly browned, about 5 minutes.

Add mushrooms; stir-fry until beginning to soften, about 2 minutes. Stir in
½ cup water, hoisin sauce, oyster sauce and sambal oelek; bring to simmer.

Add noodles and toss to combine; simmer until sauce is thickened,
2 to 3 minutes. Add snow peas and sesame oil; cook for 1 minute.

PER SERVING: about 809 cal, 38 g pro, 14 g total fat (3 g sat. fat), 125 g carb,
3 g fibre, 95 mg chol, 738 mg sodium, 467 mg potassium. % RDI: 6% calcium,
21% iron, 4% vit A, 18% vit C, 9% folate.

1 tbsp	vegetable oil
450 g	boneless skinless chicken thighs, thinly sliced
2 tsp	minced garlic
2 tsp	minced fresh ginger
2 cups	stemmed shiitake mushrooms (see tip, below), thinly sliced
¼ cup	hoisin sauce
1 tbsp	oyster sauce
1 tsp	sambal oelek or hot pepper sauce
4	pkg (each 200 g) fresh udon noodles
1 cup	snow peas, thinly sliced lengthwise
1 tsp	sesame oil

TIP FROM THE TEST KITCHEN
Shiitake mushroom stems are too tough to eat, so make
sure to trim them off completely before you slice the
caps. Save the stems for stock (see page 250), because
they're very flavourful.

QUICK CHICKEN KORMA

MAKES 4 SERVINGS

Puréed onions and toasted cashews give the sauce a creamy texture and rich flavour without adding any cream. If you love spice, don't seed the hot peppers. Serve with steamed basmati rice and a dollop of mango chutney.

⅓ cup	unsalted raw cashews
4 tsp	vegetable oil
3	onions, sliced
2	green hot peppers or jalapeño peppers, seeded and diced
3	cloves garlic, minced
1 tbsp	grated fresh ginger
1½ tsp	each ground coriander and garam masala
¼ tsp	cayenne pepper
pinch	nutmeg
pinch	salt
450 g	boneless skinless chicken thighs, quartered
1½ cups	no-salt-added chicken broth (see tip, below)
pinch	saffron threads (optional)
3 tbsp	fat-free plain Greek yogurt
1½ tsp	lime juice

In large dry skillet, toast cashews over medium heat, stirring often, until golden, 3 to 5 minutes. Transfer to food processor.

Add 2 tsp of the oil to pan; heat over medium heat. Cook onions, stirring occasionally, until golden, 12 to 15 minutes. Add to food processor; purée until smooth.

In bowl, combine hot peppers, garlic, ginger, coriander, garam masala, cayenne pepper, nutmeg and salt. Add chicken; toss to coat.

Add remaining oil to pan; heat over medium-high heat. Brown chicken, stirring occasionally, about 5 minutes.

Stir in 2 tbsp water, scraping up browned bits from bottom of pan. Stir in broth, saffron (if using) and cashew purée; simmer, stirring occasionally, until thickened and juices run clear when chicken is pierced, about 5 minutes. Stir in yogurt and lime juice; heat until warmed through but not boiling.

PER SERVING: about 307 cal, 27 g pro, 16 g total fat (3 g sat. fat), 15 g carb, 3 g fibre, 95 mg chol, 134 mg sodium, 554 mg potassium. % RDI: 8% calcium, 19% iron, 3% vit A, 18% vit C, 11% folate.

TIP FROM THE TEST KITCHEN
We've used no-salt-added broth, so this crowd-pleaser contains just 134 mg sodium per serving—a fraction of the amount found in takeout versions. If you like, you can substitute sodium-reduced or regular chicken broth.

QUICK CHICKEN AND WHITE BEAN STEW

MAKES 4 SERVINGS

Ideal to dig into on a chilly evening, this one-pot chicken stew comes together quickly.
Passata—Italian jarred tomato purée—adds full-bodied flavour and a smooth texture.
Serve the stew with crusty bread or over couscous, rice or pasta.

2	strips bacon, thinly sliced
450 g	boneless skinless chicken thighs, quartered
2 tsp	vegetable oil
1	onion, sliced
6	cloves garlic, sliced
1 tbsp	chopped fresh thyme
1	pkg (227 g) cremini or button mushrooms, sliced
1	can (540 mL) navy beans, drained and rinsed
2 cups	bottled strained tomatoes (passata)
pinch	each salt and pepper
2	green onions, sliced
2 tbsp	chopped fresh parsley
1 tsp	red wine vinegar

In Dutch oven or large heavy-bottomed saucepan, cook bacon over medium heat, stirring, until fat begins to render, about 2 minutes.

Add chicken; cook, stirring, until browned, about 4 minutes. Using slotted spoon, transfer mixture to plate; set aside.

Add oil to pan; heat over medium heat. Cook onion, stirring, until softened, about 3 minutes. Add garlic and thyme; cook, stirring, until fragrant, about 1 minute. Add mushrooms and 2 tbsp water; cook, stirring occasionally and scraping up browned bits from bottom of pan, until mushrooms are tender and no liquid remains, 4 to 5 minutes.

Return chicken mixture and any accumulated juices to pan. Stir in beans, strained tomatoes, salt, pepper and ½ cup water; bring to boil. Reduce heat, cover and simmer until stew is slightly thickened and chicken is no longer pink inside, about 8 minutes.

Remove from heat; stir in green onions, parsley and vinegar.

PER SERVING: about 449 cal, 35 g pro, 14 g total fat (5 g sat. fat), 45 g carb, 10 g fibre, 101 mg chol, 418 mg sodium, 1,204 mg potassium. % RDI: 11% calcium, 48% iron, 4% vit A, 18% vit C, 40% folate.

SKILLET CHICKEN COBBLER

MAKES 6 SERVINGS

This is just like chicken pot pie—only easier and faster. If your nonstick pan has a plastic handle, wrap it in a double layer of foil to make it ovenproof.

CHICKEN STEW: In ovenproof 10-inch (25 cm) nonstick skillet, heat oil and butter over medium-high heat; cook onion and mushrooms, stirring often, until mushrooms are lightly browned, 5 to 6 minutes.

Add chicken, garlic, salt and pepper; cook, stirring, until chicken is browned, 2 to 3 minutes. Stir in flour and cook for 1 minute. Add broth and bring to boil, stirring.

Stir in celery, carrots, bay leaf and thyme; reduce heat, cover and simmer until thickened and vegetables are tender-crisp, 3 to 5 minutes. Stir in peas. Discard bay leaf and thyme. Remove from heat and set aside.

BISCUIT TOPPING: In bowl, whisk together flour, baking powder and salt. Using pastry blender or two knives, cut in butter until crumbly. Drizzle in buttermilk, stirring just until soft sticky dough forms. Turn out onto floured surface; knead six times or just until smooth. Roll out into 6-inch (15 cm) square; brush with 2 tsp more buttermilk. Cut into six biscuits. Arrange over chicken mixture in skillet.

TO FINISH: Bake in 375°F (190°C) oven until biscuits are golden and stew is bubbly, 30 to 35 minutes. Let stand for 5 minutes before serving.

PER SERVING: about 337 cal, 21 g pro, 15 g total fat (6 g sat. fat), 30 g carb, 3 g fibre, 85 mg chol, 466 mg sodium, 481 mg potassium. % RDI: 8% calcium, 21% iron, 56% vit A, 12% vit C, 39% folate.

CHICKEN STEW:

1 tbsp	each vegetable oil and unsalted butter
1	onion, chopped
225 g	button mushrooms, quartered
450 g	boneless skinless chicken thighs, cut in bite-size pieces
1	clove garlic, minced
¼ tsp	each salt and pepper
2 tbsp	all-purpose flour
1 cup	sodium-reduced chicken broth
2	ribs celery, chopped
2	carrots, thinly sliced
1	bay leaf
1	sprig fresh thyme
1 cup	frozen peas

BISCUIT TOPPING:

1 cup + 2 tbsp	all-purpose flour
1 tsp	baking powder
¼ tsp	salt
3 tbsp	cold unsalted butter, cubed
½ cup	buttermilk (approx), see tip, left

TIP FROM THE TEST KITCHEN

Out of buttermilk? You can still make these biscuits. Pour 1 tbsp lemon juice or white vinegar into a glass measuring cup, then fill to the 1-cup mark with milk. Let stand for five minutes to thicken. Voilà—homemade buttermilk substitute.

CHEESE AND JALAPEÑO–STUFFED CHICKEN THIGHS

MAKES 4 SERVINGS

These cheesy chicken thighs taste just like Jalapeño Poppers and are the perfect fit for a family-friendly meal. Serve with steamed broccoli or a green salad.

1 cup	shredded old Cheddar cheese
⅓ cup	cream cheese, softened
2 tbsp	minced pickled jalapeño peppers
8	boneless skinless chicken thighs (about 675 g total)
1 tbsp	olive oil
1 cup	panko bread crumbs

In small bowl, stir together Cheddar, cream cheese and jalapeños; set aside.

Sandwich chicken thighs between waxed paper; using meat mallet or heavy-bottomed saucepan, pound to ¼-inch (5 mm) thickness. Drop scant tablespoonful cheese mixture onto centre of each thigh. Roll up, tucking in sides, and secure each with two toothpicks. *(Make-ahead: Refrigerate in airtight container for up to 24 hours.)*

Brush oil all over chicken. Sprinkle panko in small bowl; press all sides of chicken firmly into panko to coat. Place, seam side down, on parchment paper–lined rimmed baking sheet.

Bake in 450°F (230°C) oven until golden and instant-read thermometer inserted into centres of thighs reads 165°F (74°C), 20 to 25 minutes.

PER SERVING: about 424 cal, 37 g pro, 27 g total fat (12 g sat. fat), 6 g carb, trace fibre, 175 mg chol, 409 mg sodium, 412 mg potassium. % RDI: 22% calcium, 14% iron, 19% vit A, 18% vit C, 8% folate.

SAUCY MUSHROOM CHICKEN
MAKES 4 SERVINGS

For a change from the usual potatoes or rice, serve this savoury chicken with Israeli (pearl) couscous or orzo pasta.

Peel skin off chicken thighs and discard. In large skillet, heat oil over medium-high heat; brown chicken, 4 to 5 minutes. Using slotted spoon, transfer to plate.

Drain fat from pan; sauté mushrooms, onion, garlic, thyme, salt and pepper until mushrooms are golden and no liquid remains, about 8 minutes. Sprinkle with flour; cook, stirring, for 1 minute. Pour in milk and bring to boil, stirring and scraping up browned bits from bottom of pan.

Return chicken and any accumulated juices to pan. Stir in mustard; reduce heat, cover and simmer, turning chicken once, until juices run clear when chicken is pierced, about 20 minutes. Sprinkle with green onions.

PER SERVING: about 267 cal, 29 g pro, 12 g total fat (3 g sat. fat), 12 g carb, 2 g fibre, 111 mg chol, 481 mg sodium. % RDI: 10% calcium, 19% iron, 5% vit A, 15% vit C, 15% folate.

8	bone-in skin-on chicken thighs (900 g)
1 tbsp	vegetable oil
3 cups	sliced white or cremini mushrooms (about 250 g)
1	onion, chopped
2	cloves garlic, minced
1 tsp	dried thyme
½ tsp	salt
¼ tsp	pepper
2 tbsp	all-purpose flour
1 cup	milk
1 tbsp	Dijon mustard
2	green onions, sliced

VARIATION
Slow Cooker Saucy Mushroom Chicken
Do not remove skin from chicken thighs. After browning chicken, transfer to slow cooker. Replace milk with 1 cup chicken broth or evaporated milk; scrape mixture into slow cooker. Cover and cook on low for 4 hours. Skim off any fat. Whisk ⅓ cup water with ¼ cup all-purpose flour and stir into slow cooker; cover and cook on high until thickened, about 15 minutes. Remove skin if desired. Sprinkle with green onions.

CHICKEN SAMOSA PIE

MAKES 8 SERVINGS

Chicken thighs don't dry out when baked, so they are the most delicious choice for this main-course take on a popular appetizer. If you can't find already ground spices, such as fenugreek, grind the seeds in a clean coffee grinder. Serve with Cilantro Chutney (below).

CUMIN PASTRY:

2½ cups	all-purpose flour
1½ tsp	cumin seeds
½ tsp	salt
⅔ cup	cold butter, cubed
⅔ cup	milk

CHICKEN SAMOSA FILLING:

675 g	potatoes, peeled and diced (about 2 large)
1	carrot, diced
2 tbsp	vegetable oil
450 g	boneless skinless chicken thighs, diced
1 tsp	fennel seeds
1 tsp	cumin seeds
1 tsp	brown or black mustard seeds
½ tsp	each turmeric, ground coriander and ground fenugreek seeds
¼ tsp	cayenne pepper
1	onion, chopped
2	cloves garlic, minced
1 tbsp	grated fresh ginger
½ tsp	salt
1 cup	frozen peas
2 tbsp	chopped fresh cilantro
2 tbsp	lemon juice
1	egg, lightly beaten

CUMIN PASTRY: In food processor, combine flour, cumin seeds and salt; pulse in butter until mixture resembles fine crumbs. Pulse in milk until dough begins to clump together. Press into disc and divide in half; wrap and refrigerate for 30 minutes. *(Make-ahead: Refrigerate for up to 24 hours.)*

CHICKEN SAMOSA FILLING: While pastry is chilling, in large saucepan of boiling salted water, cook potatoes and carrot until tender, about 10 minutes. Drain and place in large bowl.

Meanwhile, in large nonstick skillet, heat 1 tbsp of the oil over medium-high heat; working in batches, cook chicken until juices run clear when chicken is pierced, about 5 minutes per batch. Add to potato mixture.

Add remaining oil to pan. Cook fennel seeds, cumin seeds, mustard seeds, turmeric, coriander, fenugreek and cayenne pepper just until cumin seeds begin to pop, 30 to 60 seconds. Add onion, garlic, ginger and salt; cook until softened, about 3 minutes. Add to chicken mixture. Stir in peas, cilantro and lemon juice; let cool.

ASSEMBLY: On lightly floured surface, roll out half of the pastry to generous ⅛-inch (3 mm) thickness; fit into 9-inch (23 cm) pie plate, trimming to rim. Spread filling in shell. Roll out remaining pastry. Brush some of the egg over pastry rim. Fit pastry over filling; trim to leave ¾-inch (2 cm) overhang. Fold overhang under pastry rim; flute to seal. Lightly brush some of the remaining egg over pastry. Cut steam vents in top. Bake on bottom rack in 400°F (200°C) oven until golden and steaming, 50 to 60 minutes.

PER SERVING: about 455 cal, 19 g pro, 22 g total fat (10 g sat. fat), 47 g carb, 4 g fibre, 108 mg chol, 636 mg sodium, 529 mg potassium. % RDI: 6% calcium, 25% iron, 34% vit A, 17% vit C, 44% folate.

Cilantro Chutney

In food processor or blender, purée together 3½ cups packed fresh cilantro leaves; ½ cup packed fresh mint leaves; 2 green onions, chopped; half green finger hot pepper, seeded; ¼ cup water; 1 tbsp lemon juice; 2 tsp extra-virgin olive oil; and ¼ tsp each granulated sugar and salt until smooth.
MAKES ½ CUP

THE ULTIMATE FRIED CHICKEN

MAKES 12 TO 16 PIECES

The longer the chicken stays in the seasoned buttermilk marinade, the better, so it's worth taking the time to let it soak overnight. Flour and potato starch work in harmony to create a tasty coating—and the double dip is the secret to the chicken's ultra-crispy exterior.

BUTTERMILK MARINADE:

2 cups	buttermilk
1½ tsp	dry mustard
1 tsp	each garlic powder and onion powder
¾ tsp	salt
½ tsp	each sweet paprika and pepper
¼ tsp	poultry seasoning
pinch	cayenne pepper

FRIED CHICKEN:

2 kg	bone-in skin-on chicken thighs, drumsticks, wings and/or breasts
2 cups	all-purpose flour
½ cup	potato starch
2 tbsp	each garlic powder and onion powder
1 tbsp	dry mustard
2 tsp	sweet paprika
1½ tsp	salt
½ tsp	pepper
	vegetable oil for deep-frying

BUTTERMILK MARINADE: In bowl, whisk together buttermilk, mustard, garlic powder, onion powder, salt, paprika, pepper, poultry seasoning and cayenne pepper.

FRIED CHICKEN: Arrange chicken in single layer in large baking dish. Pour marinade over chicken, turning to coat. Cover and refrigerate for 4 hours. *(Make-ahead: Refrigerate for up to 24 hours.)*

In large bowl, whisk together flour, potato starch, garlic powder, onion powder, mustard, paprika, salt and pepper.

Pour enough oil into large deep skillet or Dutch oven to come 3 inches (8 cm) up side. Heat until deep-fryer thermometer reads 300°F (150°C).

While oil is heating, remove chicken from buttermilk mixture, letting excess drip back into bowl; reserve remaining marinade. Pat chicken dry with paper towels. Dredge chicken in flour mixture, tapping off excess. Dip in reserved marinade, letting excess drip off. Dredge again in flour mixture, tapping off excess.

Working in batches, fry chicken, turning occasionally, until instant-read thermometer inserted into thickest part of several pieces reads 165°F (74°C), 10 to 15 minutes per batch. Drain on rack over paper towel–lined baking sheet; let stand for 5 minutes before serving.

PER EACH OF 16 PIECES: about 264 cal, 15 g pro, 15 g total fat (3 g sat. fat), 18 g carb, 1 g fibre, 45 mg chol, 314 mg sodium, 216 mg potassium. % RDI: 4% calcium, 10% iron, 4% vit A, 2% vit C, 12% folate.

TIP FROM THE TEST KITCHEN

Using a slightly lower than normal frying temperature cooks the meat all the way through without burning the coating. Do keep in mind that the temperature of the frying oil will go up and down during the cooking process. Monitor it with your deep-fryer thermometer and adjust the heat as needed to keep it steady.

BRAISED KOREAN CHICKEN STEW

MAKES 6 TO 8 SERVINGS

Braising is a surefire way to keep meats, like these drumsticks, juicy as they cook. During autumn in Korea, this stew, called *tak tchim,* is made with chestnuts, so add them if you want to indulge in this well-loved dish.

1½ cups	boiling water
10	dried shiitake mushrooms
3 tbsp	vegetable oil
1.35 kg	bone-in skin-on chicken drumsticks
5	cloves garlic, minced
1 tbsp	Korean coarse chili powder (or 1 tsp hot pepper flakes), see tip, below
½ cup	sodium-reduced soy sauce
3 tbsp	granulated sugar
2 tbsp	Chinese rice wine, sake or dry sherry
2 tbsp	lemon juice
450 g	daikon radish, peeled and cut in 1½-inch (4 cm) cubes
4	green onions, chopped
1	large Spanish onion, chopped
12	vacuum-packed peeled chestnuts, about 65 g (optional)
2	hot green peppers, seeded and sliced
2 tsp	pine nuts, toasted

In small bowl, pour boiling water over shiitake mushrooms; let stand for 30 minutes. Reserving soaking liquid, drain mushrooms; remove and discard stems.

In large skillet, heat half of the oil over medium-high heat; working in batches, brown chicken, 4 to 5 minutes per batch. Using slotted spoon, transfer to plate.

Drain all but 1 tbsp fat from pan; cook garlic and chili powder over medium-low heat for 30 seconds. Stir in ½ cup water, soy sauce, sugar, rice wine and lemon juice. Remove from heat and set aside.

In shallow Dutch oven, bring radish, green onions, Spanish onion, chestnuts (if using), mushrooms and reserved soaking liquid to boil over medium heat; cover and boil for 5 minutes.

Add chicken and soy sauce mixture; bring to boil. Reduce heat to medium-low; cover and simmer for 25 minutes, stirring occasionally.

Stir in hot peppers; simmer until radish is tender, about 15 minutes. Garnish with pine nuts.

PER EACH OF 8 SERVINGS: about 300 cal, 23 g pro, 16 g total fat (4 g sat. fat), 17 g carb, 3 g fibre, 92 mg chol, 638 mg sodium, 552 mg potassium. % RDI: 4% calcium, 14% iron, 4% vit A, 27% vit C, 16% folate.

TIP FROM THE TEST KITCHEN

Look for Korean coarse chili powder in Asian grocery stores. It is made of just dried red hot peppers, unlike Mexican chili powder, which is often a blend of spices. Hot pepper flakes make a good substitute if you can't find it.

CHICKEN FLORENTINE LASAGNA

MAKES 12 SERVINGS

Layers of sauce, pasta, spinach and cheese baked until golden and ooey-gooey make an ideal dish for entertaining. Lasagna reheats well and leftovers taste even better the next day, so feel free to make it ahead of time.

CHICKEN TOMATO SAUCE: In Dutch oven, heat 1 tbsp of the oil over medium-high heat; working in batches, brown chicken, 4 to 5 minutes per batch. Using slotted spoon, transfer to bowl. Drain fat from pan. Add remaining oil; cook onions, garlic, basil, thyme, salt and pepper over medium heat until softened, about 5 minutes.

Add tomatoes and tomato paste, mashing with potato masher; bring to boil, scraping up browned bits. Return chicken and any accumulated juices to pan; reduce heat and simmer until thickened, about 20 minutes.

CHEESE SAUCE: While tomato sauce is simmering, in large saucepan, melt butter over medium heat; cook flour, stirring, for 1 minute. Whisk in milk and bring to boil; reduce heat and simmer, whisking, until thick enough to coat back of spoon, about 10 minutes. Whisk in salt, pepper and nutmeg. Whisk in Gruyère and Parmesan; set aside.

Rinse spinach; shake off excess water. Transfer to large saucepan; cover and cook over medium heat, with just water clinging to leaves, until wilted, about 5 minutes. Drain in colander; let cool. Press out any moisture; chop and set aside.

Meanwhile, in large saucepan of boiling salted water, cook noodles according to package directions until almost tender. Drain and cool in cold water; remove and arrange in single layer on damp tea towel.

ASSEMBLY: Spread 1 cup of the tomato sauce in 13- x 9-inch (3 L) baking dish. Top with three of the noodles; spread with one-third of the remaining tomato sauce. Spread with one-third of the cheese sauce, then half of the spinach. Starting with noodles, repeat layers once.

Top with remaining noodles; spread with remaining tomato sauce and cheese sauce. Sprinkle with Gruyère and Parmesan. Cover with greased foil. *(Make-ahead: Refrigerate for up to 24 hours; add 10 minutes to baking time.)*

Bake in 375°F (190°C) oven for 30 minutes. Uncover and bake until bubbly and tip of knife inserted in centre comes out hot, 20 to 30 minutes. Let stand for 10 minutes before serving.

PER SERVING: about 404 cal, 29 g pro, 19 g total fat (9 g sat. fat), 28 g carb, 3 g fibre, 104 mg chol, 662 mg sodium. % RDI: 39% calcium, 31% iron, 60% vit A, 28% vit C, 56% folate.

CHICKEN TOMATO SAUCE:	
2 tbsp	vegetable oil
900 g	boneless skinless chicken thighs, diced
2	onions, chopped
2	cloves garlic, minced
1½ tsp	dried basil
¾ tsp	each dried thyme, salt and pepper
1	can (796 mL) whole tomatoes
¼ cup	tomato paste

CHEESE SAUCE:	
¼ cup	butter
⅓ cup	all-purpose flour
4 cups	milk
½ tsp	each salt and pepper
¼ tsp	grated nutmeg
1 cup	shredded Gruyère cheese
¼ cup	grated Parmesan cheese

2	bags (each 284 g) fresh spinach, trimmed
9	lasagna noodles
1 cup	shredded Gruyère cheese
¼ cup	grated Parmesan cheese

PIRI-PIRI BARBECUED CHICKEN

MAKES 8 SERVINGS

Traditional Portuguese piri-piri chicken is notorious for its spiciness. This version mixes a little bit of that heat with classic North American barbecue flavours. Grilling the chicken over indirect heat allows it to cook through without charring the skin.

PIRI-PIRI BARBECUE SAUCE:

⅓ cup	tomato-based chili sauce
¼ cup	Piri-Piri Spice Mix (below)
2 tbsp	extra-virgin olive oil
2 tsp	packed brown sugar
1 tsp	white wine vinegar
¼ tsp	cayenne pepper

SPICED-RUBBED CHICKEN:

½ cup	Piri-Piri Spice Mix (below)
¼ cup	extra-virgin olive oil
1 tbsp	grated lemon zest
¼ cup	lemon juice
3	cloves garlic, smashed
1	red hot pepper, sliced (or 1 tsp hot pepper flakes)
8	bone-in skin-on chicken thighs (about 1.125 kg total)
8	bone-in skin-on chicken drumsticks (about 1.125 kg total)

PIRI-PIRI BARBECUE SAUCE: Stir together chili sauce, spice mix, oil, brown sugar, vinegar and cayenne pepper. Cover and refrigerate until ready to use. *(Make-ahead: Refrigerate for up to 24 hours.)*

SPICE-RUBBED CHICKEN: Mix together spice mix, oil, lemon zest, lemon juice, garlic and hot pepper to make paste. Place chicken thighs and drumsticks in large bowl; scrape mixture over top. Toss to coat. Cover and refrigerate for 6 hours. *(Make-ahead: Refrigerate for up to 24 hours.)*

Heat one burner of two-burner barbecue or two outside burners of three-burner barbecue to medium. Grease grill over unlit burner. Remove chicken from marinade, discarding garlic and hot pepper.

Place chicken, skin side down, on greased grill; close lid and grill until grill-marked, about 25 minutes. Turn and grill until juices run clear when chicken is pierced, about 20 minutes.

Move any pieces that need more crisping or colouring over direct medium heat. Brush all over with barbecue sauce; cover and grill for 5 minutes. Transfer to platter; let stand for 5 minutes before serving.

PER SERVING: about 510 cal, 35 g pro, 37 g total fat (9 g sat. fat), 10 g carb, 4 g fibre, 148 mg chol, 555 mg sodium, 591 mg potassium. % RDI: 6% calcium, 34% iron, 30% vit A, 17% vit C, 9% folate.

Piri-Piri Spice Mix

Stir together ¼ cup sweet paprika; 2 tbsp each smoked paprika, ground cumin and ground coriander; 2 tsp each garlic powder, onion powder and packed brown sugar; and 1 tsp each salt and pepper. *(Make-ahead: Store in airtight container for up to 2 weeks.)*

MAKES ¾ CUP

SPICY ORANGE BAKED CHICKEN DRUMSTICKS

MAKES 4 SERVINGS

You can marinate and bake these glossy drumsticks all in the same casserole dish, which makes this a fast dinner that's easy on the dishwasher.

1 tbsp	grated orange zest
½ cup	orange juice
⅓ cup	liquid honey
½ tsp	hot pepper flakes
¼ tsp	each salt and pepper
8	bone-in skin-on chicken drumsticks (about 900 g), skinned (see tip, below)

In shallow casserole dish, combine orange zest, orange juice, honey, hot pepper flakes, salt and pepper; add chicken, turning to coat. *(Make-ahead: Cover and refrigerate for up to 4 hours, turning once.)*

Roast in 425°F (220°C) oven, basting twice, until glossy and golden, and juices run clear when chicken is pierced, about 30 minutes.

PER SERVING: about 249 cal, 22 g pro, 6 g total fat (2 g sat. fat), 27 g carb, 0 g fibre, 81 mg chol, 228 mg sodium. % RDI: 2% calcium, 10% iron, 3% vit A, 17% vit C, 4% folate.

TIP FROM THE TEST KITCHEN

Chicken skin can get pretty slippery when you're trying to remove it. To get a solid grip, grab it with a paper towel before trying to pull it off.

CRISPY MARINATED CHICKEN DRUMSTICKS

MAKES 12 PIECES

Golden brown and crispy, this classic is equally tasty hot or cold. It makes a wonderful addition to a summer picnic.

Place chicken in bowl; add onion, thyme sprigs and buttermilk, turning chicken to coat. Cover and refrigerate for 2 hours. *(Make-ahead: Refrigerate for up to 24 hours.)*

In separate bowl, whisk together flour, chopped thyme, salt, cayenne pepper and black pepper. Discarding marinade, press chicken into flour mixture, turning to coat. Keeping pieces separate, refrigerate on waxed paper–lined baking sheet until coating is set, about 15 minutes or for up to 1 hour.

Pour enough oil into deep-fryer or large wide heavy-bottomed pot to come at least 2½ inches (6 cm), but no more than halfway, up side of pot. Heat over medium heat until deep-fryer thermometer reads 375°F (190°C).

Working in batches, deep-fry drumsticks until crisp and juices run clear when chicken is pierced, 10 to 12 minutes per batch. Let cool on paper towel–lined platter. *(Make-ahead: Refrigerate for up to 24 hours.)*

12	bone-in skin-on chicken drumsticks (about 1.35 kg)
1	onion, chopped
12	sprigs fresh thyme
2 cups	buttermilk
1½ cups	all-purpose flour
2 tbsp	chopped fresh thyme
2 tsp	salt
1 tsp	cayenne pepper
1 tsp	coarsely ground black pepper
	canola or vegetable oil for deep-frying

PER PIECE: about 189 cal, 14 g pro, 12 g total fat (3 g sat. fat), 5 g carb, trace fibre, 62 mg chol, 219 mg sodium, 174 mg potassium. % RDI: 1% calcium, 8% iron, 2% vit A, 3% vit C, 8% folate.

OLIVE CHICKEN TAGINE
WITH DRIED FRUIT COUSCOUS

MAKES 4 SERVINGS

The fragrant spices of North African cuisine come to life in this Moroccan-style tagine. You'll find jarred preserved lemons in specialty grocery stores and the international section of many supermarkets.

OLIVE CHICKEN TAGINE: Stir together ginger, cinnamon, coriander, nutmeg and cayenne pepper; set aside half. Stir flour, salt and black pepper into remaining ginger mixture. In large bowl, sprinkle flour mixture over chicken thighs and drumsticks; toss to coat. In Dutch oven, heat oil over medium-high heat; working in batches, brown chicken, turning once, about 4 minutes per batch. Using slotted spoon, transfer to plate.

Drain all but 2 tsp fat from pan; cook onion over medium heat, stirring often, until softened and light golden, about 5 minutes. Stir in garlic and carrots; cook until garlic is softened, about 2 minutes. Stir in reserved ginger mixture; cook, stirring, until fragrant, about 30 seconds. Stir in broth; bring to boil. Stir in preserved lemon zest and bay leaf; top with chicken, skin side up for thighs.

Cover and braise in 350°F (180°C) oven until chicken is very tender and juices run clear when chicken is pierced, about 1½ hours. Transfer chicken to platter; stir olives and lemon juice into pan. Spoon vegetable mixture and sauce around chicken on platter. Discard bay leaf.

DRIED FRUIT COUSCOUS: While tagine is braising, in bowl, stir together couscous, apricots, raisins, salt and pepper; pour boiling water and lemon juice over top. Cover and let stand until liquid is absorbed, about 5 minutes. Fluff with fork; stir in cilantro. Serve alongside tagine.

PER SERVING: about 643 cal, 33 g pro, 33 g total fat (8 g sat. fat), 54 g carb, 5 g fibre, 130 mg chol, 733 mg sodium, 719 mg potassium. % RDI: 7% calcium, 23% iron, 73% vit A, 18% vit C, 20% folate.

OLIVE CHICKEN TAGINE:

1 tsp	ground ginger
¾ tsp	cinnamon
¼ tsp	ground coriander
pinch	nutmeg
pinch	cayenne pepper
2 tbsp	all-purpose flour
pinch	each salt and black pepper
4	bone-in skin-on chicken thighs (about 650 g)
4	bone-in skin-on chicken drumsticks (about 475 g)
2 tsp	vegetable oil
1	onion, chopped
3	cloves garlic, chopped
2	carrots, sliced
1 cup	sodium-reduced chicken broth
2 tbsp	thinly sliced rinsed preserved lemon zest (see tip, below)
1	bay leaf
½ cup	pitted green olives
2 tsp	lemon juice

DRIED FRUIT COUSCOUS:

1 cup	couscous
¼ cup	dried apricots, chopped
¼ cup	golden raisins
¼ tsp	each salt and pepper
1½ cups	boiling water
1 tbsp	lemon juice
⅓ cup	chopped fresh cilantro

TIP FROM THE TEST KITCHEN
For this recipe, you only need the zest from the preserved lemons. Simply rinse the lemons to get rid of any excess brine and peel the zest off, discarding the pulp. Then slice the zest and add to the recipe.

THAI GRILLED CHICKEN

MAKES 6 TO 8 SERVINGS

In southeast Asia, chicken is marinated with plenty of aromatics, including cilantro and lime, then grilled and served with a simple dipping sauce. This popular street food makes a terrific laid-back dinner at home.

DIPPING SAUCE:

¼ cup	lime juice
2 tbsp	fish sauce
1	clove garlic, minced
1½ tsp	granulated sugar
½ tsp	finely chopped Thai bird's-eye peppers (or 2 tsp finely chopped jalapeño pepper)

THAI GRILLED CHICKEN:

½ cup	chopped fresh cilantro including stems and roots (see tip, below)
4	cloves garlic, chopped
2 tbsp	fish sauce
2 tsp	grated lime zest
2 tbsp	lime juice
1½ tsp	chopped fresh ginger
1½ tsp	coriander seeds
1 tsp	packed brown sugar
½ tsp	black pepper
¼ tsp	cayenne pepper
1.8 kg	chicken pieces
	fresh cilantro sprigs

DIPPING SAUCE: Stir together lime juice, fish sauce, garlic, sugar and bird's-eye peppers; set aside.

THAI GRILLED CHICKEN: In food processor, purée together chopped cilantro, garlic, fish sauce, lime zest, lime juice, ginger, coriander seeds, brown sugar, black pepper and cayenne pepper until smooth. Pour into bowl; add chicken and turn to coat. Cover and refrigerate for 8 hours, turning often. *(Make-ahead: Refrigerate for up to 24 hours.)*

Place chicken, bone side down, on greased grill over medium-high heat; brush with marinade. Discard any remaining marinade. Close lid and grill for 15 minutes; turn and cook until juices run clear when chicken is pierced, about 30 minutes.

Garnish with cilantro sprigs; serve with dipping sauce.

PER EACH OF 8 SERVINGS: about 206 cal, 30 g pro, 8 g total fat (2 g sat. fat), 4 g carb, trace fibre, 89 mg chol, 785 mg sodium. % RDI: 3% calcium, 11% iron, 3% vit A, 5% vit C, 5% folate.

TIP FROM THE TEST KITCHEN

Cilantro roots and stems have a stronger flavour than the leaves. They can be quite gritty, though. Wash the leaves well and give the roots a brief, gentle scrub under cold running water to get rid of any traces of dirt. You can also scrape the roots clean with a paring knife before washing to make the process a bit faster.

CHICKEN DRUMSTICKS
WITH APPLE STOUT BARBECUE SAUCE
MAKES 4 TO 6 SERVINGS

This recipe makes double the sauce you need for the drumsticks.
Refrigerate the remaining sauce for up to one month to make another batch,
or slather it on any other cut of chicken you like to grill.

In saucepan, heat oil over medium-high heat; sauté onion and garlic until softened. Add stout, applesauce, maple syrup, molasses, vinegar, tomato paste and salt.

Working in batches, transfer to blender and purée until smooth. Strain through fine-mesh sieve into clean saucepan. Bring to simmer over medium heat; cook until thickened and reduced to about 3 cups, 15 to 20 minutes.

Place chicken on greased grill over medium heat. Close lid and grill, turning every 10 minutes, until juices run clear when chicken is pierced, about 30 minutes.

Brush chicken with half of the sauce; grill, uncovered and turning often, until glazed, about 5 minutes.

1 tbsp	vegetable oil
1	onion, chopped
2	cloves garlic, minced
1½ cups	stout, porter or other dark beer
1 cup	unsweetened applesauce
½ cup	each maple syrup and cooking molasses
½ cup	cider vinegar
1	can (156 mL) tomato paste
½ tsp	salt
900 g	bone-in skin-on chicken drumsticks

PER EACH OF 6 SERVINGS: about 277 cal, 17 g pro, 11 g total fat (3 g sat. fat), 27 g carb, 1 g fibre, 67 mg chol, 185 mg sodium, 601 mg potassium. % RDI: 5% calcium, 17% iron, 4% vit A, 8% vit C, 4% folate.

GARAM MASALA DRUMSTICKS
WITH ALOO GOBI
MAKES 2 SERVINGS

This Indian-inspired one-pan dish is an easy weeknight meal for two. Aloo gobi means "potato cauliflower," and it's often seasoned with garlic, onion, ginger, curry and turmeric, which lend the yellow colour.

GARAM MASALA DRUMSTICKS:

½ cup	dried bread crumbs
4 tsp	garam masala (or Homemade Garam Masala, page 96)
¼ tsp	each ground coriander, garlic powder and onion powder
pinch	cayenne pepper
pinch	salt
4	bone-in skin-on chicken drumsticks (about 450 g), skinned
1 cup	medium shredded unsweetened coconut
1	egg

ALOO GOBI:

1¼ tsp	ground cumin
¾ tsp	each ground coriander, curry powder and turmeric
½ tsp	garlic powder
¼ tsp	salt
pinch	cayenne pepper
2 tbsp	vegetable oil
2 cups	cauliflower florets
340 g	mini yellow-fleshed potatoes, scrubbed and halved

CURRY YOGURT SAUCE:

½ cup	Balkan-style plain yogurt
2 tsp	lemon juice
½ tsp	liquid honey

GARAM MASALA DRUMSTICKS: In resealable plastic bag, combine bread crumbs, garam masala, coriander, garlic powder, onion powder and cayenne pepper. Sprinkle salt over chicken; add to bread crumb mixture and shake to coat. Transfer chicken to plate.

Add coconut to bread crumb mixture in bag. In small bowl, whisk egg. Dip chicken into egg, letting excess drip back into bowl; return to bread crumb mixture and shake to coat.

ALOO GOBI: In small bowl, stir together cumin, coriander, curry powder, turmeric, garlic powder, salt and cayenne pepper; remove 1 tsp and set aside for sauce. Stir oil into remaining spice mixture.

Place cauliflower and potatoes in separate bowls. Divide oil mixture between bowls; toss to coat.

TO FINISH: Arrange chicken and potatoes on lightly greased foil-lined rimmed baking sheet; bake in 400°F (200°C) oven for 20 minutes. Turn chicken; stir potatoes.

Add cauliflower to baking sheet; bake until juices run clear when chicken is pierced and cauliflower is beginning to brown, about 20 minutes.

CURRY YOGURT SAUCE: Stir together yogurt, lemon juice, honey and reserved spice mixture. Serve with chicken and vegetables.

PER SERVING: about 592 cal, 32 g pro, 32 g total fat (11 g sat. fat), 48 g carb, 9 g fibre, 165 mg chol, 512 mg sodium, 1,410 mg potassium. % RDI: 17% calcium, 41% iron, 9% vit A, 102% vit C, 48% folate.

ROAST CHICKEN
WITH CHORIZO
MAKES 4 TO 6 SERVINGS

Espelette chili powder is a quintessential spice found in the Basque region of Spain, but it's hard to buy here. A good substitute is a mix of sweet paprika, smoked paprika and cayenne pepper, which we've used in this take on a typical Basque chicken dish.

3	sweet red peppers, halved and cored
1	sweet onion, thickly sliced
1	can (796 mL) tomatoes, drained
140 g	dry-cured chorizo (see tip, below), cut in chunks
10	cloves garlic
8	small bone-in skin-on chicken pieces (thighs, drumsticks and/or half-breasts), about 1.25 kg total
2 tbsp	olive oil
1¾ tsp	chopped fresh thyme
½ tsp	salt
½ tsp	each sweet and smoked paprika
¼ tsp	cayenne pepper

On rimmed baking sheet, broil red peppers, cut sides down, until blackened, about 12 minutes. Let cool enough to handle. Peel off blackened skins. *(Make-ahead: Refrigerate in airtight container for up to 2 days.)*

In roasting pan, combine red peppers, onion, tomatoes, chorizo and garlic.

Toss chicken with oil to coat. Combine thyme, salt, sweet paprika, smoked paprika and cayenne pepper; rub all over chicken. Place, skin side up, on vegetable mixture in pan.

Roast in 450°F (230°C) oven, basting halfway through, until juices run clear when chicken is pierced, about 45 minutes.

PER EACH OF 6 SERVINGS: about 415 cal, 28 g pro, 28 g total fat (8 g sat. fat), 14 g carb, 2 g fibre, 95 mg chol, 668 mg sodium, 690 mg potassium. % RDI: 6% calcium, 19% iron, 25% vit A, 175% vit C, 13% folate.

TIP FROM THE TEST KITCHEN
Look for dry-cured Spanish chorizo or Portuguese chouriço in the deli section of the supermarket, near the cured meat. South American fresh chorizo is an uncooked sausage; don't substitute it for the dry-cured.

ROASTED CHICKEN LEGS
WITH CORIANDER, LEMON AND FIGS
MAKES 8 SERVINGS

Chicken legs are excellent for braising because the meat doesn't dry out.
Figs add subtle sweetness to the sauce; if you don't like figs, dried apricots and
prunes make good substitutes.

Remove skin from chicken; cut drumsticks from thighs at joint. Sprinkle with
¼ tsp each of the salt and pepper.

In large shallow Dutch oven, heat oil over medium-high heat; working in
batches, brown chicken, 4 to 5 minutes per batch. Using slotted spoon,
transfer to plate.

Drain fat from pan. Add garlic, onion and remaining salt and pepper; cook
over medium heat, stirring occasionally, until softened, about 3 minutes.
Add broth, lemon zest and lemon juice; bring to boil, stirring and scraping
up browned bits from bottom of pan.

Return chicken and any accumulated juices to pan. Trim stems from figs;
add figs to pan. Add half of the cilantro; bring to simmer. Cover and braise in
325°F (160°C) oven until juices run clear when chicken is pierced, 45 to
60 minutes. Transfer chicken to deep platter.

Whisk cornstarch with cold water. Skim fat from pan juices; bring pan juices
to boil. Whisk in cornstarch mixture; cook, stirring, for 1 minute. Pour over
chicken. Sprinkle with remaining cilantro. Garnish with lemon.

8	bone-in skin-on whole chicken legs (about 1.35 kg)
½ tsp	each salt and pepper
1 tbsp	vegetable oil
3	cloves garlic, minced
1	onion, chopped
2 cups	sodium-reduced chicken broth
1 tsp	grated lemon zest
3 tbsp	lemon juice
16	dried whole figs
⅓ cup	chopped fresh cilantro
1 tbsp	cornstarch
1 tbsp	cold water
half	lemon, thinly sliced

PER SERVING: about 190 cal, 17 g pro, 6 g total fat (1 g sat. fat), 17 g carb,
3 g fibre, 58 mg chol, 358 mg sodium. % RDI: 4% calcium, 9% iron, 2% vit A,
13% vit C, 4% folate.

STICKY HONEY SESAME DRUMSTICKS
MAKES 4 SERVINGS

Five pantry staples plus a family pack of drumsticks equals one saucy, scrumptious supper. This is a weeknight superstar, ready in less than 30 minutes. Dress up your drums with pretty sliced green onions and lime wedges.

In large bowl, whisk together honey, sesame seeds, sesame oil, soy sauce and garlic. Using paper towels, pat chicken dry; toss chicken with honey mixture to coat. Arrange on parchment paper–lined rimmed baking sheet.

Bake in 400°F (200°C) oven, turning occasionally, until juices run clear when thickest part of chicken is pierced, about 25 minutes.

PER SERVING: about 377 cal, 25 g pro, 23 g total fat (5 g sat. fat), 18 g carb, 1 g fibre, 100 mg chol, 365 mg sodium, 303 mg potassium. % RDI: 2% calcium, 15% iron, 3% vit A, 2% vit C, 6% folate.

¼ cup	liquid honey
2 tbsp	sesame seeds
2 tbsp	sesame oil
2 tbsp	sodium-reduced soy sauce
4	cloves garlic, minced
900 g	bone-in skin-on chicken drumsticks

PIRI-PIRI CHICKEN LEGS

MAKES 6 SERVINGS

A little tangy, a little spicy and so good, these drumsticks are just the thing for a summer barbecue. Creamy Brussels Sprout Slaw (below) makes a fantastic side.

1.5 kg	bone-in skin-on whole chicken legs
3 tbsp	grated lemon zest
¼ cup	lemon juice
1	head garlic, minced
2 tbsp	olive oil
1 tbsp	hot pepper flakes
1 tsp	salt

Trim excess fat from chicken if necessary. In glass bowl, combine lemon zest, lemon juice, garlic, oil, hot pepper flakes and salt. Add chicken, turning to coat and pushing some of the mixture under skin. Cover and refrigerate for 8 hours. *(Make-ahead: Refrigerate for up to 24 hours.)*

Arrange chicken, skin side up, on foil-lined rimmed baking sheet. Roast in 425°F (220°C) oven, brushing once with pan drippings, until juices run clear when chicken is pierced, about 35 minutes.

PER SERVING: about 374 cal, 28 g pro, 27 g total fat (7 g sat. fat), 4 g carb, 1 g fibre, 120 mg chol, 499 mg sodium. % RDI: 3% calcium, 10% iron, 11% vit A, 17% vit C, 5% folate.

Creamy Brussels Sprout Slaw

In food processor, pulse 8 cups halved trimmed brussels sprouts (12 cups whole) until finely chopped. In large bowl, whisk together 1 cup light mayonnaise, ½ cup milk, ¼ cup prepared horseradish, 2 tbsp lemon juice, 2 tsp liquid honey, and pinch each salt and pepper. Add brussels sprouts; stir to coat. Cover and refrigerate for 1 hour. *(Make-ahead: Refrigerate for up to 2 days.)*
MAKES 12 SERVINGS

SLOW-ROASTED FENNEL CHICKEN

MAKES 4 TO 6 SERVINGS

Only seven ingredients and a long, slow roast are required to make this elegant dinner. It tastes amazing, and no one will ever know how easy it was to make.

Trim excess fat from chicken if necessary. In roasting pan, toss together chicken, tarragon, oil, salt and pepper. Arrange fennel and lemon around chicken in pan.

Roast, skin side up, in 400°F (200°C) oven, basting occasionally, until juices run clear when chicken is pierced, about 1 hour.

Transfer chicken and fennel to platter. Skim fat from pan juices and discard. Using tongs, squeeze juice from lemon into drippings; return rinds to pan and whisk to combine. Pour over chicken.

PER EACH OF 6 SERVINGS: about 315 cal, 19 g pro, 25 g total fat (6 g sat. fat), 4 g carb, 1 g fibre, 81 mg chol, 225 mg sodium, 397 mg potassium. % RDI: 3% calcium, 11% iron, 4% vit A, 15% vit C, 6% folate.

4	bone-in skin-on whole chicken legs (about 1.125 kg)
3 tbsp	chopped fresh tarragon
3 tbsp	olive oil
½ tsp	coarse salt
¼ tsp	pepper
1	fennel bulb, cut in eighths
1	lemon, quartered

MAPLE BUTTERMILK GRILLED CHICKEN

MAKES 10 TO 12 SERVINGS

Everyone will love this sweet and savoury chicken. For a juicy garnish,
cut a lime in half to grill alongside the chicken for the last 10 minutes.

In large bowl, combine buttermilk, green onions, garlic, pepper, cinnamon
and hot pepper flakes. Add chicken, turning to coat. Cover and refrigerate for
2 hours. *(Make-ahead: Refrigerate for up to 24 hours.)*

Remove chicken from marinade; discard marinade. Sprinkle chicken with salt.
Place on greased grill over medium-high heat; close lid and grill, turning
occasionally, until instant-read thermometer inserted in thickest parts of
pieces reads 165°F (74°C), about 35 minutes.

Grill, brushing with maple syrup and turning occasionally, until glossy and
coated, about 5 minutes.

PER EACH OF 12 SERVINGS: about 113 cal, 10 g pro, 5 g total fat (2 g sat. fat),
6 g carb, trace fibre, 34 mg chol, 149 mg sodium, 157 mg potassium.
% RDI: 3% calcium, 2% iron, 2% vit A, 2% folate.

2 cups	buttermilk
2	green onions, chopped
4	cloves garlic, minced
½ tsp	pepper
¼ tsp	each cinnamon and hot pepper flakes
20	small bone-in skin-on chicken pieces (about 1.125 kg), see tip, below
½ tsp	salt
¼ cup	maple syrup

TIP FROM THE TEST KITCHEN
This dish is also excellent made with a mix of
white and dark meat pieces. When cooking them
together, be sure to cut chicken breasts in half
crosswise, through the bone, to make them
similar in size to the thighs and drumsticks.
That way, everything will cook through in
the same amount of time.

ROASTED CHICKEN PIECES
WITH BALSAMIC FENNEL

MAKES 4 SERVINGS

Radishes, fennel and balsamic vinegar turn into a delightfully sweet side dish.
Make sure to use bone-in, skin-on chicken for the best flavour.

675 g	bone-in skin-on chicken thighs
675 g	bone-in skin-on chicken drumsticks
½ tsp	each salt and pepper
1 tbsp	olive oil
1	large fennel bulb, cored and thinly sliced
10	radishes, trimmed and cut in ½-inch (1 cm) wedges
2 tbsp	balsamic vinegar
2 tbsp	chopped fresh parsley

Sprinkle chicken thighs and drumsticks with half each of the salt and pepper.

In large skillet, heat 1 tsp of the oil over medium heat; working in batches, brown chicken, turning once, until golden, 4 to 5 minutes per batch. Drain fat from pan.

Meanwhile, in large bowl, whisk together remaining oil, salt and pepper; stir in fennel and radishes. Spread on large foil- or parchment paper–lined rimmed baking sheet. Top with chicken.

Bake in 400°F (200°C) oven until juices run clear when chicken is pierced, about 18 minutes. Transfer chicken to plate and cover loosely with foil.

Broil vegetables until tender-crisp, about 2 minutes; toss with vinegar. Serve with chicken. Garnish with parsley.

PER SERVING: about 576 cal, 44 g pro, 40 g total fat (11 g sat. fat), 8 g carb, 3 g fibre, 209 mg chol, 544 mg sodium, 901 mg potassium. % RDI: 7% calcium, 25% iron, 10% vit A, 32% vit C, 16% folate.

LEMON BRAISED CHICKEN
MAKES 4 SERVINGS

Use leg quarters, thighs or drumsticks for this chicken braised in a tangy sauce.
The canned anchovies add a mellow, savoury flavour without being fishy.

Starting at thigh end of chicken legs, pull skin away from flesh and, gripping with paper towel, pull downward to remove; discard skin. Cut drumsticks from thighs at joint. Trim excess fat from chicken if necessary. In shallow dish, combine flour, salt and pepper; dredge chicken in flour mixture to coat, reserving excess.

In large shallow Dutch oven, heat oil over medium-high heat; brown chicken, 4 to 5 minutes. Using slotted spoon, transfer to plate.

Drain fat from pan; reduce heat to medium. Cook garlic, onion and anchovies, stirring occasionally, until onion is softened, about 5 minutes. Add broth, wine, lemon zest and lemon juice, stirring and scraping up browned bits from bottom of pan. Return chicken to pan and top with lemon slices; bring to boil.

Cover and braise in 325°F (160°C) oven until chicken is tender and juices run clear when thickest part of thigh is pierced, 45 to 60 minutes. Transfer chicken to platter.

Skim fat from pan juices. Whisk reserved flour mixture with cold water; whisk into pan. Add olives and parsley; simmer over medium heat until thick enough to coat back of spoon, about 5 minutes. Pour over chicken.

PER SERVING: about 468 cal, 41 g pro, 26 g total fat (4 g sat. fat), 17 g carb, 4 g fibre, 162 mg chol, 1,625 mg sodium. % RDI: 9% calcium, 27% iron, 5% vit A, 52% vit C, 15% folate.

4	bone-in skin-on chicken leg quarters (1.35 kg total), see tip, below
¼ cup	all-purpose flour
¼ tsp	each salt and pepper
2 tbsp	vegetable oil
3	cloves garlic, minced
1	onion, sliced
4	anchovy fillets, chopped (or 2 tsp anchovy paste)
1 cup	chicken broth
1 cup	dry white wine or chicken broth
1 tsp	grated lemon zest
2 tbsp	lemon juice
1	lemon, thinly sliced
¼ cup	cold water
1 cup	oil-cured black olives
¼ cup	chopped fresh flatleaf parsley

TIP FROM THE TEST KITCHEN
Chicken leg quarters include a part of the back as well and are a bit bigger than whole chicken legs. They make a substantial meal.

CRISP AND JUICY BARBECUED CHICKEN

MAKES 4 TO 6 SERVINGS

There's a secret to barbecuing chicken so it's cooked through, with crispy golden skin that has everyone asking for seconds: Grill it over indirect heat until the juices run clear, then move it to direct heat to crisp and colour.

In food processor, purée onions, garlic, jalapeño peppers, basil, oil, vinegar, salt, paprika and hot pepper flakes to form paste. Scrape into large bowl.

Trim any visible fat or loose skin from chicken. If desired, cut breasts on diagonal into two pieces. Add chicken to onion mixture; toss to coat. Cover and refrigerate, turning occasionally, for 6 hours. *(Make-ahead: Refrigerate for up to 12 hours.)*

Set foil drip pan on one burner of two-burner barbecue or centre burner of three-burner barbecue. Heat remaining burner(s) to medium. Place chicken, bone side down, on greased grill over drip pan. Close lid and grill, turning halfway through, until juices run clear when thighs are pierced or breasts are no longer pink inside, about 45 minutes.

Move any pieces that need more crisping or colouring over direct medium heat; close lid and grill until golden, about 5 minutes.

PER EACH OF 6 SERVINGS: about 261 cal, 22 g pro, 18 g total fat (4 g sat. fat), 2 g carb, 1 g fibre, 80 mg chol, 453 mg sodium. % RDI: 2% calcium, 9% iron, 8% vit A, 7% vit C, 6% folate.

4	green onions, chopped
4	cloves garlic
2	jalapeño peppers, seeded and chopped
½ cup	packed fresh basil leaves
¼ cup	extra-virgin olive oil
2 tbsp	wine vinegar
1 tsp	salt
1 tsp	smoked or sweet paprika
½ tsp	hot pepper flakes
1.5 kg	bone-in skin-on chicken thighs, wings, drumsticks and/or breasts (see tip, below)

TIP FROM THE TEST KITCHEN
Use whichever chicken cuts you prefer. We like thighs because they're meaty and juicy, and there's less risk of overcooking them than with breasts.

BALSAMIC PEPPERCORN CHICKEN LEGS
MAKES 8 SERVINGS

Cooking tames the tang of vinegar and blends the robust flavours of mustard, peppercorns and garlic in this juicy, budget-friendly main dish.

8	bone-in skin-on whole chicken legs (about 2.5 kg)
¾ cup	balsamic or red wine vinegar
3 tbsp	extra-virgin olive oil
2 tbsp	Dijon mustard
6	cloves garlic, minced
1 tbsp	coarsely cracked black peppercorns
2 tsp	dried thyme
2 tsp	dried oregano
½ tsp	salt

Trim excess fat from chicken if necessary; place chicken in large shallow glass dish. In bowl, whisk together vinegar, oil, mustard, garlic, peppercorns, thyme, oregano and salt; pour over chicken. Cover and refrigerate for 2 hours, turning once. *(Make-ahead: Refrigerate for up to 8 hours.)*

Place chicken on greased grill over medium heat. Brush with marinade; discard any remaining marinade. Close lid and grill, turning once, until juices run clear when chicken is pierced, about 40 minutes.

PER SERVING: about 196 cal, 20 g pro, 12 g total fat (3 g sat. fat), 1 g carb, 0 g fibre, 92 mg chol, 119 mg sodium. % RDI: 1% calcium, 9% iron, 3% vit A, 4% folate.

JERK CHICKEN
WITH GRILLED BANANAS
MAKES 4 SERVINGS

Jerk chicken, covered in a mouthwatering, spice-infused sauce, is a Jamaican favourite. Here, it's accompanied by grilled bananas, which stand in for the traditional plantains.

Trim excess fat from chicken if necessary; place chicken in shallow dish. Combine garlic, cumin, paprika, ginger, curry paste, allspice, pepper, thyme, salt and cayenne pepper; rub all over chicken. Cover and refrigerate for 2 hours. *(Make-ahead: Refrigerate for up to 24 hours.)*

Place chicken on greased grill over medium-high heat; close lid and grill, turning halfway through, until juices run clear when chicken is pierced, about 25 minutes.

Meanwhile, peel and cut each banana diagonally into thirds; brush with oil. Add to grill; cook, turning often, until golden, about 6 minutes. Sprinkle with lemon juice; serve with chicken.

PER SERVING: about 406 cal, 32 g pro, 18 g total fat (5 g sat. fat), 32 g carb, 3 g fibre, 105 mg chol, 393 mg sodium. % RDI: 6% calcium, 31% iron, 16% vit A, 17% vit C, 9% folate.

4	bone-in skin-on chicken leg quarters or 8 bone-in skin-on chicken thighs, trimmed (about 1.35 kg)
2	cloves garlic, minced
1 tbsp	each ground cumin and sweet paprika
1 tbsp	minced fresh ginger
1 tbsp	curry paste or powder
2 tsp	each ground allspice and pepper
1 tsp	dried thyme
½ tsp	salt
¼ tsp	cayenne pepper
4	firm bananas (see tip, below)
1 tsp	vegetable oil
2 tsp	lemon juice

TIP FROM THE TEST KITCHEN
Look for bananas with a green tinge to the peel to ensure they're firm enough to stand up to grilling. They will be a little more starchy than fully ripe bananas—perfect with the spicy chicken.

**INDIAN-SPICED WINGS
WITH CUCUMBER CILANTRO DIP**
(PAGE 163)

CHAPTER 4

WINGS, BURGERS & MORE

BUFFALO-STYLE WINGS
WITH BLUE CHEESE DIP AND CRUDITÉS
MAKES ABOUT 30 PIECES

This is the most widely enjoyed and recognized style of chicken wing.
Frank's RedHot Original Cayenne Pepper Sauce is the classic hot sauce used to make this
recipe, but feel free to experiment with other sauces, adjusting the quantity as desired.

BLUE CHEESE DIP:

⅔ cup	light sour cream
½ cup	crumbled blue cheese (about 60 g)
⅓ cup	light mayonnaise
1 tsp	white wine vinegar
¼ tsp	pepper

BUFFALO-STYLE WINGS:

⅓ cup	butter
⅔ cup	Frank's RedHot Original hot sauce
4 tsp	cider vinegar
½ tsp	salt
1.35 kg	whole chicken wings
	vegetable oil for deep-frying
6 cups	vegetable crudités

BLUE CHEESE DIP: In food processor or blender, blend sour cream, blue
cheese, mayonnaise, vinegar and pepper until smooth. Transfer to bowl; cover
and refrigerate for 30 minutes. *(Make-ahead: Refrigerate for up to 24 hours.)*

BUFFALO-STYLE WINGS: In small saucepan, melt butter over medium heat;
stir in hot sauce, vinegar and salt. Set aside and keep warm. Remove tips
from chicken wings; separate wings at joint.

Pour enough oil into deep fryer or large wide heavy-bottomed pot to come
at least 2½ inches (6 cm), but no more than halfway, up side. Heat on
medium until deep-fryer thermometer reads 375°F (190°C). Working in
two batches, deep-fry wings until crisp, floating and juices run clear when
wings are pierced, 10 to 12 minutes per batch. Using slotted spoon, transfer to
paper towel–lined bowl.

Discard paper towels; pour sauce over wings, tossing to coat. Serve with
vegetables and blue cheese dip.

PER PIECE: about 90 cal, 5 g pro, 7 g total fat (3 g sat. fat), 2 g carb,
trace fibre, 24 mg chol, 320 mg sodium. % RDI: 3% calcium, 2% iron,
13% vit A, 7% vit C, 3% folate.

TIP FROM THE TEST KITCHEN
For extra-crispy wings, toss them with sauce and
roast on foil-lined rimmed baking sheet in 400°F
(200°C) oven until sauce is set, about 8 minutes.

PARMESAN ROSEMARY CHICKEN WINGS

MAKES ABOUT 8 PIECES

No need for messy deep-frying to get these crunchy baked wings. They make a fun meal for two—just add some sliced baby cukes, carrots and cherry tomatoes.

2 tbsp	butter, melted
2 tbsp	Dijon mustard
450 g	separated trimmed chicken wings (see tip, below)
¾ cup	grated Parmesan cheese
¼ cup	dried bread crumbs
½ tsp	chopped fresh rosemary
¼ tsp	pepper

In large bowl, whisk butter with mustard until smooth. Pat chicken wings dry with paper towels. Add wings to butter mixture along with Parmesan, bread crumbs, rosemary and pepper; toss to coat. Arrange on parchment paper–lined rimmed baking sheet.

Bake in 425°F (220°C) oven, turning once, until juices run clear when wings are pierced, about 25 minutes.

PER PIECE: about 107 cal, 8 g pro, 8 g total fat (3 g sat. fat), 2 g carb, trace fibre, 31 mg chol, 136 mg sodium, 60 mg potassium. % RDI: 5% calcium, 3% iron, 3% vit A, 1% vit C, 1% folate.

TIP FROM THE TEST KITCHEN

Already separated and trimmed chicken wings are a real time-saver. If you can't find them, cut tips off whole chicken wings, and then cut wings at remaining joint.

CHILI CHICKEN WINGS

MAKES ABOUT 12 PIECES

These saucy grilled wings are covered with a delicious mix of chili powder and spices, and then dunked in a savoury-sweet homemade barbecue sauce. They're totally addictive.

ANCHO TOMATO SAUCE: In saucepan, heat oil over medium heat; cook onion and garlic, stirring occasionally, until softened, about 3 minutes. Stir in ketchup, molasses, vinegar, ancho chili powder, mustard and hot pepper sauce; reduce heat and simmer, stirring occasionally, until bubbly, about 5 minutes. Let cool.

CHILI CHICKEN WINGS: While sauce is cooking, mix together chili powder, paprika, brown sugar, cumin, garlic powder, salt and pepper. Straighten each chicken wing; push skewer through length from base to tip. Rub all over with spice mixture. Cover and let stand for 30 minutes. *(Make-ahead: Refrigerate for up to 24 hours, turning occasionally.)*

Place wings on greased grill over medium heat; close lid and grill, turning once, for 10 minutes. Baste with sauce; grill, basting and turning occasionally, until crisp and juices run clear when wings are pierced, 15 to 25 minutes.

PER PIECE: about 233 cal, 18 g pro, 13 g total fat (3 g sat. fat), 10 g carb, trace fibre, 53 mg chol, 343 mg sodium. % RDI: 3% calcium, 13% iron, 15% vit A, 8% vit C, 3% folate.

ANCHO TOMATO SAUCE:

1 tbsp	vegetable oil
¼ cup	minced onion
2	cloves garlic, minced
¾ cup	ketchup or tomato-based chili sauce
2 tbsp	fancy molasses
1 tbsp	cider vinegar
2 tsp	ancho chili powder
1 tsp	dry mustard
1 tsp	hot pepper sauce

CHILI CHICKEN WINGS:

1½ tbsp	chili powder
1 tbsp	sweet paprika
1 tbsp	packed brown sugar
1½ tsp	ground cumin
½ tsp	garlic powder
¼ tsp	each salt and pepper
1.35 kg	whole chicken wings

TIP FROM THE TEST KITCHEN
Any kind of long skewer will work for this recipe, but if you use metal ones, you can skip the step of soaking them for 30 minutes. Wooden or bamboo skewers need to be soaked so they don't char on the grill.

GRILLED HONEY-GARLIC CHICKEN WINGS

MAKES ABOUT 24 PIECES

Chicken wings are a guaranteed hit with crowds, but they don't always come off the grill super crispy. Our solution: Render out some of the fat in the oven before grilling.

Sprinkle chicken wings with salt and pepper. Arrange on greased rack on rimmed baking sheet; bake in 325°F (160°C) oven until juices run clear when wings are pierced, about 20 minutes. *(Make-ahead: Let cool; cover and refrigerate for up to 24 hours. Reheat on grill before continuing.)*

Meanwhile, in bowl, stir together honey, garlic and soy sauce.

Place wings on greased grill over medium-high heat; grill wings, turning and brushing with honey mixture often, until browned, about 5 minutes.

900 g	separated trimmed chicken wings (see tip, page 158)
¼ tsp	each salt and pepper
¼ cup	liquid honey (see tip, below)
4	cloves garlic, minced
2 tbsp	sodium-reduced soy sauce

PER PIECE: about 53 cal, 4 g pro, 3 g total fat (1 g sat. fat), 3 g carb, 0 g fibre, 12 mg chol, 86 mg sodium, 33 mg potassium. % RDI: 1% iron, 1% vit A.

TIP FROM THE TEST KITCHEN
A light, flavourful honey, such as clover or wildflower, would be perfect for this recipe. Buckwheat honey might be a bit too strong— save it for baking.

BEER BARBECUE SAUCE WINGS
WITH MUSTARD DIP AND CRUDITÉS
MAKES ABOUT 30 PIECES

The malty sweetness of beer makes an enticing marinade.
Any beer will do, but a strong-flavoured wheat beer or ale is the best.

BEER-MARINATED WINGS:

1.35 kg	whole chicken wings
¾ cup	wheat beer or ale
1 tsp	Worcestershire sauce
½ tsp	celery seed

BARBECUE SAUCE:

⅓ cup	ketchup
4 tsp	wine vinegar
1 tbsp	molasses
2 tsp	extra-virgin olive oil
¾ tsp	sweet paprika
pinch	each salt and pepper

MUSTARD DIP:

1 cup	light mayonnaise
2 tbsp	grainy mustard
6 cups	vegetable crudités

BEER-MARINATED WINGS: Remove tips from chicken wings; separate wings at joint. In large bowl, mix together beer, Worcestershire sauce and celery seed; add wings, tossing to coat. Cover and refrigerate for 12 hours. *(Make-ahead: Refrigerate for up to 24 hours.)*

Reserving marinade, place wings on rack on foil-lined rimmed baking sheet. Roast in 400°F (200°C) oven, turning once, until juices run clear when wings are pierced, about 45 minutes.

BARBECUE SAUCE: While wings are roasting, in small saucepan, bring reserved marinade, ketchup, vinegar, molasses, oil, paprika, salt and pepper to boil; reduce heat, partially cover and simmer, stirring occasionally, until thickened and reduced to ¾ cup, about 10 minutes. Remove ¼ cup and set aside for dip.

In bowl, toss wings with sauce. Return to rack-lined rimmed baking sheet; roast until sauce is set, about 8 minutes.

MUSTARD DIP: Combine reserved sauce, mayonnaise and mustard. Serve with wings and vegetables.

PER PIECE: about 85 cal, 5 g pro, 6 g total fat (1 g sat. fat), 3 g carb, trace fibre, 15 mg chol, 122 mg sodium. % RDI: 1% calcium, 3% iron, 10% vit A, 7% vit C, 3% folate.

INDIAN-SPICED WINGS
WITH CUCUMBER CILANTRO DIP

MAKES ABOUT 30 PIECES

The yogurt in this curry-flavoured marinade contributes to the wings' tenderness, while mango chutney adds a welcome hint of sweetness.

INDIAN-SPICED WINGS: Remove tips from chicken wings; separate wings at joint. In large bowl, mix together yogurt, chutney, curry paste, lemon juice, garlic and salt; add wings, tossing to coat. Cover and refrigerate for 4 hours. *(Make-ahead: Refrigerate for up to 24 hours.)*

CUCUMBER CILANTRO DIP: While wings are chilling, mix together yogurt, cucumber, cilantro, lemon juice and salt; cover and refrigerate for 1 hour.

TO FINISH: Place wings on rack on foil-lined rimmed baking sheet. Roast in 400°F (200°C) oven, turning once, until juices run clear when wings are pierced, about 45 minutes. Serve with vegetables and dip.

PER PIECE about 68 cal, 5 g pro, 4 g total fat (1 g sat. fat), 3 g carb, trace fibre, 14 mg chol, 121 mg sodium. % RDI: 2% calcium, 2% iron, 10% vit A, 7% vit C, 3% folate.

INDIAN-SPICED WINGS:

1.35 kg	whole chicken wings
¼ cup	Balkan-style plain yogurt
¼ cup	mango chutney
2 tbsp	mild or medium curry paste
2 tbsp	lemon juice
2	cloves garlic, minced
½ tsp	salt

CUCUMBER CILANTRO DIP:

¾ cup	Balkan-style plain yogurt
½ cup	finely chopped seeded peeled cucumber
¼ cup	chopped fresh cilantro
1 tsp	lemon juice
pinch	salt
6 cups	vegetable crudités

TIP FROM THE TEST KITCHEN
If your mango chutney is chunky, chop the solids before adding it to the recipe.

GARLIC GINGER CHICKEN WINGS

MAKES ABOUT 25 PIECES

Aromatic ginger and garlic are terrific partners for chicken. Here, they're even tastier in the company of a salty-sweet sauce accented with hot pepper.

1.35 kg	separated trimmed chicken wings (see tip, page 158)
1 tsp	five-spice powder
3 tbsp	soy sauce
3 tbsp	unseasoned rice vinegar or white vinegar
2 tbsp	packed brown sugar
4 tsp	finely chopped garlic (about 3 cloves)
4 tsp	finely chopped fresh ginger
4 tsp	vegetable oil
pinch	pepper
1	small hot pepper (such as Thai bird's-eye pepper), finely chopped
3	green onions, chopped

In bowl, sprinkle chicken wings with five-spice powder; toss with 1 tbsp of the soy sauce. Arrange on rack on foil-lined rimmed baking sheet; bake in 425°F (220°C) oven, turning once, until crisp, golden and juices run clear when wings are pierced, 40 to 45 minutes.

In large bowl, stir together remaining soy sauce, vinegar, brown sugar, garlic, ginger, oil, pepper and hot pepper; add wings and toss to coat. To serve, sprinkle with green onions.

PER PIECE: about 73 cal, 6 g pro, 5 g total fat (1 g sat. fat), 2 g carb, trace fibre, 17 mg chol, 90 mg sodium, 56 mg potassium. % RDI: 1% calcium, 3% iron, 1% vit A, 2% vit C, 1% folate.

CRISPY FLOUR-DUSTED WINGS
WITH PARSLEY DIP AND CRUDITÉS

MAKES ABOUT 30 PIECES

These are the ultimate in crunchy wings. Eat them hot and juicy straight from the oven or enjoy them sprinkled with lemon juice and a touch of hot sauce.

PARSLEY DIP:

½ cup	each light sour cream and light mayonnaise
¼ cup	chopped fresh parsley
1 tsp	grated lemon zest
dash	hot pepper sauce

CRISPY WINGS:

1.35 kg	whole chicken wings
	vegetable oil for deep-frying
½ cup	all-purpose flour
¾ tsp	each sweet paprika and ground coriander
¾ tsp	each salt and pepper
6 cups	vegetable crudités

PARSLEY DIP: Stir together sour cream, mayonnaise, parsley, lemon zest and hot pepper sauce; cover and refrigerate for 30 minutes. *(Make-ahead: Refrigerate for up to 24 hours.)*

CRISPY WINGS: While dip is chilling, remove tips from chicken wings; separate wings at joint. Pour enough oil into deep fryer or large wide heavy-bottomed pot to come at least 2½ inches (6 cm), but no more than halfway, up side. Heat over medium heat until deep-fryer thermometer reads 375°F (190°C).

In bowl, stir together flour, paprika, coriander, salt and pepper. Dredge wings to coat all over; shake off any excess.

Working in two batches, deep-fry wings until crisp, floating and juices run clear when wings are pierced, 10 to 12 minutes per batch. Using slotted spoon, transfer to paper towel–lined bowl. Serve with dip and vegetables.

PER PIECE: about 72 cal, 4 g pro, 5 g total fat (1 g sat. fat), 3 g carb, trace fibre, 13 mg chol, 81 mg sodium. % RDI: 2% calcium, 3% iron, 10% vit A, 9% vit C, 4% folate.

CHINESE STICKY CHICKEN WINGS

MAKES ABOUT 12 PIECES

Fragrant five-spice powder and a sweet-tart caramel glaze make these wings irresistible. The hot pepper is optional, but it gives the chicken a nice bite.

In heavy-bottomed saucepan, heat sugar over medium heat, swirling occasionally but not stirring, until melted, clear and nutty brown. Remove from heat.

Averting face, stir in soy sauce and vinegar until bubbles subside; stir in five-spice powder. If mixture clumps, stir over low heat until almost melted (any remainder will melt in cooking). Set caramel mixture aside.

Sprinkle chicken wings with pepper. In wok or skillet, heat oil over medium-high heat; working in two batches, fry wings until golden and juices run clear when wings are pierced, about 6 minutes per batch. Drain in sieve over heatproof bowl.

Reserving 1½ tbsp, drain oil from wok; wipe clean. Return reserved oil to wok and heat over medium-high heat; fry green onions and garlic until fragrant, about 30 seconds.

Add wings, and hot pepper (if using); stir-fry for 1 minute. Add caramel mixture; stir-fry until reduced and wings are coated, about 2 minutes.

½ cup	granulated sugar
3 tbsp	sodium-reduced soy sauce or tamari
1 tbsp	unseasoned rice vinegar or cider vinegar
¾ tsp	five-spice powder (see tip, below)
675 g	separated trimmed chicken wings (see tip, page 158)
¼ tsp	white pepper
1 cup	vegetable oil
3	green onions, cut in 1½-inch (4 cm) pieces
2	cloves garlic, minced
1	hot red pepper (optional), seeded and thinly sliced

PER PIECE: about 99 cal, 6 g pro, 5 g total fat (1 g sat. fat), 10 g carb, 1 g fibre, 21 mg chol, 171 mg sodium, 76 mg potassium. % RDI: 1% calcium, 4% iron, 2% vit A, 9% vit C, 2% folate.

TIP FROM THE TEST KITCHEN
If you don't have five-spice powder, you can substitute a mixture of ½ tsp cinnamon and pinch each ground cloves and pepper.

NACHO WINGS
WITH GUACAMOLE DIP AND CRUDITÉS

MAKES ABOUT 30 PIECES

Nothing could be better than two pub-food favourites—nachos and chicken wings— rolled into one. These wings are delicious hot, at room temperature and even cold. Pair with your favourite hot sauce for an extra kick.

MARINATED WINGS: Remove tips from chicken wings; separate wings at joint. In glass baking dish, whisk together buttermilk, egg, hot pepper sauce, salt and pepper; add wings, tossing to coat. Cover and refrigerate for 4 hours. *(Make-ahead: Refrigerate for up to 24 hours.)*

GUACAMOLE DIP: While wings are chilling, scoop avocado flesh into bowl; mash until fairly smooth. Stir in sour cream, red onion, cilantro, lime juice, salt and pepper; cover and refrigerate for 1 hour.

NACHO COATING: In food processor, finely grind tortilla chips to make about 2 cups crumbs; transfer to bowl. Stir in oregano, chili powder and cumin.

TO FINISH: Remove wings from marinade; discard marinade. Press wings into coating, turning to coat all over. Roast on rack on foil-lined rimmed baking sheet in 400°F (200°C) oven, turning once, until crisp and juices run clear when wings are pierced, 45 minutes. Serve with dip and vegetables.

PER PIECE: about 108 cal, 5 g pro, 7 g total fat (2 g sat. fat), 7 g carb, 1 g fibre, 19 mg chol, 97 mg sodium. % RDI: 3% calcium, 4% iron, 10% vit A, 9% vit C, 7% folate.

MARINATED WINGS:

1.35 kg	whole chicken wings
⅔ cup	buttermilk
1	egg
2 tsp	hot pepper sauce
¼ tsp	each salt and pepper

GUACAMOLE DIP:

1	large ripe avocado (see tip, page 75)
⅓ cup	light sour cream
¼ cup	finely chopped red onion
¼ cup	chopped fresh cilantro
1 tbsp	lime juice
¼ tsp	each salt and pepper

NACHO COATING:

225 g	plain salted tortilla chips (about 8 cups)
1½ tsp	dried oregano
1½ tsp	ancho or other chili powder
1 tsp	ground cumin
6 cups	vegetable crudités

MOJO WINGS

MAKES ABOUT 12 PIECES

Popular in Cuba, citrus juice–based mojo marinades give robust flavour to chicken. Barbecuing whole wings is easy because they won't fall through the grill grate.

⅓ cup	orange juice
2 tbsp	lime juice
2 tbsp	lemon juice
1 tsp	dried oregano
1 tsp	ground cumin
1 tsp	each salt and pepper
2	cloves garlic, minced
1.35 kg	whole chicken wings

In large bowl, whisk together orange juice, lime juice, lemon juice, oregano, cumin, salt, pepper and garlic. Add chicken wings; toss to coat. Cover and refrigerate for 4 hours, turning often. *(Make-ahead: Refrigerate for up to 24 hours.)*

Place on greased grill over medium heat; close lid and grill, turning occasionally, until golden and juices run clear when wings are pierced, about 30 minutes.

PER PIECE: about 148 cal, 14 g pro, 10 g total fat (3 g sat. fat), 1 g carb, trace fibre, 42 mg chol, 176 mg sodium. % RDI: 1% calcium, 6% iron, 3% vit A, 4% vit C, 2% folate.

TIP FROM THE TEST KITCHEN

This mojo marinade is tasty on all cuts of chicken. It's especially good at helping chicken breasts stay moist when grilled.

CILANTRO CHICKEN WINGS

MAKES ABOUT 12 PIECES

Running two parallel skewers through each whole wing is a nifty way
of keeping wings stable and making them easier to turn on the barbecue.

If cilantro stems have roots, scrape roots clean with paring knife (see tip,
page 136). In mini chopper or small food processor, purée together cilantro,
fish sauce, ginger, salt, peppercorns and sugar. Scrape into large bowl;
stir in garlic.

Cut tips off chicken wings. Add wings to marinade; toss to coat. Cover and
refrigerate for 8 hours. *(Make-ahead: Refrigerate for up to 24 hours.)*

Arrange three wings on work surface. Thread one metal skewer through left
side of each of the three wings; thread second metal skewer through right
side. Repeat with remaining wings.

Place on greased grill over medium heat; brush with remaining marinade.
Close lid and grill, turning occasionally, until golden and juices run clear
when wings are pierced, 30 minutes.

4	cilantro stems (with or without roots)
¼ cup	fish sauce
1½ tsp	grated fresh ginger
1 tsp	salt
1 tsp	black peppercorns
1 tsp	granulated sugar
4	cloves garlic, minced
1.35 kg	whole chicken wings

PER PIECE: about 116 cal, 11 g pro, 8 g total fat (2 g sat. fat), 1 g carb,
trace fibre, 32 mg chol, 687 mg sodium. % RDI: 1% calcium, 5% iron, 3% vit A,
1% vit C, 24% folate.

SMART SPAGHETTI AND MEATBALLS

MAKES 6 SERVINGS

We've lightened up this classic Italian dish by using extra-lean ground chicken instead of the usual beef-and-pork combination. Whole wheat pasta and bread crumbs add an extra hit of fibre. Serve with a tossed green salad for a satisfying, complete meal.

TOMATO SAUCE: In saucepan, heat oil over medium heat; cook carrot, celery, onion, garlic, Italian herb seasoning and salt, stirring occasionally, until softened, about 7 minutes.

Add wine; cook for 2 minutes. Add strained tomatoes and ¾ cup water; bring to boil. Reduce heat, cover and simmer, stirring occasionally, until slightly thickened, about 40 minutes.

CHICKEN MEATBALLS: While sauce is simmering, in large bowl, stir bread crumbs, egg, Parmesan, garlic, Italian herb seasoning, salt and hot pepper flakes; stir in chicken until combined. Shape by scant 1 tbsp into 30 meatballs. Bake on parchment paper–lined rimmed baking sheet in 375°F (190°C) oven until instant-read thermometer inserted into centre of several meatballs reads 165°F (74°C), about 15 minutes. Add to sauce.

TO FINISH: While meatballs are baking, in large pot of boiling salted water, cook pasta according to package directions; drain. Serve topped with meatballs and sauce. Garnish with basil.

PER SERVING: about 555 cal, 31 g pro, 13 g total fat (4 g sat. fat), 81 g carb, 9 g fibre, 90 mg chol, 881 mg sodium, 609 mg potassium. % RDI: 13% calcium, 46% iron, 25% vit A, 8% vit C, 17% folate.

TOMATO SAUCE:

1 tbsp	olive oil
1	carrot, finely chopped
1	rib celery, finely chopped
half	small sweet onion, finely diced
3	cloves garlic, minced
½ tsp	Italian herb seasoning
¼ tsp	salt
¼ cup	dry white or red wine
1	bottle (680 mL) strained tomatoes (passata)

CHICKEN MEATBALLS:

½ cup	fresh whole wheat bread crumbs
1	egg
⅓ cup	grated Parmesan cheese
2	cloves garlic, minced
½ tsp	Italian herb seasoning
¼ tsp	salt
pinch	hot pepper flakes
450 g	extra-lean ground chicken

565 g	whole wheat spaghetti
¼ cup	torn fresh basil leaves

POZOLE CHILI

MAKES 12 SERVINGS

This stick-to-your-ribs chili has all the best flavours of a traditional Mexican soup called pozole. Add extra jalapeños or use hot green salsa for a spicier dish. Serve topped with sour cream, julienned radish, cubed avocado, fresh cilantro and a lime wedge.

4	serrano, poblano or Cubanelle peppers, halved and seeded
1	jalapeño pepper, halved and seeded
1 tbsp	vegetable oil
1.125 kg	lean ground chicken
1	large onion, chopped
½ tsp	each ground cumin and ground coriander
¼ tsp	salt
3½ cups	sodium-reduced chicken broth
1½ cups	mild green salsa
2	cans (each 540 mL) white kidney beans, drained and rinsed
2 cups	frozen corn kernels
1 cup	packed fresh cilantro, coarsely chopped

On foil-lined rimmed baking sheet, rub serrano and jalapeño peppers with 2 tsp of the oil. Broil, skin side up, until blistered and beginning to blacken, about 5 minutes. Let cool enough to handle. Remove charred skin; coarsely chop peppers.

Meanwhile, in Dutch oven or large pot, heat remaining oil over high heat; cook chicken, breaking up with spoon, until browned and no liquid remains, about 15 minutes.

Reduce heat to medium-high; sauté onion until beginning to soften, about 3 minutes. Stir in cumin, coriander and salt.

Stir in broth, salsa and chopped peppers, scraping up any browned bits from bottom of pan. Add beans and corn; bring to boil.

Reduce heat to medium-low; simmer, stirring occasionally, until thickened, about 30 minutes. Stir in cilantro.

PER SERVING: about 308 cal, 22 g pro, 15 g total fat (4 g sat. fat), 21 g carb, 6 g fibre, 71 mg chol, 715 mg sodium, 352 mg potassium. % RDI: 5% calcium, 15% iron, 5% vit A, 8% vit C, 17% folate.

30-MINUTE CHICKEN CHILI

MAKES 4 SERVINGS

Pull this mildly seasoned chili together in minutes.
The leftovers make a nutritious and satisfying lunch.

1 tbsp	vegetable oil
1	onion, diced
3	cloves garlic, minced
450 g	extra-lean ground chicken
1	carrot, diced
1	rib celery, diced
1	pkg (227 g) cremini or button mushrooms, diced
half	sweet red pepper, diced
4 tsp	chili powder
1 tsp	each ground cumin and ground coriander
½ tsp	dried oregano
½ tsp	salt
1	can (796 mL) whole tomatoes, crushed by hand (see tip, right)
2 tbsp	tomato paste
1	can (540 mL) chickpeas, drained and rinsed
4 cups	lightly packed baby spinach

In Dutch oven, heat oil over medium-high heat; sauté onion and garlic until just beginning to soften, about 3 minutes. Stir in chicken, carrot, celery, mushrooms and red pepper; sauté, breaking up chicken with spoon, until chicken is browned, about 5 minutes. Stir in chili powder, cumin, coriander, oregano and salt; sauté for 2 minutes.

Stir in tomatoes and tomato paste; bring to boil. Reduce heat and simmer, stirring occasionally, for 10 minutes.

Add chickpeas and spinach; cook, stirring occasionally, for 5 minutes.

PER SERVING: about 401 cal, 30 g pro, 16 g total fat (3 g sat. fat), 38 g carb, 11 g fibre, 89 mg chol, 890 mg sodium, 1,290 mg potassium. % RDI: 18% calcium, 51% iron, 78% vit A, 105% vit C, 51% folate.

TIP FROM THE TEST KITCHEN
Crushing canned whole tomatoes by hand, rather than mashing or dicing them, creates a chunky texture that's really nice in rustic stews and soups.

BOCCONCINI CHICKEN BURGERS

MAKES 4 SERVINGS

Grinding the chicken thighs yourself gives these patties wonderful texture and rich flavour. If you're in a hurry, substitute 450 g lean ground chicken.

In food processor, pulse chicken until coarsely ground; set aside.

In large bowl, beat egg with 1 tbsp water; stir in onion, garlic, Parmesan, bread crumbs, chopped basil, sun-dried tomatoes, salt and pepper. Mix in chicken. Shape into four ¾-inch (2 cm) thick patties.

Place patties on greased grill over medium heat; close lid and grill, turning once (see tip, below), until instant-read thermometer inserted sideways into centre of several patties reads 165°F (74°C), 12 to 14 minutes.

Sandwich patties, bocconcini, tomato and basil leaves in buns.

PER SERVING: about 499 cal, 39 g pro, 20 g total fat (8 g sat. fat), 40 g carb, 3 g fibre, 170 mg chol, 904 mg sodium, 534 mg potassium. % RDI: 35% calcium, 29% iron, 12% vit A, 15% vit C, 40% folate.

450 g	boneless skinless chicken thighs
1	egg
half	onion, grated
2	cloves garlic, minced
⅓ cup	grated Parmesan cheese
¼ cup	dried bread crumbs
2 tbsp	chopped fresh basil
2 tbsp	chopped drained oil-packed sun-dried tomatoes
¼ tsp	each salt and pepper
4	slices bocconcini cheese (one 115 g ball)
1	plum tomato, sliced
4	fresh basil leaves
4	hamburger buns

TIP FROM THE TEST KITCHEN

Chicken burgers can be a little more delicate and crumbly than beef burgers. To flip them on the grill without breaking them, use one spatula over top and one underneath to support each patty as you turn it.

SWEET-AND-SOUR CHICKEN BURGERS

MAKES 4 SERVINGS

Ground chicken is a lighter-tasting alternative to beef in grilled burgers, and this simple sweet-and-sour barbecue sauce keeps the patties moist and flavourful.

SWEET-AND-SOUR BARBECUE SAUCE: In small saucepan, heat oil over medium heat; cook onion and garlic, stirring occasionally, until tender and light golden, about 5 minutes.

Stir in strained tomatoes, chipotle pepper, tomato paste, vinegar, sugar and salt; bring to boil. Reduce heat and simmer until thickened, 10 to 12 minutes. Let cool slightly. Using immersion blender, purée until smooth; set aside.

CHICKEN BURGERS: While barbecue sauce is cooling, stir together chicken, bread crumbs, egg, chili powder, salt and pepper until combined. Shape into four ½-inch (1 cm) thick patties.

Place patties on greased grill over medium-high heat; brush with half of the barbecue sauce. Close lid and grill, turning once (see tip, opposite) and brushing with remaining sauce, until instant-read thermometer inserted sideways into centre of several patties reads 165°F (74°C), 10 to 12 minutes.

Sandwich patties, avocado, cucumber, radishes and lettuce in buns.

PER SERVING: about 527 cal, 30 g pro, 24 g total fat (5 g sat. fat), 49 g carb, 6 g fibre, 128 mg chol, 872 mg sodium, 829 mg potassium. % RDI: 11% calcium, 38% iron, 8% vit A, 18% vit C, 60% folate.

SWEET-AND-SOUR BARBECUE SAUCE:

2 tsp	vegetable oil
1	onion, finely diced
2	cloves garlic, minced
⅔ cup	bottled strained tomatoes (passata)
1	canned chipotle pepper in adobo sauce, chopped
2 tbsp	tomato paste
1 tbsp	red wine vinegar
2 tsp	packed brown sugar
pinch	salt

CHICKEN BURGERS:

450 g	lean ground chicken
¼ cup	fresh bread crumbs
1	egg
1 tsp	chili powder
½ tsp	salt
¼ tsp	pepper
1	avocado, pitted, peeled and sliced
½ cup	sliced cucumber
3	radishes, sliced
1 cup	shredded iceberg lettuce
4	onion buns, halved

BUTTER CHICKEN BURGERS

MAKES 4 SERVINGS

Torn between butter chicken and burgers tonight? Why not have both?
Serve these patties in kaiser rolls and top with plain Greek yogurt,
sliced tomatoes and cucumbers, and lettuce leaves.

1	egg
2	cloves garlic, minced
¼ cup	dried bread crumbs
2 tbsp	butter chicken curry paste (see tip, below)
1 tbsp	lemon juice
2 tsp	grated fresh ginger
¾ tsp	garam masala or Homemade Garam Masala (page 96)
¼ tsp	each salt and pepper
450 g	ground chicken

In bowl, stir together egg, garlic, bread crumbs, curry paste, lemon juice, ginger, garam masala, salt and pepper. Add chicken; mix just until combined. Divide into quarters; with wet hands, gently press to form four ¾-inch (2 cm) thick patties.

Place patties on greased grill over medium-high heat; close lid and grill, turning once (see tip, page 179), until instant-read thermometer inserted sideways into centre of several patties reads 165°F (74°C), 10 to 12 minutes.

PER SERVING: about 260 cal, 22 g pro, 14 g total fat (4 g sat. fat), 9 g carb, 1 g fibre, 121 mg chol, 388 mg sodium, 251 mg potassium. % RDI: 4% calcium, 15% iron, 6% vit A, 7% vit C, 10% folate.

TIP FROM THE TEST KITCHEN
Be sure to use thick butter chicken curry paste (not sauce) to keep the burgers moist but not sloppy.

JERK CHICKEN BURGERS

MAKES 4 SERVINGS

Jerk barbecue sauce adds a zesty, spicy note to simple grilled chicken burgers. This sauce is less fiery than jerk marinade, which you can substitute (in a smaller amount) to make prep even speedier, if you like.

1	egg
½ cup	finely diced sweet green pepper
¼ cup	dried bread crumbs
2 tbsp	jerk barbecue sauce (or 1 tbsp jerk marinade)
1 tbsp	soy sauce
2	cloves garlic, minced
1 tsp	dried thyme
pinch	ground allspice
450 g	lean ground chicken
4	slices cored peeled fresh pineapple
1 tbsp	vegetable oil

In bowl, beat egg; stir in green pepper, bread crumbs, jerk barbecue sauce, soy sauce, garlic, thyme and allspice. Add chicken; mix just until combined. Shape into four ¾-inch (2 cm) thick patties. *(Make-ahead: Layer between waxed paper in airtight container and refrigerate for up to 24 hours or freeze for up to 1 month. Thaw in refrigerator.)*

Place patties on greased grill over medium heat; close lid and grill, turning once (see tip, page 179), until instant-read thermometer inserted sideways into centre of several patties reads 165°F (74°C), about 15 minutes.

Meanwhile, brush pineapple with oil; grill until marked, about 5 minutes. Serve on burgers.

PER SERVING: about 355 cal, 23 g pro, 21 g total fat (5 g sat. fat), 18 g carb, 2 g fibre, 134 mg chol, 524 mg sodium. % RDI: 5% calcium, 18% iron, 7% vit A, 43% vit C, 10% folate.

PESTO CHICKEN BURGERS

MAKES 4 SERVINGS

Fragrant basil, crunchy walnuts and salty Parmesan cheese give these burgers all the wonderful flavours of pesto without requiring you to actually make pesto. Easy-peasy!

In large bowl, beat egg with 2 tbsp water; stir in basil, bread crumbs, onion, Parmesan, walnuts, garlic, salt and pepper. Add chicken; mix just until combined. Shape into four ¾-inch (2 cm) thick patties.

Place patties on greased grill over medium heat; close lid and grill, turning once (see tip, page 179), until instant-read thermometer inserted sideways into centre of several patties reads 165°F (74°C), 12 to 14 minutes.

Sandwich patties and tomato in buns.

PER SERVING: about 492 cal, 31 g pro, 23 g total fat (6 g sat. fat), 39 g carb, 3 g fibre, 139 mg chol, 886 mg sodium. % RDI: 21% calcium, 30% iron, 10% vit A, 17% vit C, 37% folate.

1	egg
½ cup	chopped fresh basil
¼ cup	dried bread crumbs
¼ cup	finely chopped onion
¼ cup	grated Parmesan cheese
1 tbsp	finely chopped walnuts or pecans
2	cloves garlic, minced
½ tsp	salt
¼ tsp	pepper
450 g	ground chicken
4	slices tomato
4	hamburger buns

HERB AND CRANBERRY CHICKEN BURGERS
WITH CARAWAY COLESLAW

MAKES 4 SERVINGS

Adding a bit of water to the burger mix helps keep the lean chicken juicy.
There's no need for condiments when you have this crunchy coleslaw topping.
If you don't want the bun, just serve the burger on a bed of slaw.

CHICKEN BURGERS: In large bowl, stir together oats, green onions, cranberries, egg, garlic, parsley, mustard, vinegar, rosemary, salt, pepper and 2 tbsp water. Add chicken; mix just until combined. Shape into four ¾-inch (2 cm) thick patties.

Place patties on greased grill over medium-high heat; close lid and grill, turning once (see tip, page 179), until instant-read thermometer inserted sideways into centre of several patties reads 165°F (74°C), 10 to 12 minutes. Sandwich patties in buns.

CARAWAY COLESLAW: While burgers are grilling, in large bowl, whisk together vinegar, oil, mustard, honey, caraway seeds, pepper and salt. Toss with coleslaw mix and parsley. Serve some on burgers and remainder on the side.

PER SERVING: about 480 cal, 30 g pro, 18 g total fat (4 g sat. fat), 52 g carb, 6 g fibre, 135 mg chol, 636 mg sodium, 458 mg potassium. % RDI: 15% calcium, 36% iron, 24% vit A, 57% vit C, 56% folate.

CHICKEN BURGERS:

½ cup	quick-cooking rolled oats (not instant)
3	green onions, thinly sliced
¼ cup	dried cranberries, chopped
1	egg
1	clove garlic, grated or pressed
2 tbsp	chopped fresh parsley
1 tbsp	Dijon mustard
1 tbsp	cider vinegar
½ tsp	chopped fresh rosemary
¼ tsp	each salt and pepper
450 g	ground chicken
4	hamburger buns

CARAWAY COLESLAW:

3 tbsp	cider vinegar
1 tbsp	olive oil
1 tbsp	Dijon mustard
1 tbsp	liquid honey
¼ tsp	caraway seeds
¼ tsp	pepper
pinch	salt
8 cups	coleslaw mix or broccoli slaw (about one 397 g pkg)
2 tbsp	chopped fresh parsley

SALSA CHICKEN MEAT LOAF

MAKES 6 SERVINGS

Adding salsa to the chicken mixture, as well as spreading it over top, boosts the flavour of the mild meat. The melted cheese garnish gives each slice the appeal of chicken tacos in a less-messy package.

2	eggs
¾ cup	medium chunky salsa
½ cup	dried Italian bread crumbs
half	onion, grated
half	sweet green pepper, finely diced
½ tsp	each chili powder and salt
¼ tsp	each dried thyme and pepper
675 g	lean or extra-lean ground chicken
½ cup	shredded Monterey Jack cheese

In bowl and using fork, beat eggs. Mix in ¼ cup of the salsa, the bread crumbs, onion, green pepper, chili powder, salt, thyme and pepper. Mix in chicken.

Pat evenly into 8- x 4-inch (1.5 L) loaf pan. Spread remaining salsa over top. Bake in 375°F (190°C) oven until instant-read thermometer inserted in centre reads 165°F (74°C), about 1 hour and 20 minutes.

Sprinkle Monterey Jack over top; bake until melted, about 5 minutes. Let stand for 5 minutes; drain off fat.

PER SERVING: about 278 cal, 26 g pro, 15 g total fat (5 g sat. fat), 9 g carb, 1 g fibre, 154 mg chol, 557 mg sodium. % RDI: 11% calcium, 15% iron, 9% vit A, 23% vit C, 9% folate.

CONFETTI CHICKEN MEAT LOAF

MAKES 6 SERVINGS

Colourful diced veggies boost the fibre content—and tastiness—of this family-friendly main dish. Good old-fashioned Chive and Parsley Mashed Potatoes (page 207) are the obvious choice for a side, but rice or baguette slices are great, too.

In skillet, heat oil over medium heat; cook onions, garlic, carrot, celery, and red and green peppers, stirring often, until softened, about 7 minutes. Let cool slightly.

In large bowl, beat eggs with bread crumbs. Add vegetable mixture, chicken, one-third of the tomato sauce, the parsley, salt, basil, pepper and thyme; mix well.

Line 8- x 4-inch (1.5 L) loaf pan with foil, leaving 2-inch (5 cm) overhang. Press meat mixture into pan; spread remaining tomato sauce over top. Bake in 350°F (180°C) oven until instant-read thermometer inserted in centre reads 165°F (74°C), about 1½ hours. Let stand in pan for 10 minutes.

Using foil overhang, lift loaf out of pan, allowing juices to drip back into pan. Transfer to warmed serving plate; remove foil. If desired, skim fat off juices in pan and spoon juices over loaf.

2 tbsp	vegetable oil
2	onions, chopped
2	cloves garlic, minced
1	each carrot and rib celery, diced
1	each sweet red and green pepper, diced
2	eggs
½ cup	dried bread crumbs
450 g	lean ground chicken
1	can (213 mL) tomato sauce
¼ cup	chopped fresh parsley
1 tsp	salt
½ tsp	dried basil
¼ tsp	each pepper and dried thyme

PER SERVING: about 275 cal, 19 g pro, 15 g total fat (3 g sat. fat), 17 g carb, 3 g fibre, 121 mg chol, 726 mg sodium. % RDI: 5% calcium, 16% iron, 37% vit A, 88% vit C, 19% folate.

CHICKEN MEAT LOAF FLORENTINE

MAKES 4 SERVINGS

Wilted baby spinach and sautéed leek add a touch of elegance to this chicken meat loaf. If you can't find Fontina cheese, any mild-tasting buttery cheese will do, such as Havarti or mozzarella.

1 tbsp	extra-virgin olive oil
1	leek (white and light green parts only), quartered and thinly sliced
4 cups	lightly packed baby spinach
2	cloves garlic, minced
1 tsp	Italian herb seasoning
½ tsp	each salt and pepper
pinch	hot pepper flakes
1 cup	fresh bread crumbs
1	egg, lightly beaten
¾ cup	shredded Fontina cheese
1 tsp	Dijon mustard
450 g	extra-lean ground chicken
⅓ cup	bottled strained tomatoes (passata)

In skillet, heat oil over medium heat; cook leek, stirring occasionally, until softened, about 6 minutes.

Stir in spinach, garlic, Italian herb seasoning, salt, pepper and hot pepper flakes; cook, stirring occasionally, until spinach is wilted and no liquid remains, about 3 minutes. Transfer to large bowl; let stand for 10 minutes.

Stir in bread crumbs, egg, ½ cup of the Fontina and mustard; mix in chicken. Shape into 7- x 4-inch (18 x 10 cm) log; place on foil-lined rimmed baking sheet. Brush all over with strained tomatoes.

Bake in 375°F (190°C) oven until instant-read thermometer inserted in centre reads 165°F (74°C), about 45 minutes. Sprinkle with remaining Fontina; let stand for 10 minutes before slicing.

PER SERVING: about 358 cal, 29 g pro, 21 g total fat (8 g sat. fat), 12 g carb, 2 g fibre, 156 mg chol, 709 mg sodium, 513 mg potassium. % RDI: 19% calcium, 29% iron, 42% vit A, 10% vit C, 36% folate.

VARIATION
Greek-Style Chicken Meat Loaf

Omit spinach. Replace Italian herb seasoning with dried oregano. Decrease salt to ¼ tsp. Replace Fontina cheese with crumbled feta cheese. Stir ⅓ cup chopped pitted green olives into chicken mixture.

MUSTARDY CHICKEN AND CAULIFLOWER SALAD

MAKES 4 SERVINGS

This salad is also excellent if you swap broccoli florets for the cauliflower. Use leftover grilled chicken from another meal, or cube rotisserie chicken from the grocery store.

3 cups	cauliflower florets (see tip, below)
4 tsp	olive oil
1 tbsp	Dijon mustard
1 tbsp	lemon juice
pinch	each salt and pepper
5 cups	packed fresh baby spinach
3 cups	cubed grilled chicken

In large pot of boiling salted water, blanch cauliflower until tender-crisp, about 3 minutes. Using slotted spoon, immediately transfer to bowl of ice water. Chill; drain well and set aside.

Meanwhile, in large bowl, whisk together oil, mustard, lemon juice, salt and pepper. Add spinach, chicken and cauliflower; toss to coat.

PER SERVING: about 270 cal, 33 g pro, 13 g total fat (3 g sat. fat), 5 g carb, 3 g fibre, 93 mg chol, 368 mg sodium, 584 mg potassium. % RDI: 6% calcium, 19% iron, 37% vit A, 77% vit C, 52% folate.

TIP FROM THE TEST KITCHEN
To save time later in the week, cut an entire head of cauliflower into florets when you're prepping this recipe. Blanch it all as directed and save the extras to use in other salads or for an easy side.

MOROCCAN CHICKEN AND COUSCOUS SALAD

MAKES 4 TO 6 SERVINGS

Couscous is one of the easiest starches to prepare and requires only boiling a kettle. Here, it's matched up with chicken, veggies, herbs and a simple dressing laced with typical Moroccan spices.

COUSCOUS SALAD: In large heatproof bowl, stir couscous with boiling water; cover and let stand until absorbed, about 5 minutes. Fluff with fork; let cool to room temperature. Add chicken, tomatoes, orange and red peppers, cucumber, almonds, green onions, cilantro and mint.

DRESSING: Whisk together oil, lemon juice, honey, cumin, salt, cinnamon, chili powder, black pepper and cayenne pepper. Drizzle over salad; toss gently to combine.

PER EACH OF 6 SERVINGS: about 362 cal, 21 g pro, 17 g total fat (3 g sat. fat), 34 g carb, 6 g fibre, 42 mg chol, 265 mg sodium, 362 mg potassium. % RDI: 5% calcium, 19% iron, 10% vit A, 75% vit C, 10% folate.

COUSCOUS SALAD:

1 cup	whole wheat couscous
1 cup	boiling water
2 cups	diced cooked chicken
1 cup	grape tomatoes, halved lengthwise
half	each sweet orange and red pepper, diced
half	English cucumber, chopped
⅓ cup	salted dry-roasted almonds, coarsely chopped
2	green onions, thinly sliced
2 tbsp	each chopped fresh cilantro and mint

DRESSING:

¼ cup	olive oil
¼ cup	lemon juice
1 tbsp	liquid honey
½ tsp	each ground cumin and salt
¼ tsp	each cinnamon and chili powder
¼ tsp	each black pepper and cayenne pepper

SPICY CHIPOTLE CHICKEN PIZZAS

MAKES 4 SERVINGS

Chipotle peppers are simply ripe red jalapeños that have been smoked until they shrivel up like raisins. You can buy them dry or canned in adobo sauce—here, the saucy canned variety is best. They add a smoky, savoury heat to these mini-pizzas.

In food processor, purée pizza sauce with chipotle pepper until smooth. Arrange pitas on rimmed baking sheet; spread sauce over pitas. Top with chicken, Monterey Jack, red pepper and green onions.

Bake in 450°F (230°C) oven until cheese is bubbly and golden, about 10 minutes.

PER SERVING: about 357 cal, 22 g pro, 13 g total fat (7 g sat. fat), 41 g carb, 6 g fibre, 50 mg chol, 632 mg sodium, 455 mg potassium. % RDI: 24% calcium, 22% iron, 13% vit A, 53% vit C, 15% folate.

1 cup	prepared pizza sauce or Tomato Pizza Sauce (page 37)
1	canned chipotle pepper in adobo sauce
4	whole wheat pitas
1 cup	shredded cooked chicken
1 cup	shredded Monterey Jack cheese
half	sweet red pepper, thinly sliced
2	green onions, chopped

CHICKEN AND
SWEET POTATO POT PIE
MAKES 4 SERVINGS

This fast version of pot pie is another great way to use up leftover roast, grilled or rotisserie chicken. It is quicker to make than a regular pot pie because the ready-made pastry bakes as the filling simmers.

half	pkg (450 g pkg) frozen rolled butter puff pastry, thawed
1	egg, lightly beaten
2 tbsp	butter
1	onion, chopped
1	rib celery, chopped
1	large sweet potato, peeled and cubed
¼ tsp	each salt and pepper
⅓ cup	all-purpose flour
2 cups	sodium-reduced chicken broth
3 cups	shredded cooked chicken
2 tbsp	thinly sliced fresh sage
pinch	nutmeg
2 cups	baby spinach
½ cup	10% cream

On parchment paper, unroll pastry; cut lengthwise then crosswise to make four equal sections. Brush with egg. Transfer paper with pastry onto baking sheet; bake in 400°F (200°C) oven until puffed and golden, 16 to 18 minutes.

Meanwhile, in Dutch oven or large saucepan, melt butter over medium heat; cook onion, celery, sweet potato, salt and pepper until sweet potato is tender, 7 to 8 minutes.

Stir in flour; cook, stirring, for 1 minute. Gradually stir in broth and bring to boil; reduce heat and simmer until thickened, about 8 minutes.

Stir in chicken, sage and nutmeg; cook until chicken is hot, about 4 minutes. Stir in spinach and cream; cook until spinach is wilted. Ladle into bowls; top with puff pastry.

PER SERVING: about 611 cal, 34 g pro, 31 g total fat (15 g sat. fat), 47 g carb, 5 g fibre, 165 mg chol, 793 mg sodium, 568 mg potassium. % RDI: 11% calcium, 29% iron, 151% vit A, 22% vit C, 27% folate.

MIDDLE EASTERN COUSCOUS BOWL

MAKES 4 SERVINGS

This zesty bowl dresses up leftover roast or grilled chicken. It's great for using up last night's cooked couscous too. If you don't have any, just prepare 1 cup couscous according to the package directions—it will double in volume.

In large bowl, whisk together lemon zest, lemon juice, oil, cumin, ginger, salt, pepper and cinnamon.

Add couscous, chicken, red pepper, olives and raisins; toss to coat. Sprinkle with green onion; garnish with mint (if using).

PER SERVING: about 337 cal, 19 g pro, 15 g total fat (3 g sat. fat), 31 g carb, 2 g fibre, 46 mg chol, 305 mg sodium, 331 mg potassium. % RDI: 3% calcium, 13% iron, 12% vit A, 113% vit C, 12% folate.

1 tsp	grated lemon zest
3 tbsp	lemon juice
3 tbsp	olive oil
¼ tsp	each ground cumin and ground ginger
¼ tsp	each salt and pepper
pinch	cinnamon
2 cups	cooked couscous
2 cups	shredded cooked chicken
1 cup	diced sweet red or orange pepper
¼ cup	mixed olives (green and black)
3 tbsp	raisins (see tip, below)
1	green onion, sliced small fresh mint leaves (optional)

TIP FROM THE TEST KITCHEN
If you don't have raisins in the pantry, substitute sliced dried apricots and add a crunchy garnish of toasted sliced almonds.

POMEGRANATE CHICKEN
(PAGE 215)

CHAPTER 5

WHOLE CHICKENS

MUSTARD AND PANCETTA ROAST CHICKEN

MAKES 4 TO 6 SERVINGS

Stuffing crispy pancetta and grainy mustard under the skin of the chicken infuses the meat with loads of flavour. Instead of thyme, you can use whatever fresh herb you like, such as rosemary or sage.

10	thin slices pancetta (about 85 g), diced (see tip, below)
1 tbsp	grainy mustard
1	whole chicken (1.8 to 2.25 kg)
10	sprigs fresh thyme
8	cloves garlic
pinch	each salt and pepper

In small skillet, cook pancetta over medium heat, stirring often, until golden and crisp, about 7 minutes. Drain on paper towel–lined plate. In small bowl, mix pancetta with mustard; set aside.

Remove giblets and neck (if any) from chicken; remove any excess fat and skin. Place thyme and garlic in cavity. Using fingers, gently loosen skin from breast meat, being careful not to tear skin. Evenly distribute pancetta mixture under skin to cover breast. Sprinkle with salt and pepper; tuck wings under back.

Place chicken, breast side up, on greased rack in roasting pan. Roast in 400°F (200°C) oven until starting to brown, about 30 minutes. Reduce heat to 375°F (190°C); roast until instant-read thermometer inserted in thickest part of thigh reads 185°F (85°C), about 40 minutes.

Discard contents of cavity; tip chicken to pour juices into pan drippings. Transfer chicken to platter; cover loosely with foil and let rest for 15 minutes before carving. Skim fat from pan drippings; serve jus with chicken.

PER EACH OF 6 SERVINGS: about 296 cal, 32 g pro, 18 g total fat (5 g sat. fat), trace carb, trace fibre, 122 mg chol, 320 mg sodium, 298 mg potassium. % RDI: 2% calcium, 11% iron, 5% vit A, 3% vit C, 2% folate.

TIP FROM THE TEST KITCHEN

Pancetta is unsmoked cured pork belly, so it's similar to bacon but lacks the smoky flavour. It's easy to find in rolls at the deli counter, where you can have it sliced to whatever thickness you prefer.

GARLIC ROAST CHICKEN
WITH MATZO STUFFING
MAKES 4 TO 6 SERVINGS

Matzo is a Passover staple, but you don't need to celebrate the holiday to enjoy this juicy chicken. Toasted whole wheat matzo gives the stuffing wonderful flavour and texture; if you use Chicken Schmaltz (page 291) instead of oil, it will be even tastier.

MATZO STUFFING:

2	sheets whole wheat matzo
2 tbsp	vegetable oil or Chicken Schmaltz (page 291)
1	large onion, chopped
2	ribs celery, chopped
1	clove garlic, minced
¼ cup	chopped walnuts, toasted
¼ cup	raisins
	boiling water
1 cup	chicken broth
1	egg
¼ tsp	each salt and pepper

CHICKEN AND GRAVY:

1	whole chicken (1.5 to 2.25 kg)
2 tbsp	olive oil
2	cloves garlic, minced
1 tbsp	chopped fresh thyme
1 tsp	each salt and sweet paprika
½ tsp	pepper
2 tbsp	potato flour
1 cup	chicken broth

MATZO STUFFING: Break matzo into bite-size pieces; spread on baking sheet. Bake in 400°F (200°C) oven until lightly toasted, about 4 minutes. Transfer to bowl. In skillet, heat oil over medium-high heat; sauté onion, celery and garlic until golden, about 10 minutes. Add to bowl along with walnuts.

Meanwhile, soak raisins in boiling water for 5 minutes. Drain and add to bowl. Whisk together broth, egg, salt and pepper; stir into matzo mixture until combined. Let stand for 30 minutes.

CHICKEN AND GRAVY: Remove giblets and neck (if any) from chicken; remove any excess fat and skin. Stir together oil, garlic, thyme, salt, paprika and pepper; rub over inside and outside of chicken. Fill cavity with stuffing. Tie legs together with kitchen string; tuck wings under back. Place, breast side up, on greased rack in roasting pan. Pour ¾ cup water into pan. Place any additional stuffing in 4-cup (1 L) baking dish.

Roast chicken in 375°F (190°C) oven, basting occasionally, until instant-read thermometer inserted in thickest part of thigh reads 185°F (85°C), 2 to 2¼ hours, adding up to 1½ cups more water if pan is dry. Bake additional stuffing, uncovered, for 30 minutes, basting once with pan juices.

Spoon stuffing from cavity into bowl; cover and set aside. Transfer chicken to platter; cover loosely with foil and let rest for 20 minutes before carving.

Skim fat from pan juices. Sprinkle with potato flour; cook for 1 minute. Pour in broth and any juices from chicken; boil, stirring, until thickened, about 2 minutes. Pour into warmed gravy boat. Serve with chicken and stuffing.

PER EACH OF 6 SERVINGS (WITHOUT SKIN): about 288 cal, 11 g pro, 15 g total fat (3 g sat. fat), 29 g carb, 3 g fibre, 46 mg chol, 548 mg sodium, 495 mg potassium. % RDI: 4% calcium, 17% iron, 35% vit A, 15% vit C, 13% folate.

LEMON SAFFRON ROTISSERIE CHICKEN

MAKES 4 TO 6 SERVINGS

This simple recipe is a tasty introduction to roasting meats on a rotisserie. The addition of just a few simple seasonings and time spent turning over the flames are the keys to succulent chicken.

Using mortar and pestle or small food processor, mash together garlic, lemon zest, thyme, pepper, salt and saffron until pasty and golden. Mix in oil.

Remove giblets and neck (if any) from chicken. Cut off and discard wing tips; remove any excess fat and skin. Place chicken in large bowl; add saffron mixture; with fingers, rub all over inside and outside of chicken. Cover and refrigerate for 2 hours. *(Make-ahead: Refrigerate for up to 12 hours.)*

Place bay leaves and one of the lemon halves in cavity. Skewer neck and body cavities closed. Tie legs together with kitchen string; tie chicken around wings and breast.

According to manufacturer's instructions, secure chicken on rotisserie skewer, and prepare and heat barbecue to medium-high. Fit skewer onto rotisserie; start motor. Close lid and grill until skin is crisp and golden, juices run clear when chicken is pierced and instant-read thermometer inserted in thickest part of thigh reads 185°F (85°C), about 1¾ hours.

Transfer to carving board; remove rotisserie skewer and forks. Cover chicken loosely with foil; let rest for 10 to 15 minutes.

Remove skewers, string, bay leaves and lemon. Using kitchen scissors, poultry shears or knife, cut chicken into eight pieces. Cut remaining lemon into wedges to squeeze over chicken.

PER EACH OF 6 SERVINGS: about 216 cal, 22 g pro, 13 g total fat (3 g sat. fat), 2 g carb, trace fibre, 79 mg chol, 260 mg sodium. % RDI: 1% calcium, 7% iron, 3% vit A, 7% vit C, 3% folate.

4	cloves garlic, minced
1 tbsp	grated lemon zest
2 tsp	chopped fresh thyme (or ½ tsp dried)
1 tsp	coarsely ground pepper
½ tsp	salt
¼ tsp	crumbled saffron threads
2 tbsp	extra-virgin olive oil
1	whole chicken (about 1.5 kg)
2	bay leaves
1	lemon, halved

TIP FROM THE TEST KITCHEN

Every rotisserie is different, so we advise you to read the instructions for yours carefully when you set it up. This ensures fewer headaches and guarantees delicious results.

BASIC BRINED ROTISSERIE CHICKEN

MAKES 4 TO 6 SERVINGS

Brining is an excellent way to ensure juicy meat and golden skin when cooking a whole chicken on the barbecue. Use these basic proportions for salt, sweetener and water as a guide, and then create your own brines with different herbs or citrus fruit instead of apple.

Remove giblets and neck (if any) from chicken; pat dry inside and out. Remove any excess fat and skin. Set chicken aside.

In very large heatproof bowl or container large enough to hold 20 cups, combine boiling water, salt and maple syrup, stirring until salt is dissolved.

Add cold water, peppercorns, bay leaves, apple, onion and sage; add chicken, breast side down. Cover and refrigerate for 12 to 24 hours.

Remove chicken from brine; pat dry. Place on rack on rimmed baking sheet; refrigerate, uncovered, until skin is dry and tacky, about 3 hours.

According to manufacturer's instructions, secure chicken on rotisserie skewer, and prepare and heat barbecue to medium. Tuck wings under back; tie legs together with kitchen string. Fit skewer onto rotisserie; start motor. Close lid and grill until instant-read thermometer inserted in thickest part of thigh reads 185°F (85°C), about 1 hour.

Transfer to carving board; remove rotisserie skewer and forks, and string. Cover chicken loosely with foil; let rest for 10 minutes before carving.

1	whole chicken (about 1.35 kg)
2 cups	boiling water
¼ cup	coarse sea salt
2 tbsp	maple syrup or packed brown sugar
6 cups	cold water
1 tsp	black peppercorns
4	bay leaves
1	red apple, sliced
half	onion, sliced
6 to 8	sprigs fresh sage

PER EACH OF 6 SERVINGS: about 207 cal, 22 g pro, 13 g total fat (4 g sat. fat), 1 g carb, 0 g fibre, 79 mg chol, 302 mg sodium, 246 mg potassium. % RDI: 1% calcium, 5% iron, 4% vit A, 2% folate.

TIP FROM THE TEST KITCHEN

No rotisserie? Try indirect heat. Set a foil drip pan on one burner of a two-burner barbecue, or on the centre burner of a three-burner barbecue; heat the remaining burner(s) to medium. Place the chicken, breast side up, on a greased grill over the drip pan. Close the lid and grill as directed.

THE ULTIMATE ROAST CHICKEN
WITH GRAVY
MAKES 4 SERVINGS

Crispy herb-flecked skin? Check. Tender, juicy meat? Check. Rich, full-bodied gravy? It's got that, too. Our foolproof take on the classic Sunday supper is so good— and so easy—you might be tempted to make it on weeknights.

GARLIC BUTTER:

4 tsp	butter, softened
2	cloves garlic, pressed or finely grated
2 tsp	chopped fresh thyme
1 tsp	chopped fresh rosemary
¼ tsp	each salt and pepper

ROAST CHICKEN:

1	whole chicken (1.5 kg)
¼ tsp	each salt and pepper
1	small onion, quartered
4	sprigs fresh thyme
1	sprig fresh rosemary

GRAVY:

2 tbsp	all-purpose flour
4 tsp	butter, softened
¼ cup	dry white wine
1 cup	sodium-reduced chicken broth
pinch	pepper
	boiling water (optional)

GARLIC BUTTER: In small bowl, stir together butter, garlic, thyme, rosemary, salt and pepper. Set aside.

ROAST CHICKEN: Remove giblets and neck (if any) from chicken; remove any excess fat and skin. Sprinkle cavity with salt and pepper; place onion, thyme and rosemary in cavity. Rub chicken all over with garlic butter. Place chicken, breast side up, on greased rack in roasting pan; tuck wings under back.

Roast in 375°F (190°C) oven for 45 minutes; baste and continue to roast, basting occasionally, until instant-read thermometer inserted in thickest part of thigh reads 185°F (85°C), about 30 more minutes. Discard contents of cavity. Using tongs, tip chicken to pour juices into pan. Transfer chicken to platter; cover loosely with foil and let rest for 20 minutes before carving.

GRAVY: Meanwhile, tilt pan so juices collect at one end. Skim fat from surface, reserving 1 tbsp.

In small bowl, stir together flour, butter and reserved fat; set aside. Place pan over medium heat; whisk in wine. Cook, whisking and scraping up browned bits from bottom of pan, until reduced by half, about 1 minute.

Whisk in broth; bring to boil. Gradually whisk in butter mixture, 2 tsp at a time, until smooth. Cook, whisking constantly, until thickened, about 2 minutes. Strain through fine-mesh sieve; stir in pepper.

If necessary, stir in enough boiling water to loosen and make 1 cup gravy. Serve with chicken.

PER SERVING: about 435 cal, 37 g pro, 29 g total fat (11 g sat. fat), 4 g carb, trace fibre, 152 mg chol, 601 mg sodium, 431 mg potassium. % RDI: 2% calcium, 11% iron, 13% vit A, 2% vit C, 6% folate.

TIP FROM THE TEST KITCHEN
The trick to rich lump-free gravy is to whisk the butter and flour mixture into the pan a little at a time. The flour gradually thickens the gravy as the butter melts.

ROAST SPICED CHICKEN

MAKES 4 TO 6 SERVINGS

A North African–inspired blend of fragrant spices flavours this chicken. For an extra spicy kick, add another ½ tsp cayenne pepper to the dry rub. Chive and Parsley Mashed Potatoes (below) are tasty with this—or any other—roast chicken.

Stir together cumin, ginger, cinnamon, cayenne pepper, nutmeg, salt and pepper. Remove giblets and neck (if any) from chicken; pat dry inside and out. Remove any excess fat and skin. Rub chicken all over with spice mixture; cover and refrigerate for 2 hours. *(Make-ahead: Refrigerate for up to 12 hours.)*

Place lemon and garlic in cavity; tuck wings under back. Place chicken, breast side up, on greased rack in roasting pan.

Roast in 400°F (200°C) oven, brushing with butter three times, until starting to brown, about 30 minutes. Reduce heat to 375°F (190°C); roast until instant-read thermometer inserted in thickest part of thigh reads 185°F (85°C), about 40 more minutes.

Discard contents of cavity; tip chicken to pour juices into pan drippings. Transfer chicken to platter; cover loosely with foil and let rest for 15 minutes before carving. Skim fat from pan drippings; serve jus with chicken.

2 tsp	ground cumin
1 tsp	ground ginger
½ tsp	each cinnamon and cayenne pepper
pinch	each nutmeg, salt and pepper
1	whole chicken (1.8 to 2.25 kg)
1	lemon, quartered
8	cloves garlic
2 tbsp	butter, melted

PER EACH OF 6 SERVINGS: about 314 cal, 29 g pro, 21 g total fat (7 g sat. fat), 1 g carb, trace fibre, 122 mg chol, 135 mg sodium, 326 mg potassium.
% RDI: 2% calcium, 15% iron, 9% vit A, 8% vit C, 3% folate.

Chive and Parsley Mashed Potatoes

In large pot of boiling salted water, cook 1.5 kg russet potatoes, peeled and cubed, until tender, about 10 minutes. Drain and return to pot; heat over low heat until dry, about 30 seconds. Using potato masher, mash until smooth. In small saucepan, heat together ¼ cup whipping cream (35%), 2 tbsp each chopped fresh chives and fresh parsley, 1 tbsp butter, ½ tsp salt and ¼ tsp pepper until steaming. Pour over potatoes and mash until smooth. Scrape into serving bowl. *(Make-ahead: Let cool for 30 minutes. Refrigerate, uncovered, until cold. Cover and refrigerate for up to 24 hours. Reheat in microwaveable bowl on high for 5 minutes.)*

MAKES 8 SERVINGS

BARBECUED LEMON FENNEL CHICKEN
MAKES 4 OR 5 SERVINGS

Cooking a whole chicken over indirect heat converts your barbecue into an oven and cooks the interior through without charring the exterior.

1	whole chicken (1.8 kg)
1	small onion, quartered
half	lemon
½ tsp	each salt and pepper
2 tsp	grated lemon zest
¼ cup	lemon juice
¼ cup	vegetable oil
½ tsp	fennel seeds, crushed (see tip, below)

Remove giblets and neck (if any) from chicken; pat chicken dry inside and out. Remove any excess fat and skin. Place onion and lemon half in cavity; sprinkle cavity with a pinch each of the salt and pepper. Tie legs together with kitchen string; tuck wings under back.

Stir together lemon zest, lemon juice, oil, fennel seeds and remaining salt and pepper; set aside.

Set foil drip pan on one burner of two-burner barbecue or centre burner of three-burner barbecue; heat remaining burner(s) to medium. Place chicken, breast side up, on greased grill over drip pan; brush with one-third of the lemon mixture. Close lid and grill for 20 minutes. Brush with half of the remaining lemon mixture; close lid and grill for 20 minutes.

Brush chicken with remaining lemon mixture; close lid and grill until instant-read thermometer inserted in thickest part of thigh reads 185°F (85°C), 40 to 60 more minutes. Transfer to carving board; cover loosely with foil and let rest for 10 minutes before carving.

PER EACH OF 5 SERVINGS: about 294 cal, 26 g pro, 20 g total fat (3 g sat. fat), 1 g carb, trace fibre, 98 mg chol, 313 mg sodium. % RDI: 1% calcium, 7% iron, 3% vit A, 11% vit C, 3% folate.

TIP FROM THE TEST KITCHEN
A mortar and pestle is a great tool for crushing fennel seeds. All you need to do is press down on the seeds a few times to crush them to the right coarse texture. You can also spread the seeds on a cutting board and crush them with the bottom of a heavy saucepan.

BEER-CAN CHICKEN
WITH GREEK SPICES
MAKES 6 SERVINGS

This is a classic barbecue method that's no-muss, no-fuss. If you're not into using the can, you can substitute a specialized standup roasting pan that has a built-in holder for the beer and chicken juices.

Stir together oregano, mint, cumin, pepper, salt and cinnamon; set aside.

Remove giblets and neck (if any) from chicken; pat chicken dry inside and out. Cut off and discard wing tips; remove any excess fat and skin. Sprinkle 2 tsp of the spice mixture inside body and neck cavities. Rub 1 tbsp of the remaining spice mixture over chicken.

Open can of beer and pour off ⅓ cup. Using can opener, make five holes in top of can. Spoon remaining spice mixture through holes in can. Holding chicken upright with opening of body cavity down, insert beer can into cavity.

Set foil drip pan on one burner of two-burner barbecue or centre burner of three-burner barbecue; heat remaining burner(s) to medium. Stand chicken on greased grill over unlit burner, spreading legs apart to support chicken if necessary.

Close lid and grill, keeping temperature between 250°F and 300°F (120°C and 150°C) and using oven thermometer if necessary, until juices run clear when chicken is pierced and instant-read thermometer inserted in thickest part of thigh reads 185°F (85°C), 1 to 1¼ hours.

Using tongs, lift chicken and beer can off grill and transfer to large bowl. Cover chicken with foil; let rest for 10 minutes.

Holding chicken upright with tongs and wearing oven mitts, remove beer can, being careful not to spill beer. Discard remaining beer and can. Transfer chicken to carving board and carve.

1 tbsp	dried oregano
2 tsp	dried mint
1 tsp	ground cumin
1 tsp	pepper
¾ tsp	salt
¾ tsp	cinnamon
1	whole chicken (1.5 kg)
1	can (355 mL) beer (see tip, below)

PER SERVING: about 169 cal, 25 g pro, 7 g total fat (2 g sat. fat), 1 g carb, trace fibre, 75 mg chol, 244 mg sodium. % RDI: 2% calcium, 11% iron, 2% vit A, 3% folate.

TIP FROM THE TEST KITCHEN
Any beer will work in this recipe. Some cooks joke that you need the cheapest brew you can find, but a nice fruity ale or a beer that has been aged in oak barrels would be spectacular. Don't worry too much about the fancy factor, though— just buy a beer you'll enjoy drinking with the tender chicken.

LEMONY CHICKEN
WITH CRISPY HERBED SKIN
MAKES 4 TO 6 SERVINGS

The classic combination of lemon, garlic and fresh herbs makes this
chicken recipe the perfect candidate for a homey family meal.

3 tbsp	butter, softened
2½ tsp	minced fresh thyme (see tip, below)
4	cloves garlic, grated or pressed
1 tsp	grated lemon zest
¼ tsp	each salt and pepper
1	whole chicken (1.8 to 2.25 kg)
1	lemon, quartered
1	onion, quartered

In small bowl, mix together butter, thyme, garlic, lemon zest and a pinch
each of the salt and pepper.

Remove giblets and neck (if any) from chicken; place lemon in cavity.
Remove any excess fat and skin. Using fingers, gently loosen skin from breast
meat, being careful not to tear skin. Evenly distribute butter mixture under
skin to cover breast. Sprinkle remaining salt and pepper over chicken; tuck
wings under back.

Place chicken, breast side up, on greased rack in roasting pan; arrange onion
in pan around rack. Roast in 400°F (200°C) oven until starting to brown,
about 30 minutes. Reduce heat to 375°F (190°C); roast until instant-read
thermometer inserted in thickest part of thigh reads 185°F (85°C), about
40 more minutes.

Discard contents of cavity; tip chicken to pour juices into pan drippings.
Transfer chicken to platter; cover loosely with foil and let rest for 15 minutes
before carving. Skim fat from pan drippings; serve jus with chicken.

PER EACH OF 6 SERVINGS: about 330 cal, 29 g pro, 23 g total fat (8 g sat. fat),
2 g carb, trace fibre, 127 mg chol, 243 mg sodium, 318 mg potassium.
% RDI: 2% calcium, 12% iron, 10% vit A, 10% vit C, 3% folate.

TIP FROM THE TEST KITCHEN
Vary the herbs depending on what you have on
hand—especially if it's summertime and you have
a herb garden in your backyard or on your
balcony. Fresh parsley, basil or marjoram are
other tasty options.

GARLIC ROAST CHICKENS
WITH SHERRY VINEGAR
MAKES 8 SERVINGS

Cooking two chickens at once makes plenty of servings for a dinner party or a big family meal. Plus, leftovers make great sandwiches. What sets these roast chickens apart is the garlic paste smeared under the skin, infusing the birds with its seductive flavour.

GARLIC PASTE: On cutting board and using chef's knife, mince garlic; sprinkle with salt. With flat side of knife, mash to form paste; place in bowl. Stir in vinegar, mustard, paprika, thyme and pepper.

CHICKENS AND GRAVY: Remove giblets and neck (if any) from chickens; remove any excess fat and skin. Starting at neck end of each chicken and using fingers, gently loosen skin from breast meat, being careful not to tear skin. Loosen skin from thigh and leg meat. Using fingers, spread half of the garlic paste over breast beneath skin of each chicken, working forward to legs and smoothing paste. Tie legs together with kitchen string; tuck wings under back. Place, breast side up, on greased rack in large roasting pan. Cover and refrigerate for 8 hours. *(Make-ahead: Refrigerate for up to 24 hours.)*

Roast in 400°F (200°C) oven for 45 minutes. Pour vinegar over chickens. Roast until instant-read thermometer inserted in thickest part of thigh reads 185°F (85°C), about 45 more minutes. Transfer to carving board; cover loosely with foil and let rest for 10 minutes before carving.

Skim fat from pan juices. Sprinkle flour over juices; cook, stirring, over medium-high heat for 1 minute. Whisk in broth; reduce heat and simmer, whisking, until thickened, about 5 minutes. Strain and serve with chicken.

PER SERVING: about 313 cal, 35 g pro, 16 g total fat (4 g sat. fat), 6 g carb, trace fibre, 126 mg chol, 661 mg sodium. % RDI: 3% calcium, 16% iron, 8% vit A, 2% vit C, 9% folate.

GARLIC PASTE:

8	cloves garlic
1 tsp	salt
2 tbsp	sherry vinegar or cider vinegar (see tip, below)
4 tsp	Dijon mustard
2 tsp	each sweet paprika and dried thyme
1 tsp	pepper

CHICKENS AND GRAVY:

2	whole chickens (each 1.5 kg)
½ cup	sherry vinegar or cider vinegar
¼ cup	all-purpose flour
2 cups	chicken broth

TIP FROM THE TEST KITCHEN
Sherry vinegar is a mellow, slightly sweet-edged vinegar that's ideal for this dish and for salad dressings. Cider vinegar is great, too, and will give the chicken and gravy a little extra tang.

MUSTARD ROAST CHICKEN

MAKES 4 OR 5 SERVINGS

A blend of Dijon mustard, soy sauce, ginger and garlic adds a slightly spicy zip to the crisp skin and seals in the juices as the chicken roasts. It also lends a salty, rich edge to the homemade gravy. Yum!

1	whole chicken (1.5 kg)
⅓ cup	Dijon mustard
2 tsp	soy sauce
1 tsp	minced fresh ginger
1	clove garlic, minced
2 cups	chicken broth
4 tsp	all-purpose flour

Remove giblets and neck (if any) from chicken; pat chicken dry inside and out. Remove any excess fat and skin. Tie legs together with kitchen string; tuck wings under back. Place, breast side up, on greased rack in roasting pan.

Stir together mustard, soy sauce, ginger and garlic; brush all over chicken. Pour in 1½ cups of the broth. Roast in 325°F (160°C) oven, basting every 30 minutes, until instant-read thermometer inserted in thickest part of thigh reads 185°F (85°C), 1¾ to 2 hours. Transfer to warmed platter; cover loosely with foil and let rest for 10 minutes before carving.

Skim fat from pan juices. Sprinkle flour over juices; cook, stirring, over medium-high heat for 1 minute. Whisk in remaining broth; boil, whisking, until smooth and thickened. Strain and serve with chicken.

PER EACH OF 5 SERVINGS: about 259 cal, 28 g pro, 14 g total fat (4 g sat. fat), 3 g carb, 1 g fibre, 98 mg chol, 786 mg sodium. % RDI: 3% calcium, 10% iron, 3% vit A, 5% folate.

TIP FROM THE TEST KITCHEN

No one likes lumpy gravy. Constantly whisking the flour with the pan juices is the key to developing that silky, smooth texture. But sometimes, no matter how hard you try, you might find the odd lump. The solution: Always strain the gravy through a fine-mesh sieve before serving. It takes out the lumps like magic.

POMEGRANATE CHICKEN

MAKES 8 SERVINGS

Tart-sweet pomegranate molasses adds a tangy flavour and rich mahogany colour to the chicken. Look for it in Middle Eastern food stores or substitute thawed cranberry cocktail concentrate.

Remove giblets and neck (if any) from chicken; pat chicken dry inside and out. Remove any excess fat and skin. Tie legs together with string; tuck wings under back. Place, breast side up, on greased rack in roasting pan. Stir together butter, cumin, coriander and ¼ tsp each of the salt and pepper; brush over chicken.

Roast in 325°F (160°C) oven for 1½ hours. Stir together pomegranate molasses, honey, orange zest and orange juice; brush over chicken. Roast until instant-read thermometer inserted in thickest part of thigh reads 185°F (85°C), about 25 more minutes. Transfer to carving board; cover loosely with foil and let rest for 10 minutes before carving.

Meanwhile, skim fat from pan juices. Place pan over high heat. Add ¾ cup of the broth and wine; bring to boil, stirring and scraping up browned bits from bottom of pan. Reduce heat and simmer for 2 minutes.

In bowl, whisk together cornstarch and remaining salt, pepper and broth; whisk into pan juices and boil, whisking, until thickened, about 2 minutes. Strain and serve with chicken.

1	large whole chicken (about 2.7 kg)
1 tbsp	butter, melted
1 tsp	each ground cumin and ground coriander
½ tsp	each salt and pepper
¼ cup	pomegranate molasses
2 tbsp	liquid honey
1 tbsp	grated orange zest
1 tbsp	orange juice
1 cup	chicken broth
¼ cup	white wine
1 tsp	cornstarch

PER SERVING: about 302 cal, 29 g pro, 15 g total fat (5 g sat. fat), 12 g carb, trace fibre, 108 mg chol, 348 mg sodium. % RDI: 3% calcium, 13% iron, 5% vit A, 3% vit C, 4% folate.

ROAST CHICKEN
WITH ONIONS AND FIGS
MAKES 4 TO 6 SERVINGS

One of the simplest tricks when roasting chicken is to add lemon to the cavity.
It keeps the meat juicy and adds a citrusy taste; here, that's a wonderful contrast to the
sweet figs and pearl onions. Roasted squash is an excellent, easy side dish.

2 tbsp	vegetable oil
2 tsp	liquid honey
¼ tsp	each salt and pepper
1	whole chicken (about 1.5 kg)
1	small onion
4	cloves garlic
half	lemon
2	sprigs fresh thyme
4 cups	pearl onions (about two 284 g pkg), peeled
2 cups	dried whole Calimyrna figs
1 tbsp	all-purpose flour
½ cup	white wine
1 cup	chicken broth

Whisk together 1 tbsp of the oil, 1 tsp of the honey, salt and pepper; set aside.

Remove giblets and neck (if any) from chicken; pat chicken dry inside and out. Remove any excess fat and skin. Place onion, garlic, lemon and thyme in cavity. Tie legs together with kitchen string; tuck wings under back. Place, breast side up, on greased rack in roasting pan. Toss pearl onions with remaining oil; add to pan.

Roast in 375°F (190°C) oven for 30 minutes; brush with honey mixture. Roast until instant-read thermometer inserted in thickest part of thigh reads 185°F (85°C), about 30 more minutes.

Remove pearl onions and set aside. Discard onion, garlic, lemon and thyme from cavity; tip chicken to pour juices into pan drippings. Transfer chicken to warmed platter; cover loosely with foil and let rest for 20 minutes before carving.

While chicken is resting, trim hard stems off figs; set figs aside.

Skim fat from pan juices. Whisk in flour; cook, whisking, for 1 minute. Add wine; boil, whisking, until most of the liquid is evaporated, about 1 minute. Add broth, stirring and scraping up any browned bits from bottom of pan; simmer, whisking, until smooth, slightly thickened and glossy. Add pearl onions, figs and remaining honey; simmer, stirring, until figs are hot, about 2 minutes. Serve with chicken.

PER EACH OF 6 SERVINGS: about 449 cal, 25 g pro, 17 g total fat (4 g sat. fat), 51 g carb, 9 g fibre, 81 mg chol, 304 mg sodium. % RDI: 11% calcium, 19% iron, 5% vit A, 17% vit C, 7% folate.

SPICED SPATCHCOCK CHICKEN

MAKES 4 SERVINGS

Spatchcock chickens are split and flattened by removing the backbone and pressing on the breastbone. Opening the bird decreases grilling or roasting time, which keeps the meat moist, and allows the thighs, legs and breasts to cook evenly at the same time.

2 tbsp	extra-virgin olive oil
1½ tsp	turmeric
1 tsp	pepper
¾ tsp	ground allspice
½ tsp	each cinnamon and salt
¼ tsp	cayenne pepper
1	whole chicken (1.35 kg)
	lime wedges

In large bowl, stir together oil, turmeric, pepper, allspice, cinnamon, salt and cayenne pepper; set aside.

Remove giblets and neck (if any) from chicken. Using kitchen shears, cut chicken down each side of backbone; remove backbone. Turn chicken breast side up; press firmly on breastbone to flatten. Add to bowl and rub all over with spice mixture.

Set foil drip pan on one burner of two-burner barbecue or centre burner of three-burner barbecue; heat remaining burner(s) to medium. Place chicken, bone side down, on greased grill over drip pan. Close lid and grill, turning once, until instant-read thermometer inserted in thickest part of thigh reads 185°F (85°C). (Or roast in roasting pan in 375°F/190°C oven for 1 hour.) Transfer to cutting board; cover loosely with foil and let rest for 10 minutes before cutting into pieces. Serve with lime wedges.

PER SERVING: about 373 cal, 32 g pro, 26 g total fat (6 g sat. fat), 1 g carb, 1 g fibre, 119 mg chol, 390 mg sodium, 401 mg potassium. % RDI: 2% calcium, 12% iron, 6% vit A, 2% vit C, 4% folate.

TIP FROM THE TEST KITCHEN

Indirect heat is the easiest method for barbecuing spatchcock chickens, because it keeps the skin from burning. If you do grill over direct heat, keep the burners on low and watch carefully for temperature changes and doneness cues.

SPATCHCOCK BARBECUE CHICKEN
WITH FRESH HERBS
MAKES 4 SERVINGS

Your summertime herb garden can come in handy for this recipe. A mix of chopped fresh herbs, garlic and orange zest makes a bright, fresh seasoning paste that complements the tender meat. Serve with Herbed Israeli Couscous (below).

In food processor, pulse together oil, garlic, tarragon, marjoram, rosemary, thyme, bay leaves, orange zest, salt and pepper to make paste. Transfer to large bowl.

Remove giblets and neck (if any) from chicken. Using kitchen shears, cut chicken down each side of backbone; remove backbone. Turn chicken breast side up; press firmly on breastbone to flatten. Add to bowl and rub all over with herb mixture. Cover and refrigerate for 1 hour.

Set foil drip pan on one burner of two-burner barbecue or centre burner of three-burner barbecue; heat remaining burner(s) to medium. Place chicken, bone side down, on greased grill over drip pan. Close lid and grill, turning once, until instant-read thermometer inserted in thickest part of thigh reads 185°F (85°C). Transfer to cutting board; cover loosely with foil and let rest for 10 minutes before cutting into pieces.

2 tbsp	olive oil
2	cloves garlic, minced
1 tbsp	each chopped fresh tarragon, marjoram, rosemary and thyme
2	bay leaves
1 tbsp	grated orange zest
½ tsp	salt
¼ tsp	pepper
1	whole chicken (1.35 kg)

PER SERVING: about 374 cal, 33 g pro, 26 g total fat (6 g sat. fat), 2 g carb, trace fibre, 119 mg chol, 389 mg sodium, 390 mg potassium. % RDI: 3% calcium, 12% iron, 8% vit A, 5% vit C, 5% folate.

Herbed Israeli Couscous
In saucepan, bring 1¾ cups water to boil; add 1½ cups Israeli (pearl) couscous. Cover and simmer until no liquid remains, about 8 minutes. Stir in ¼ cup chopped fresh parsley, 2 tbsp butter or olive oil, 1 tbsp chopped fresh mint and ¼ tsp each salt and pepper.
MAKES 4 SERVINGS

SPATCHCOCK CHICKEN
WITH MUSTARD-GLAZED PARSNIPS AND CRISPY KALE

MAKES 4 SERVINGS

Talk about a complete meal—meat, starch and veggies all together in one tasty, super-nutritious package. To turn the crisp-edged kale into chips, simply bake it for a few more minutes until each piece is crunchy throughout.

CHICKEN AND PARSNIPS: Stir together butter, honey, herbes de Provence, and ¼ tsp salt and pepper. Remove giblets and neck (if any) from chicken. Using kitchen shears, cut chicken down each side of backbone; remove backbone. Turn chicken breast side up; press firmly on breastbone to flatten. Place, bone side down, on large rimmed baking sheet; brush with butter mixture.

Halve parsnips lengthwise; cut each half into quarters. Toss together parsnips, oil, and a pinch each of salt and pepper. Spread around chicken on baking sheet. Roast on bottom rack in 375°F (190°C) oven, turning parsnips and basting chicken with any pan juices halfway through, until instant-read thermometer inserted in thickest part of chicken thigh reads 185°F (85°C), about 1 hour.

Remove parsnips; toss with mustard. Transfer chicken to cutting board; cover loosely with foil and let rest for 10 minutes before cutting into pieces.

CRISPY KALE: While chicken and parsnips are roasting, toss together kale, oil, salt and pepper; spread in single layer on parchment paper–lined rimmed baking sheet. Bake on top rack in 375°F (190°C) oven until edges are crispy, about 15 minutes. Serve with chicken and parsnips.

CHICKEN AND PARSNIPS:

2 tbsp	butter, melted
2 tsp	liquid honey
½ tsp	herbes de Provence
¼ tsp	each salt and pepper (approx)
1	whole chicken (about 1.35 kg)
900 g	parsnips
2 tsp	olive oil
2 tbsp	grainy mustard

CRISPY KALE:

8 cups	torn stemmed kale
1 tsp	olive oil
pinch	each salt and pepper

PER SERVING: about 574 cal, 36 g pro, 28 g total fat (9 g sat. fat), 51 g carb, 10 g fibre, 119 mg chol, 451 mg sodium, 1,663 mg potassium. % RDI: 25% calcium, 34% iron, 196% vit A, 272% vit C, 71% folate.

GRILLED SPATCHCOCK CHICKEN
WITH BUTTERY BARBECUE SAUCE

MAKES 4 TO 6 SERVINGS

Butter gives this simple barbecue sauce a glossy look and a rich flavour.
And because you can store it for a month in the fridge, you may want to make
extra to brush over drumsticks, ribs or other grilled meats.

BUTTERY BARBECUE SAUCE:

¼ cup	butter
2 cups	finely diced onion
¼ cup	cider vinegar
1	clove garlic, minced
⅔ cup	ketchup
¼ cup	liquid honey
2 tbsp	packed brown sugar
2 tsp	dry mustard
1 tsp	smoked hot paprika (see tip, below)
¼ tsp	cayenne pepper

SPATCHCOCK CHICKEN:

1	whole chicken (about 1.35 kg)
1 tbsp	butter, melted
½ tsp	each salt and pepper

BUTTERY BARBECUE SAUCE: In saucepan, heat 1 tbsp of the butter over medium heat; cook onion, stirring often, until golden, about 8 minutes. Add vinegar and garlic; cook until no liquid remains, about 30 seconds.

Stir in ketchup, honey, brown sugar, mustard, paprika and cayenne pepper; bring to boil. Reduce heat and simmer, stirring occasionally, until as thick as ketchup, about 25 minutes. Remove from heat. Stir in remaining butter. *(Make-ahead: Refrigerate in airtight container for up to 1 month; warm gently before using.)*

SPATCHCOCK CHICKEN: Remove giblets and neck (if any) from chicken. Using kitchen shears, cut chicken down each side of backbone; remove backbone. Turn chicken breast side up; press firmly on breastbone to flatten.

Brush chicken with butter; sprinkle with salt and pepper. Place, bone side down, on greased grill over medium heat; close lid and grill, turning once, for 35 minutes. Grill, brushing with ½ cup of the barbecue sauce, until instant-read thermometer inserted in thickest part of thigh reads 185°F (85°C), 10 to 15 more minutes. Transfer to cutting board; cover loosely with foil and let rest for 10 minutes before cutting into pieces.

PER EACH OF 6 SERVINGS: about 297 cal, 22 g pro, 18 g total fat (7 g sat. fat), 12 g carb, 1 g fibre, 93 mg chol, 417 mg sodium, 340 mg potassium. % RDI: 2% calcium, 7% iron, 10% vit A, 3% vit C, 4% folate.

TIP FROM THE TEST KITCHEN
Smoked paprika comes in hot and mild varieties. We've used the hot here to give the barbecue sauce a bit of bite, but you can substitute mild if you like.

CHICKEN UNDER BRICKS

MAKES 4 SERVINGS

Barbecued chicken doesn't get any juicier than this. Weighing the grilling bird down with a foil-wrapped brick is a fun Italian cooking method (called *pollo al mattone*). The brick compresses the meat, allowing it to cook more evenly.

Stir together oil, garlic, oregano, salt, pepper and hot pepper flakes; set aside.

Remove giblets and neck (if any) from chicken. Using kitchen shears, cut chicken down each side of backbone; remove backbone. Turn chicken breast side up; press firmly on breastbone to flatten. Place in shallow dish; tuck wings behind back. Brush with oil mixture; cover and refrigerate for 4 hours. *(Make-ahead: Refrigerate for up to 24 hours.)*

Wrap two bricks in foil. Place chicken, skin side down, on greased grill over medium heat. Place bricks on chicken; close lid and grill for 20 minutes. Wearing oven mitts, remove bricks and turn chicken over. Replace bricks; grill until instant-read thermometer inserted in thickest part of thigh reads 185°F (85°C), about 20 more minutes, wrapping wings in foil if browning too quickly.

Transfer to cutting board; cover loosely with foil and let rest for 10 minutes before cutting chicken into two breast and two leg portions.

¼ cup	extra-virgin olive oil
4	cloves garlic, minced
2 tbsp	finely chopped fresh oregano (or 1 tsp dried)
1 tsp	each salt and pepper
½ tsp	hot pepper flakes
1	whole chicken (1.35 kg)

PER SERVING: about 452 cal, 41 g pro, 31 g total fat (7 g sat. fat), 1 g carb, trace fibre, 132 mg chol, 552 mg sodium. % RDI: 3% calcium, 15% iron, 8% vit A, 2% vit C, 4% folate.

VARIATIONS

Cornish Hens Under Bricks

Use 2 Cornish hens (1.35 kg total); reduce cooking time by about 10 minutes, watching carefully to avoid flare-ups. Cut each hen in half to serve.

Herbed Chicken Under Bricks

Omit oregano and hot pepper flakes. Use 2 tbsp chopped fresh sage (or 2 tsp dried) and 1 tbsp chopped fresh rosemary (or 1 tsp dried).

ROASTED LEMON
AND THYME CHICKEN
WITH CARROTS AND POTATOES

MAKES 4 SERVINGS

Parboiling the vegetables ensures they roast up to a tender golden brown while the chicken cooks. Make sure your baking sheets are large enough for everything to brown evenly.

4	potatoes, scrubbed and cut in 8 wedges each
4	carrots, cut in 1½-inch (4 cm) pieces
3 tbsp	olive oil
1 tbsp	chopped fresh thyme
½ tsp	each salt and pepper
1	lemon
1	whole chicken (1.35 kg), quartered (see tip, below)

In large pot of boiling lightly salted water, cook potatoes for 1 minute. Add carrots; cook until potatoes are slightly softened, about 8 minutes. Drain well.

In large bowl, combine potato mixture, 1 tbsp of the oil, and ¼ tsp each of the thyme, salt and pepper; toss to coat. Spread on large foil-lined rimmed baking sheet.

Finely grate lemon to make 1 tbsp zest; juice lemon. In large bowl, mix together lemon zest, lemon juice and remaining thyme and olive oil. Add chicken; turn to coat.

Discarding lemon mixture, arrange chicken, skin side up, on separate rimmed baking sheet; sprinkle with remaining salt and pepper.

Roast chicken on top rack and vegetables on bottom rack in 425°F (220°C) oven, basting chicken with pan juices and tossing vegetables occasionally, until vegetables are golden and instant-read thermometer inserted in thickest part of chicken thigh reads 185°F (85°C), about 40 minutes.

Remove vegetables from oven. Broil chicken until golden, about 1 minute. Serve with vegetables.

PER SERVING: about 559 cal, 37 g pro, 26 g total fat (6 g sat. fat), 44 g carb, 6 g fibre, 119 mg chol, 796 mg sodium, 1,480 mg potassium. % RDI: 6% calcium, 24% iron, 134% vit A, 40% vit C, 30% folate.

TIP FROM THE TEST KITCHEN
To quarter a chicken, cut down both sides of the backbone with kitchen shears (discarding the backbone), and then cut the chicken into two breast portions and two leg portions.

SPATCHCOCK CORIANDER LEMON CHICKEN

MAKES 4 SERVINGS

Ground coriander has a light, citrusy aroma that works well with lemon. These two partners mix with other spices and aromatics to create a complex-tasting (but easy-to-make) spice rub on this yummy barbecued chicken.

2 tbsp	extra-virgin olive oil
1 tbsp	each grated lemon zest and lemon juice
2 tsp	ground coriander
1 tsp	fennel seeds, crushed (see tip, page 208)
¾ tsp	salt
pinch	each turmeric and cayenne pepper
2	cloves garlic, minced
1	shallot, minced
1	whole chicken (1.35 kg)

Stir together oil, lemon zest, lemon juice, coriander, fennel seeds, salt, turmeric, cayenne pepper, garlic and shallot; set aside.

Remove giblets and neck (if any) from chicken. Using kitchen shears, cut chicken down each side of backbone; remove backbone. Turn chicken breast side up; press firmly on breastbone to flatten. Place in shallow glass dish; tuck wings behind back. Brush with lemon mixture; cover and refrigerate for 1 hour. *(Make-ahead: Refrigerate for up to 24 hours.)*

Set foil drip pan on one burner of two-burner barbecue or centre burner of three-burner barbecue; heat remaining burner(s) to medium. Place chicken, bone side down, on greased grill over drip pan. Close lid and grill, turning once, until instant-read thermometer inserted in thickest part of thigh reads 185°F (85°C), about 45 minutes.

Transfer to cutting board; cover loosely with foil and let rest for 10 minutes before cutting into pieces.

PER SERVING: about 377 cal, 33 g pro, 26 g total fat (6 g sat. fat), 2 g carb, 1 g fibre, 119 mg chol, 533 mg sodium, 407 mg potassium. % RDI: 3% calcium, 10% iron, 6% vit A, 7% vit C, 4% folate.

CHICKEN IN ROASTED RED PEPPER SAUCE

MAKES 4 TO 6 SERVINGS

You can use jarred roasted peppers if you want to make this dish faster. Roasted red peppers are handy to have on hand, though, and they freeze well, so make a double batch and save some for later.

Broil red peppers, turning occasionally, until softened and charred, 10 to 15 minutes. Let cool. Peel, seed and core. In food processor, purée peppers with tomato paste until smooth.

Meanwhile, remove giblets and neck (if any) from chicken; discarding backbone, cut chicken into eight pieces, cutting each breast in half. Toss with paprika and salt. In Dutch oven, heat 1 tbsp of the oil over medium-high heat; working in batches, brown chicken, about 8 minutes per batch. Using slotted spoon, transfer to plate.

Drain fat from pan; wipe clean with paper towel. Add remaining oil; sauté onion and garlic until softened, about 5 minutes. Add pancetta and hot pepper flakes; cook, stirring, for 2 minutes. Return chicken to pan.

Add tomatoes and bring to boil; stir in red pepper mixture. Cover and simmer over medium-low heat until thickened and juices run clear when chicken is pierced, about 20 minutes. Stir in parsley.

3	sweet red peppers
1 tbsp	tomato paste
1	whole chicken (about 1.35 kg)
1 tbsp	smoked or sweet paprika
½ tsp	salt
2 tbsp	olive oil
1	onion, chopped
2	cloves garlic, minced
85 g	pancetta or cured ham, cubed
¼ tsp	hot pepper flakes
2 cups	chopped tomatoes
3 tbsp	minced fresh parsley

PER EACH OF 6 SERVINGS (WITHOUT SKIN): about 255 cal, 25 g pro, 13 g total fat (5 g sat. fat), 10 g carb, 3 g fibre, 88 mg chol, 368 mg sodium, 587 mg potassium. % RDI: 3% calcium, 15% iron, 36% vit A, 183% vit C, 12% folate.

CHICKEN IN MOREL SAUCE

MAKES 4 TO 6 SERVINGS

Oh, what a creamy, decadent treat! This sauce is so incredibly tasty, laced with sherry and rich morel mushrooms—and it's impressive for a dinner party.

1½ cups	sodium-reduced chicken broth
1	pkg (14 g) dried morel mushrooms (see tip, below)
1	whole chicken (about 1.8 kg), cut in pieces
1 tsp	each salt and pepper
¼ cup	all-purpose flour
2 tbsp	vegetable oil
¼ cup	butter
⅓ cup	chopped shallots
2	cloves garlic, minced
1 cup	dry sherry
½ cup	whipping cream (35%)
1	sprig fresh thyme
2 tbsp	chopped fresh parsley

In small saucepan, bring broth to boil. Remove from heat. Add mushrooms; let stand for 30 minutes to rehydrate.

Meanwhile, sprinkle chicken with salt and pepper; dredge in flour, shaking off excess. In large skillet or Dutch oven, heat oil over medium heat; working in batches, brown chicken, about 8 minutes per batch. Using slotted spoon, transfer to plate.

Drain fat from skillet. Add butter; melt over medium heat. Cook shallots and garlic until softened, about 2 minutes. Pour in sherry, scraping up browned bits from bottom of skillet; bring to boil. Boil for 2 minutes.

Stir in cream, thyme and mushrooms with soaking liquid, being careful not to add any grit from bottom of saucepan. Return chicken and any accumulated juices to skillet; bring to boil. Reduce heat and simmer until juices run clear when chicken is pierced and sauce is thickened, about 45 minutes. Sprinkle with parsley.

PER EACH OF 6 SERVINGS (WITHOUT SKIN): about 428 cal, 33 g pro, 20 g total fat (10 g sat. fat), 28 g carb, 3 g fibre, 146 mg chol, 690 mg sodium, 545 mg potassium. % RDI: 4% calcium, 19% iron, 16% vit A, 8% vit C, 20% folate.

TIP FROM THE TEST KITCHEN
Small packages of dried morel mushrooms are usually on display in the produce section of the supermarket. They have a smoky, woodsy flavour that shines in this sauce.

ROAST CHICKEN
WITH OLIVES AND PRUNES

MAKES 4 SERVINGS

Olives add a wonderful saltiness to this dish, and prunes balance it with their natural sweetness, while sherry vinegar and lemons give the whole thing a bit of tartness.

Remove giblets and neck (if any) from chicken. Discarding backbone, cut chicken into 10 pieces. In roasting pan, toss together chicken, prunes, olives, vinegar, oil, garlic, salt, pepper and lemon.

Roast, skin side up, in 450°F (230°C) oven, basting occasionally with pan drippings, until juices run clear when chicken is pierced, about 40 minutes.

Transfer chicken to platter. Remove lemon and squeeze juice into drippings; return lemon rinds to pan and whisk to combine. Pour over chicken.

PER SERVING (WITHOUT SKIN): about 437 cal, 33 g pro, 24 g total fat (5 g sat. fat), 23 g carb, 3 g fibre, 125 mg chol, 694 mg sodium, 615 mg potassium. % RDI: 4% calcium, 16% iron, 6% vit A, 13% vit C, 4% folate.

1	whole chicken (about 1.35 kg)
¾ cup	pitted prunes
½ cup	pitted green olives
3 tbsp	sherry vinegar or cider vinegar
2 tbsp	olive oil
3	cloves garlic, smashed
½ tsp	salt
¼ tsp	pepper
1	lemon, quartered

TIP FROM THE TEST KITCHEN
To save prep time, you can also use the same weight of chicken pieces, drumsticks or bone-in, skin-on chicken thighs.

CHICKEN AND CORNMEAL BUTTERMILK DUMPLINGS

MAKES 6 TO 8 SERVINGS

Chicken and dumplings are spectacular comfort food. Starting with a whole chicken is economical, and cutting it into pieces is easier than you might think. Plus, you can save the wing tips and back to make Slow Cooker Chicken Stock (page 248).

CHICKEN STEW:

1	whole chicken (1.35 kg)
1 tbsp	vegetable oil
2	carrots, cut in chunks
2	ribs celery, cut in chunks
1	onion, chopped
2	cloves garlic, minced
1 cup	sodium-reduced chicken broth
2	bay leaves
1 tsp	dried thyme
½ tsp	each salt and pepper
¼ tsp	dried marjoram
2	potatoes, peeled and cut in 1-inch (2.5 cm) cubes
⅓ cup	cold water
3 tbsp	all-purpose flour

BUTTERMILK DUMPLINGS:

¾ cup	all-purpose flour
¼ cup	yellow cornmeal
1 tsp	baking powder
¼ tsp	baking soda
pinch	salt
2 tbsp	cold butter, cubed
⅔ cup	buttermilk (see tip, page 121)
2 tbsp	chopped fresh parsley

CHICKEN STEW: Remove giblets and neck (if any) from chicken. Discarding backbone, cut into eight pieces. Remove skin and discard; set chicken aside.

In shallow Dutch oven, heat oil over medium heat; cook carrots, celery, onion and garlic, stirring occasionally, until onion is softened, about 5 minutes.

Add 1½ cups water, broth, bay leaves, thyme, salt, pepper and marjoram; bring to boil. Add chicken; reduce heat, cover and simmer for 20 minutes. Add potatoes; cover and simmer for 5 minutes. Whisk cold water with flour; whisk into broth mixture.

BUTTERMILK DUMPLINGS: While stew is simmering, in bowl, whisk flour, cornmeal, baking powder, baking soda and salt. Using pastry blender, cut in butter until in coarse crumbs. Stir in buttermilk and parsley to make sticky spoonable dough. Drop dough, in eight evenly spaced mounds, onto stew.

TO FINISH: Cover and cook, without lifting lid, until dumplings are no longer doughy underneath and juices run clear when chicken is pierced, about 15 minutes. Discard bay leaves.

PER EACH OF 8 SERVINGS: about 264 cal, 20 g pro, 8 g total fat (3 g sat. fat), 28 g carb, 2 g fibre, 59 mg chol, 409 mg sodium, 485 mg potassium. % RDI: 7% calcium, 13% iron, 37% vit A, 12% vit C, 25% folate.

BRAISED CHICKEN, CHESTNUTS AND SHIITAKE MUSHROOMS

MAKES 4 TO 6 SERVINGS

Even though fresh shiitake mushrooms are for sale in virtually all supermarkets, the dried ones provide more flavour. Choose the biggest and most uniformly shaped shiitakes. They're more expensive but worth it for this showy dish.

Cut X into flat side of each chestnut. In small saucepan of boiling water, cook chestnuts, four at a time, until skins are easy to peel off, about 2 minutes. In saucepan, cover peeled chestnuts with water and bring to boil; cover and simmer until tender, about 5 minutes. Drain and set aside.

In bowl, soak mushrooms in warm water until tender, about 30 minutes. Reserving liquid, drain mushrooms; remove stems and discard.

While mushrooms are soaking, using kitchen shears, cut chicken down each side of backbone; discard backbone. Cut off wing tips. Cut chicken in half along breastbone. Cut each half between thigh and breast. Cut each breast in half crosswise. Cut each leg at joint between drumstick and thigh.

Cut white and light green parts of onions into 1-inch (2.5 cm) long pieces; finely chop dark green parts. Set aside separately. Thinly slice ginger and stack slices; cut into diamond shapes and set aside.

In large shallow Dutch oven, heat oil over medium-high heat; working in batches, brown chicken, about 8 minutes per batch. Using slotted spoon, transfer to plate.

Drain all but 1 tbsp fat from pan. Add white and light green onion pieces and ginger to pan; stir-fry for 30 seconds. Add mushrooms and carrots; stir-fry for 1 minute. Stir in reserved mushroom soaking liquid, soy sauce, sugar and wine; bring to boil. Return chicken and any accumulated juices to pan; reduce heat, cover and simmer for 30 minutes.

Add chestnuts, Szechuan pepper and white pepper; simmer, uncovered, over medium heat until juices run clear when chicken is pierced, about 10 minutes.

Meanwhile, in large pot of boiling salted water, blanch bok choy just until tender, about 2 minutes. Drain and toss with sesame oil; arrange on warm platter. Using slotted spoon, arrange chicken on platter; surround with carrots, mushrooms and chestnuts. Add reserved dark green parts of green onions to sauce; pour over chicken.

450 g	fresh chestnuts
16	large dried shiitake mushrooms
1½ cups	warm water
1	whole chicken (1.35 kg)
3	green onions
1	piece (1½ inches/ 4 cm) fresh ginger
2 tbsp	vegetable oil
2	carrots, sliced
¼ cup	soy sauce
2 tbsp	granulated sugar
2 tbsp	Chinese rice wine, sake or dry sherry
½ tsp	Szechuan or black pepper
¼ tsp	white pepper
450 g	baby or Shanghai bok choy, halved lengthwise
¼ tsp	sesame oil

PER EACH OF 6 SERVINGS: about 481 cal, 30 g pro, 25 g total fat (6 g sat. fat), 34 g carb, 7 g fibre, 105 mg chol, 1,037 mg sodium. % RDI: 12% calcium, 29% iron, 86% vit A, 65% vit C, 36% folate.

CHICKEN FRICOT

MAKES 8 SERVINGS

Fricot is a traditional Acadian stew made with meat or fish. Fluffy dumplings, also called doughboys, are cooked atop the stew, making it the ultimate comfort food. It's a favourite of many New Brunswickers, whether or not they're of Acadian heritage.

CHICKEN STEW: Remove giblets and neck (if any) from chicken. Discarding backbone, cut chicken into six pieces; set aside.

In large Dutch oven, sauté salt pork over medium-high heat until golden, about 4 minutes. Using slotted spoon, transfer pork to plate; set aside.

Add chicken pieces to pan; brown all over, about 8 minutes. Transfer to plate; set aside. Drain all but 2 tbsp fat from pan. Reduce heat to medium; cook carrots, celery and onion, stirring occasionally, until onion is softened but not coloured, about 3 minutes.

Stir in potatoes, savory, salt and pepper; cook, stirring, for 2 minutes. Return chicken and salt pork to pan; stir in 6 cups water. Bring just to boil, skimming foam from surface as needed. Reduce heat, cover and simmer for 45 minutes.

Place ice cubes in glass measure. Pour in enough of the cooking liquid to make ⅔ cup; let cool.

Meanwhile, using slotted spoon, transfer chicken to plate; let cool enough to handle. Pull meat from bones; discard bones and skin. Shred or coarsely chop chicken. Skim any fat from cooking liquid; return chicken to pan and bring to simmer.

DUMPLINGS: While chicken is returning to simmer, in bowl, whisk together flour, baking powder, parsley and salt. Stir egg yolks into reserved cooled cooking liquid; drizzle over flour mixture. With fork, toss to make sticky, stretchy dough.

TO FINISH: Increase heat to medium. Drop dough, in eight evenly spaced mounds, onto stew; cover and simmer until puffed and no longer doughy underneath, and knife inserted into centre of dumpling comes out clean, 8 to 10 minutes.

PER SERVING: about 395 cal, 20 g pro, 16 g total fat (4 g sat. fat), 42 g carb, 3 g fibre, 110 mg chol, 757 mg sodium, 640 mg potassium. % RDI: 9% calcium, 19% iron, 53% vit A, 15% vit C, 35% folate.

CHICKEN STEW:

1	whole chicken (about 1.35 kg)
115 g	salt pork, diced
3	carrots, chopped
3	ribs celery, chopped
1	large onion, chopped
900 g	yellow-fleshed potatoes, peeled and chopped
2 tsp	dried savory
¾ tsp	salt
½ tsp	pepper
2	ice cubes

DUMPLINGS:

1½ cups	all-purpose flour
1 tbsp	baking powder
1 tbsp	chopped fresh parsley
½ tsp	salt
2	egg yolks

NORMANDY-STYLE ROAST CORNISH HENS

MAKES 6 SERVINGS

Roasting with apples, Calvados and generous amounts of cream and butter brings out the best in Cornish hens.

3	Cornish hens (about 2.25 kg total), see tip, below
1½ tsp	salt
½ tsp	pepper
2	bay leaves
6	sprigs fresh thyme (or 1 tsp dried)
2	apples (unpeeled and uncored), halved and thinly sliced
1	onion, thinly sliced
⅓ cup	butter
¼ cup	Calvados or brandy
½ cup	sodium-reduced chicken broth
⅓ cup	whipping cream (35%)

Remove giblets and neck (if any) from hens; trim ends of wings. Trim off excess fat and skin. Mix salt with pepper; sprinkle about one-third inside cavities. Divide bay leaves and thyme between cavities. Mix apples with onion; place handful inside each hen, setting remaining mixture aside. Skewer cavity closed; tie legs together with kitchen string and tuck wings under back.

In large ovenproof skillet, melt butter over medium heat; brown hens all over, about 12 minutes. Transfer to plate.

Add remaining apple mixture to skillet; top with hens, breast side up. Sprinkle with remaining salt mixture. Roast in 375°F (190°C) oven, basting every 10 minutes, until instant-read thermometer inserted in thickest part of thigh reads 185°F (85°C), 1 to 1¼ hours. Untie and add contents of cavities to skillet. Halve hens and transfer to serving platter; keep warm.

Place skillet over medium-high heat; cook until almost no liquid remains. Add Calvados; holding skillet at arm's length, ignite liquid. Let flames subside. Stir in broth; cook until reduced by half. Stir in cream; bring to boil. Strain through fine-mesh sieve, pressing on solids. Serve with hens.

PER SERVING: about 634 cal, 40 g pro, 47 g total fat (18 g sat. fat), 7 g carb, trace fibre, 275 mg chol, 841 mg sodium. 632 mg potassium. % RDI: 4% calcium, 14% iron, 19% vit A, 5% vit C, 4% folate.

TIP FROM THE TEST KITCHEN
Guinea hens—game birds that are similar to Cornish hens— make a nice substitute in this recipe and the one on the opposite page. Use two guinea hens (about 2 kg total) in place of the three Cornish hens.

BRAISED CORNISH HENS
WITH ONIONS
MAKES 6 SERVINGS

Cornish hens become fall-off-the-bone tender and saturated with Mediterranean-inspired flavours in this recipe. Serve with roasted root vegetables.

In large saucepan of boiling water, blanch onions for 1 minute; drain and transfer to bowl of ice water. Let cool slightly. Peel, trimming root end if necessary. Set aside.

Remove giblets and neck (if any) from hens. Trim ends of wings; trim off excess fat and skin. Pat hens dry; cut each in half. In bowl, mix flour, salt and pepper; dredge hens in mixture, shaking off excess.

In wide Dutch oven, heat 1 tbsp of the oil over medium-high heat. Working in batches and using remaining oil, sear hens all over until golden brown, about 6 minutes. Transfer to plate.

In same pan, cook anchovies, garlic and hot pepper flakes until garlic is light golden, about 1 minute. Add ½ cup of the broth and vinegar; bring to boil, scraping up any browned bits from bottom of pan.

Return hens and any accumulated juices to pan; add sage and remaining broth and bring to boil. Cover and transfer to 300°F (150°C) oven; braise for 30 minutes.

Stir in onions; cover and cook for 30 minutes. Uncover and cook until juices run clear when hens are pierced and onions are tender, about 15 minutes. Using slotted spoon, transfer hens and onions to platter and keep warm.

Skim off any fat from braising liquid; bring to boil over high heat. Boil until slightly thickened and reduced to 1½ cups, about 12 minutes. *(Make-ahead: Cover and refrigerate hens and sauce in separate airtight containers for up to 2 days.)*

Spoon some of the sauce over hens and onions; serve remaining sauce on the side.

2	pkg (each 284 g) cipollini and/or red pearl onions
3	Cornish hens (about 2.25 kg total), see tip, opposite
⅓ cup	all-purpose flour
1 tsp	salt
½ tsp	pepper
2 tbsp	vegetable oil
3	anchovy fillets, minced
3	cloves garlic, sliced
¼ tsp	hot pepper flakes
2½ cups	sodium-reduced chicken broth
1 tbsp	white wine vinegar
2 tbsp	chopped fresh sage

PER SERVING: about 568 cal, 43 g pro, 37 g total fat (9 g sat. fat), 13 g carb, 2 g fibre, 233 mg chol, 844 mg sodium, 685 mg potassium. % RDI: 5% calcium, 18% iron, 6% vit A, 8% vit C, 12% folate.

ROASTED STUFFED CORNISH HENS

MAKES 8 SERVINGS

Little Cornish hens take less time to bake than a large bird—and there is no finicky carving. Just cut each hen in half and arrange over the mounded stuffing.

RICE STUFFING:

2 tbsp	butter
3	leeks (white parts only), sliced
1	rib celery, thinly sliced
2	cloves garlic, minced
1½ cups	long-grain rice
2½ cups	sodium-reduced chicken broth
1 tbsp	chopped fresh tarragon
1 tsp	grated lemon zest
¼ tsp	each salt and pepper

ROASTED CORNISH HENS:

2 tbsp	butter, melted
½ tsp	grated lemon zest
4	Cornish hens (about 2.7 kg total)
¼ tsp	salt
pinch	pepper

RICE STUFFING: In saucepan, melt butter over medium-high heat; cook leeks, celery and garlic, stirring occasionally, until softened, about 5 minutes.

Add rice, stirring to coat. Add broth, tarragon, lemon zest, salt and pepper; bring to boil. Reduce heat, cover and simmer until rice is tender and no liquid remains, about 18 minutes. Remove from heat and let stand for 10 minutes. *(Make-ahead: Let cool for 30 minutes; refrigerate in airtight container for up to 24 hours, adding 10 minutes to cooking time for baking dish.)*

ROASTED CORNISH HENS: Stir butter with lemon zest; set aside. Remove giblets and neck (if any) from hens. Trim ends of wings; trim off excess fat and skin. Fill each cavity with about ½ cup of the stuffing. Brush hens with butter mixture; sprinkle with salt and pepper. Place remaining stuffing in greased 8-inch (2 L) square baking dish.

Place hens, breast side up, on greased rack in shallow roasting pan. Bake in 400°F (200°C) oven for 45 minutes, basting occasionally. Add stuffing; bake, uncovering halfway through, until stuffing is hot and instant-read thermometer inserted into thickest part of hen thigh reads 185°F (85°C), about 30 minutes.

Transfer hens to cutting board; let rest for 10 minutes before cutting in half.

PER SERVING: about 613 cal, 40 g pro, 35 g total fat (12 g sat. fat), 32 g carb, 1 g fibre, 225 mg chol, 505 mg sodium, 583 mg potassium. % RDI: 5% calcium, 17% iron, 10% vit A, 7% vit C, 9% folate.

PIRI-PIRI CORNISH HEN

MAKES 2 SERVINGS

A single Cornish hen makes a delectable main dish for a romantic dinner for two. Or, for a dinner party, simply multiply the recipe.

1	Cornish hen (about 675 g)
1 tbsp	chopped pimiento (see tip, below) or roasted red pepper
2	cloves garlic
½ tsp	salt
2 tbsp	extra-virgin olive oil
1 tsp	sweet paprika
1 tsp	hot pepper sauce
½ tsp	grated orange zest
¼ tsp	dried thyme
¼ tsp	pepper

Using kitchen shears, cut along each side of backbone of hen; discard backbone. Trim ends of wings; trim off excess fat and skin. Cut hen in half; set aside.

On cutting board, finely mince together pimiento, garlic and salt; scrape into small bowl. Add 1 tbsp of the oil, paprika, hot pepper sauce, orange zest, thyme and pepper; mix well. Rub all over each half of hen. Refrigerate for 10 minutes. *(Make-ahead: Cover and refrigerate for up to 24 hours.)*

In ovenproof skillet, heat remaining oil over medium-high heat; brown hen, skin side down, about 5 minutes. Turn over; transfer to 400°F (200°C) oven. Bake, basting once, until juices run clear when hen is pierced, 20 to 25 minutes.

PER SERVING: about 427 cal, 26 g pro, 35 g total fat (8 g sat. fat), 2 g carb, 1 g fibre, 150 mg chol, 664 mg sodium. % RDI: 3% calcium, 13% iron, 11% vit A, 12% vit C, 2% folate.

TIP FROM THE TEST KITCHEN

Pimientos are mild red Spanish peppers. You usually see them stuffed into pitted green olives, but they are sold in jars by themselves as well. Look for them in the pickle aisle of the supermarket.

ROSEMARY GARLIC CORNISH HENS

MAKES 4 SERVINGS

Cornish hens may sound fussy, but they are excellent for weeknights because they roast so quickly. Serve this easy recipe with Cranberry Pistachio Pilaf (below) and a salad.

On cutting board and using chef's knife, mince garlic; sprinkle with ¼ tsp of the salt. With flat side of knife, mash to form paste; place in bowl. Mince enough of the rosemary to make 1 tsp; add to garlic paste along with butter. Mash to combine.

Remove giblets and neck (if any) from hens. Trim ends of wings; trim off excess fat and skin. Starting at neck end and using fingers, gently loosen skin over hen breasts, being careful not to tear skin; evenly spread butter mixture under skin to cover breasts. Sprinkle with pepper and remaining salt; drizzle with oil.

Place remaining rosemary on greased rack in small roasting pan; top with hens, breast side up. Roast in 400°F (200°C) oven, basting often, until juices run clear when hens are pierced, 25 to 35 minutes. Cut hens in half to serve.

1	clove garlic
½ tsp	salt
1	bunch fresh rosemary
2 tbsp	butter, softened
2	Cornish hens (about 1.35 kg total), halved
¼ tsp	pepper
1 tbsp	olive oil

PER SERVING: about 379 cal, 26 g pro, 30 g total fat (10 g sat. fat), trace carb, trace fibre, 165 mg chol, 401 mg sodium, 287 mg potassium. % RDI: 2% calcium, 8% iron, 9% vit A, 2% vit C, 1% folate.

Cranberry Pistachio Pilaf

In saucepan, melt 1 tbsp butter over medium heat. Add 1 shallot, minced, and pinch each salt and pepper; cook until softened, about 1 minute. Stir in 1½ cups each basmati rice, sodium-reduced chicken broth and water; bring to boil. Reduce heat, cover and simmer until rice is tender and no liquid remains, about 15 minutes. Let stand, covered, for 5 minutes. Stir in 2 tbsp each chopped toasted pistachios, chopped dried cranberries and minced fresh parsley.

MAKES 4 SERVINGS

LEMON PEPPER CORNISH HENS
MAKES 4 SERVINGS

Lemon and pepper may take the lead on these juicy hens, but a mélange of aromatic spices gives them a slightly exotic taste.

Using kitchen shears, cut along each side of backbone of each hen; discard backbones. Cut hens in half; trim ends of wings. Trim off excess fat and skin; set hens aside.

Mix together lemon zest, lemon juice, garlic, pepper, brown sugar, ginger, oregano, salt, cumin and cloves; add hens, turning to coat. Cover and refrigerate for 2 hours. *(Make-ahead: Refrigerate for up to 1 day.)* Bring to room temperature.

Brush hens lightly with oil. Place, bone side down, on greased grill over medium heat; close lid and grill, turning once and basting with more oil, until juices run clear when hens are pierced and skin is crisp, 25 to 30 minutes.

PER SERVING: about 454 cal, 32 g pro, 33 g total fat (8 g sat. fat), 6 g carb, 1 g fibre, 186 mg chol, 668 mg sodium. % RDI: 4% calcium, 16% iron, 5% vit A, 17% vit C, 3% folate.

2	Cornish hens (about 1.35 kg total)
1½ tsp	grated lemon zest
¼ cup	lemon juice
3	cloves garlic, pressed
1 tbsp	pepper
2 tsp	packed brown sugar
2 tsp	grated fresh ginger
1½ tsp	dried oregano, crumbled
1 tsp	salt
½ tsp	ground cumin
¼ tsp	ground cloves
	extra-virgin olive oil

SOUTHWEST CORNISH HENS

MAKES 8 SERVINGS

Ground ancho and chipotle chili peppers add wonderful heat to these hens. If you substitute regular chili powder for them, you may want to add a pinch of cayenne pepper, too.

2 tbsp	ground ancho chili pepper or chili powder
2 tsp	each dried oregano and ground cumin
1 tsp	ground chipotle chili pepper or chili powder
1 tsp	celery salt
1 tsp	each salt and pepper
3 tbsp	extra-virgin olive oil
2	cloves garlic, minced
4	Cornish hens (about 2.7 kg total)

In small bowl, stir together ancho chili pepper, oregano, cumin, chipotle chili pepper, celery salt, salt and pepper; stir in oil and garlic. Set aside.

Using kitchen shears, cut along each side of backbone of each hen; discard backbones. Cut hens in half; trim ends of wings. Trim off excess fat and skin.

Place hens, skin side up, on foil-lined rimmed baking sheet. Rub spice mixture all over hens. Cover and refrigerate for 30 minutes. *(Make-ahead: Cover and refrigerate for up to 24 hours.)*

Transfer to greased rack in roasting pan. Pour 1 cup water into pan. Roast in 375°F (190°C) oven for 30 minutes; baste with pan juices. Roast until instant-read thermometer inserted into thickest part of thigh reads 185°F (85°C), 30 to 35 minutes.

PER SERVING: about 424 cal, 32 g pro, 31 g total fat (8 g sat. fat), 2 g carb, 1 g fibre, 185 mg chol, 549 mg sodium, 410 mg potassium. % RDI: 4% calcium, 16% iron, 11% vit A, 3% vit C, 3% folate.

TIP FROM THE TEST KITCHEN

If you'd prefer to barbecue the hens rather than roast them, set a foil drip pan on one burner of a two-burner barbecue, or on the centre burner of a three-burner barbecue; heat the remaining burner(s) to medium. Set the hens, bone side down, on a greased grill over the drip pan. Close the lid and grill until the bottom is grill-marked, about 25 minutes. Turn and grill until the juices run clear when the thickest part of the thigh is pierced, about 20 minutes. Move any pieces that need more crisping or colouring over direct heat. Close the lid and grill until golden, about 3 minutes.

TUSCAN CORNISH HENS

MAKES 4 SERVINGS

These hens are cooked with traditional Tuscan seasonings of fennel, garlic and rosemary. Fresh rosemary has a grassier, fresher flavour than dried, which makes it better suited to this recipe.

In shallow glass dish, whisk together lemon juice, oil, garlic, rosemary, fennel seeds, salt and pepper; set aside.

Using kitchen shears, cut along each side of backbone of each hen; discard backbones. Turn breast side up. Press firmly on breastbone to flatten; tuck wings behind back. Add to lemon juice mixture, turning to coat. Cover and refrigerate for 4 hours. (*Make-ahead: Refrigerate, turning occasionally, for up to 24 hours.*)

Place hens, skin side down, on greased grill over medium heat; close lid and grill for 15 minutes. Turn and grill until juices run clear when hens are pierced, about 20 minutes.

Transfer to cutting board; cover loosely with foil and let rest for 10 minutes. Cut hens in half to serve.

⅓ cup	lemon juice
¼ cup	extra-virgin olive oil
4	cloves garlic, minced
1 tbsp	chopped fresh rosemary
2 tsp	fennel seeds, crushed (see tip, page 208)
½ tsp	each salt and pepper
4	Cornish hens (about 1.8 kg total)

PER SERVING: about 586 cal, 45 g pro, 43 g total fat (11 g sat. fat), 2 g carb, trace fibre, 262 mg chol, 274 mg sodium. % RDI: 3% calcium, 15% iron, 7% vit A, 5% vit C, 2% folate.

HOMESTYLE CHICKEN NOODLE SOUP
(PAGE 262)

CHAPTER 6

STOCKS, SOUPS & STUFFINGS

SLOW COOKER CHICKEN STOCK

MAKES 12 CUPS

You will never want to buy commercial broth again after tasting this incredibly delicious, yet simple, homemade chicken stock. Add whatever vegetables or scraps you have in the fridge, such as the green tops of leeks, shallots, herb stems and celery leaves.

900 g	chicken bones (about 3 carcasses) and/or pieces, such as wings and necks
2	onions, coarsely chopped
3	ribs celery, coarsely chopped
3	carrots, coarsely chopped
10	sprigs fresh parsley (or parsley stems)
2	bay leaves
½ tsp	black peppercorns
12 cups	cold water

In slow cooker, combine chicken bones, onions, celery, carrots, parsley, bay leaves and peppercorns; pour in water. Cover and cook on low for 12 to 24 hours.

Line fine-mesh sieve with damp cheesecloth; strain stock into large bowl, pressing vegetables to extract liquid. Let cool for 30 minutes.

Refrigerate, uncovered, until fat hardens on surface, about 8 hours. Save fat for another use or discard. *(Make-ahead: Refrigerate in airtight containers for up to 3 days or freeze for up to 2 months.)*

PER 1 CUP: about 39 cal, 5 g pro, 1 g total fat (trace sat. fat), 1 g carb, 0 g fibre, 1 mg chol, 32 mg sodium, 200 mg potassium. % RDI: 1% calcium, 4% iron, 2% folate.

TIP FROM THE TEST KITCHEN
Homemade stock with no added salt is far more delicious than store-bought—and it gives you better control over the amount of sodium you add to your recipes.

STOVE-TOP CHICKEN BROTH

MAKES 8 CUPS

This slow-simmered broth has wonderfully rich chicken flavour. Make a double batch if you have time, and freeze any leftovers in recipe-friendly portions for another day.

1	stewing hen (or 1 whole chicken, 1.35 kg)
3	small carrots (unpeeled), coarsely chopped
3	small onions (unpeeled), coarsely chopped
3	ribs celery, coarsely chopped
1 cup	sliced mushrooms (stems and/or caps)
3	cloves garlic, smashed
10	sprigs fresh parsley
½ tsp	salt
½ tsp	black peppercorns
2	bay leaves
8 cups	cold water

In large stockpot, combine hen, carrots, onions, celery, mushrooms, garlic, parsley, salt, peppercorns and bay leaves; pour in water. Cover and cook over low heat for 4 hours.

Discard hen. Line fine-mesh sieve with damp cheesecloth; strain broth into large bowl, pressing vegetables to extract liquid.

Refrigerate, uncovered, until fat hardens on surface, about 8 hours. Save fat for another use or discard. *(Make-ahead: Refrigerate in airtight containers for up to 3 days or freeze for up to 2 months.)*

PER 1 CUP: about 39 cal, 5 g pro, 1 g total fat (trace sat. fat), 1 g carb, 0 g fibre, 1 mg chol, 175 mg sodium. % RDI: 1% calcium, 4% iron, 2% folate.

TIP FROM THE TEST KITCHEN

To extract maximum flavour, stocks and broths need to simmer for hours. This means the leftover meat won't have any taste left. Discard it and cook fresh chicken to make the most delicious soups.

OLD-FASHIONED CLEAR CHICKEN SOUP

MAKES 8 TO 10 SERVINGS

Chicken bones are the best choice for making tasty soup. This is the base you need for a batch of soul-satisfying Matzo Ball Soup (page 255).

Cut leek lengthwise in half; spread leaves and rinse under running water to remove grit.

In soup pot, bring chicken backs and cold water to boil; skim off foam. Add leek, carrots, parsnip, turnip (if using), celery, onion, parsley, thyme, bay leaf, 1 tsp salt and peppercorns; return to boil. Reduce heat, cover and simmer for 1 hour.

Using slotted spoon, transfer carrots, parsnip and turnip to bowl; let cool. Simmer soup, covered, for 1 hour, adding dill (if using) in last 10 minutes.

Line fine-mesh sieve with damp cheesecloth; strain soup into large bowl. Skim off fat. Dice cooled vegetables and return to soup. Season with more salt if desired.

PER EACH OF 10 SERVINGS: about 56 cal, 5 g pro, 2 g total fat (trace sat. fat), 5 g carb, 1 g fibre, 1 mg chol, 271 mg sodium, 294 mg potassium. % RDI: 2% calcium, 5% iron, 26% vit A, 5% vit C, 7% folate.

1	leek
1.35 kg	chicken backs or other chicken bones (see tip, below)
14 cups	cold water
2	carrots, peeled
1	parsnip, peeled
1	white turnip (optional), peeled
3	ribs celery with leaves, chopped
1	onion, quartered
	fresh parsley sprigs
	fresh thyme sprigs (or ½ tsp dried thyme)
1	bay leaf
1 tsp	salt (approx)
½ tsp	black peppercorns
3	sprigs fresh dill (optional)

TIP FROM THE TEST KITCHEN

This soup is a great way to use up leftover chicken backs and trimmings. Keep a bag in the freezer and add parts as you have them. Freeze for up to one month, sealing well to protect the meat from freezer burn (which is the enemy of fresh-tasting stock).

CHICKEN CONSOMMÉ
WITH CHIVE CRÊPES
MAKES 8 SERVINGS

This lovely clear soup makes an elegant appetizer for Easter dinner; garnish with a more chopped chives if you like. Enjoy leftover crêpes with cream cheese and smoked salmon.

8 cups	Stove-Top Chicken Broth (page 250) or Slow Cooker Chicken Stock (page 248)
1	each carrot and rib celery
1	onion (unpeeled)
225 g	white mushrooms
2 tbsp	Chicken Schmaltz (page 291), optional
6	egg whites
1 tsp	salt
1 tsp	black peppercorns
½ tsp	dried thyme
2	Chive Crêpes (page 50)

In Dutch oven, bring broth to boil.

Meanwhile, in food processor, mince together carrot, celery, onion and mushrooms. Pulse in schmaltz (if using), egg whites, salt, peppercorns and thyme; add to hot broth. Return to gentle boil, stirring occasionally to prevent egg from sticking to bottom of pot, until "raft" forms on surface, 10 minutes.

Make small hole in raft. Simmer gently over medium-low heat, stirring and without boiling, until broth is clear and raft begins to sink, 40 to 45 minutes. Let cool for 10 minutes.

Line fine-mesh sieve with damp cheesecloth; place over large heatproof glass measure. Using ladle, break raft and gently ladle (not pour) liquid through cheesecloth to make 6 cups, adding up to ¾ cup water if necessary. Discard raft. *(Make-ahead: Let cool; refrigerate in airtight container for up to 2 days or freeze for up to 1 month.)*

Roll up crêpes; slice ¼-inch (5 mm) thick. Divide among soup bowls; pour in consommé.

PER SERVING: about 63 cal, 6 g pro, 3 g total fat (1 g sat. fat), 3 g carb, 1 g fibre, 16 mg chol, 483 mg sodium, 215 mg potassium. % RDI: 2% calcium, 5% iron, 2% vit A, 5% folate.

TIP FROM THE TEST KITCHEN
The raft is the reason this soup comes out crystal clear. As the egg white mixture cooks, it gathers up all the particles that could cloud the broth so they can be removed completely.

SHERRIED CHICKEN CONSOMMÉ

MAKES 8 SERVINGS

Good homemade broth is the key to this rich, clear soup.
Consommé is an elegant addition to a special menu. Serve it with
your favourite garnishes (see tip, below) and a glass of sherry.

8 cups	Stove-Top Chicken Broth (page 250) or Slow Cooker Chicken Stock (page 248)
1	each carrot, rib celery and onion (unpeeled)
225 g	white mushrooms
2 tbsp	Chicken Schmaltz (page 291), optional
6	egg whites
1 tsp	each salt and black peppercorns
½ tsp	dried thyme
3 tbsp	dry sherry

In Dutch oven, bring broth to boil.

Meanwhile, in food processor, mince together carrot, celery, onion and mushrooms. Pulse in schmaltz (if using), egg whites, salt, peppercorns and thyme. Add to hot broth. Return to gentle boil, stirring occasionally to prevent egg from sticking to bottom of pot, until "raft" forms on surface, 10 minutes.

Make small hole in raft. Simmer gently over medium-low heat, stirring and without boiling, until broth is clear and raft begins to sink, 40 to 45 minutes. Let cool for 10 minutes.

Line fine-mesh sieve with damp cheesecloth; place over large heatproof glass measure. Using ladle, break raft and gently ladle (not pour) liquid through cheesecloth to make 6 cups, adding up to ¾ cup water if necessary. Discard raft. *(Make-ahead: Let cool; refrigerate in airtight container for up to 2 days or freeze for up to 1 month.)*

Pour into clean saucepan; add sherry and heat through.

PER SERVING: about 46 cal, 5 g pro, 1 g total fat (trace sat. fat), 2 g carb, 0 g fibre, 1 mg chol, 462 mg sodium, 205 mg potassium. % RDI: 1% calcium, 4% iron, 2% folate

TIP FROM THE TEST KITCHEN

This consommé is lovely with all sorts of accents. Add garnishes—such as cooked rice or small pasta, small cooked filled pasta, thinly sliced mushrooms, sautéed leeks, enoki mushrooms, chopped chives or sprigs of watercress—to bowls before ladling hot consommé over top.

MATZO BALL SOUP

MAKES 8 SERVINGS

Matzo balls are comfort food on a grand scale. You start with cold soup because some of it goes into the matzo balls to flavour them while the rest is warmed to serve as the base.

In large bowl, whisk together eggs, schmaltz, ⅔ cup of the soup and salt; whisk in matzo meal. Cover and refrigerate for 1 hour.

Bring large pot of salted water to boil. With wet hands and using about 3 tbsp for each, form matzo mixture into balls; slide into water. Reduce heat, cover and simmer for 30 minutes.

Meanwhile, in large saucepan, bring remaining soup to boil; reduce heat to low and keep warm. Using slotted spoon, transfer matzo balls to soup; simmer for 20 minutes before serving.

PER SERVING: about 279 cal, 13 g pro, 12 g total fat (3 g sat. fat), 29 g carb, 2 g fibre, 123 mg chol, 887 mg sodium, 442 mg potassium. % RDI: 4% calcium, 15% iron, 38% vit A, 5% vit C, 30% folate.

5	eggs
¼ cup	Chicken Schmaltz (page 291)
1	batch cold Old-Fashioned Clear Chicken Soup (page 251)
1½ tsp	salt
1⅔ cups	matzo meal

CORNISH HEN BROTH
WITH WATERCRESS
MAKES 6 TO 8 SERVINGS

Cornish hens make a wonderfully light and clear, yet flavourful, stock.
It is a delicious match for tender watercress, one of the delights of spring.

In large pot, bring watercress stems, Cornish hen, celery, onion, parsley, peppercorns, bay leaf, ginger, garlic and 8 cups water to boil over medium-high heat, skimming off foam. Reduce heat, cover and simmer for 1 hour.

Remove hen; let cool enough to handle. Discard skin and bones; finely shred meat and set aside. Line fine-mesh sieve with damp cheesecloth; place over large heatproof glass measure. Strain stock to make 8 cups. *(Make-ahead: Refrigerate broth and meat in separate airtight containers for up to 3 days.)*

In saucepan, bring broth and salt to boil over medium-high heat. Divide watercress leaves, shredded meat and pasta among bowls; pour broth over top. Serve with lemon wedges.

PER EACH OF 8 SERVINGS: about 129 cal, 16 g pro, 4 g total fat (1 g sat. fat), 6 g carb, 1 g fibre, 45 mg chol, 206 mg sodium. % RDI: 3% calcium, 8% iron, 6% vit A, 8% vit C, 10% folate.

4 cups	lightly packed watercress, stems and leaves separated
1	Cornish hen (about 675 g)
2	ribs celery with leaves, chopped
1	onion, halved
4	sprigs fresh parsley
8	black peppercorns
1	bay leaf
2	slices fresh ginger
1	clove garlic, smashed
½ tsp	salt
1 cup	cooked tiny pasta or rice (⅓ cup uncooked)
	lemon wedges

VIETNAMESE CHICKEN NOODLE SOUP

MAKES 4 TO 6 SERVINGS

Arrange bean sprouts, basil, chilies and limes on a platter with small bowls of hot sauce and fish sauce to serve with this aromatic soup. Then diners can garnish and season their bowlfuls according to taste.

SOUP:

8 cups	Stove-Top Chicken Broth (page 250), Slow Cooker Chicken Stock (page 248) or sodium-reduced chicken broth
3	slices fresh ginger
1	whole star anise
4	whole cloves
half	cinnamon stick, broken
2 tsp	black peppercorns
2	bone-in skin-on chicken breasts
2 tbsp	fish sauce
450 g	dried rice stick noodles (about ¼ inch/5 mm wide)
4	green onions, thinly sliced
½ cup	fresh cilantro leaves

GARNISHES:

2 cups	bean sprouts
1	bunch Thai or regular basil (see tip, right)
2	limes, cut in wedges
8	small red or green hot peppers
	sriracha
	fish sauce or hoisin sauce

SOUP: In Dutch oven, bring broth, ginger, star anise, cloves, cinnamon and peppercorns to boil. Add chicken; reduce heat and simmer until no longer pink inside, about 20 minutes. Remove chicken and let cool enough to handle. Remove meat from skin and bones in large chunks; slice and set aside. Discard skin and bones.

Line fine-mesh sieve with damp cheesecloth; strain broth into clean pot, pressing solids gently to extract liquid. Bring to boil; add chicken and fish sauce. Reduce heat and simmer until heated through.

While broth mixture is simmering, prepare noodles according to package instructions. Drain and rinse under cold water; toss to drain well. Divide among large soup bowls.

Ladle soup over noodles. Sprinkle with green onions and cilantro.

GARNISHES: Serve soup with separate bowls of bean sprouts, basil, limes and chilies. Season with sriracha and fish sauce as desired.

PER EACH OF 6 SERVINGS: about 426 cal, 20 g pro, 7 g total fat (2 g sat. fat), 69 g carb, 4 g fibre, 33 mg chol, 771 mg sodium. % RDI: 4% calcium, 14% iron, 11% vit A, 45% vit C, 23% folate.

TIP FROM THE TEST KITCHEN
Thai basil has green leaves and pretty dark purple flowers. It has a lovely licorice-tinged flavour that's terrific in Asian soups like this.
If you can't find it, regular Italian basil is a good substitute.

SPRINGTIME ITALIAN CHICKEN SOUP
MAKES 6 SERVINGS

Classic Italian stracciatella soup—threaded with delicate cooked egg—is the inspiration for this recipe. Made with a savoury homemade stock, it's light, lemony and full of flavour.

ITALIAN CHICKEN STOCK: In stockpot, combine chicken, onions, celery, tomatoes, carrot, parsley, thyme, bay leaves, garlic and peppercorns. Pour in 12 cups water; bring to boil. Reduce heat and simmer, skimming occasionally, for 4 hours.

Line fine-mesh sieve with damp cheesecloth; place over large heatproof glass measure. Strain stock, pressing solids to extract liquid and make about 8 cups. Refrigerate, uncovered, until fat solidifies on surface, about 8 hours. Lift off fat and discard. *(Make-ahead: Refrigerate in airtight container for up to 3 days or freeze for up to 1 month.)*

SOUP: Set aside ¼ cup of the stock. In large saucepan, bring remaining stock to boil; add salt and boil until reduced to 6 cups, about 13 minutes.

Meanwhile, whisk together eggs, Parmesan, semolina, parsley, lemon zest and reserved stock. Gradually pour into boiling stock, stirring constantly, until eggs break into strands, about 1 minute.

PER SERVING: about 114 cal, 10 g pro, 6 g total fat (3 g sat. fat), 5 g carb, trace fibre, 121 mg chol, 468 mg sodium. % RDI: 10% calcium, 5% iron, 6% vit A, 5% vit C, 11% folate.

ITALIAN CHICKEN STOCK:

900 g	chicken backs, necks and wing tips
2	onions, chopped
2	large ribs celery (with leaves), chopped
2	plum tomatoes, quartered
1	carrot, chopped
8	sprigs fresh parsley
4	sprigs fresh thyme
2	bay leaves
2	cloves garlic
½ tsp	black peppercorns

SOUP:

¾ tsp	salt
3	eggs
½ cup	finely grated Parmesan cheese
3 tbsp	semolina or cornmeal
3 tbsp	finely chopped fresh parsley
1½ tsp	grated lemon zest

HOMESTYLE CHICKEN NOODLE SOUP

MAKES 6 TO 8 SERVINGS

Put down that can opener: Once you've had a bowl of this comforting soup—bursting with tender carrots, noodles and chicken— you'll never eat commercial chicken noodle again.

1 tbsp	vegetable oil
1	onion, chopped
2	each small carrots and ribs celery, sliced
¾ cup	sliced mushrooms
1	clove garlic, chopped
½ tsp	each salt and pepper
¼ tsp	dried thyme
1	bay leaf
8 cups	Stove-Top Chicken Broth (page 250), Slow Cooker Chicken Stock (page 248) or sodium-reduced chicken broth
2	bone-in skin-on chicken breasts
¾ cup	green beans, chopped
1 cup	egg noodles
2 tbsp	chopped fresh parsley

In Dutch oven, heat oil over medium-high heat; cook onion, carrots, celery, mushrooms, garlic, salt, pepper, thyme and bay leaf, stirring often, until softened, about 10 minutes.

Add broth; bring to boil. Add chicken and return to boil; reduce heat and simmer until chicken is no longer pink inside, about 20 minutes. Remove chicken; let cool enough to handle. Remove meat from skin and bones; dice and return to soup. Discard skin and bones.

Add green beans to soup; cook until tender, about 7 minutes. Discard bay leaf. *(Make-ahead: Let cool for 30 minutes; refrigerate in airtight container for up to 3 days or freeze for up to 4 months.)*

Meanwhile, in saucepan of boiling water, cook noodles according to package instructions. Drain and add to soup along with parsley.

PER EACH OF 8 SERVINGS: about 147 cal, 13 g pro, 6 g total fat (1 g sat. fat), 8 g carb, 1 g fibre, 29 mg chol, 352 mg sodium. % RDI: 3% calcium, 8% iron, 27% vit A, 5% vit C, 8% folate.

CHICKEN SOUP
WITH WONTONS
MAKES 4 SERVINGS

This light yet satisfying soup is perfect for chasing away the chills.
When making the stock, add a few slices of fresh ginger and a couple
of green onions for extra flavour.

In saucepan large enough for wontons to move freely, bring water to boil.
Add wontons and boil until cooked through and floating, about 5 minutes.
Using slotted spoon, transfer to soup bowls; keep warm. Discard water.

Add broth, sesame oil and pepper to pan; bring to boil. Boil for 1 minute.

Add bok choy; cook until tender, about 1 minute. Ladle over wontons;
sprinkle with green onion.

PER SERVING: about 346 cal, 18 g pro, 4 g total fat (1 g sat. fat), 58 g carb,
3 g fibre, 10 mg chol, 848 mg sodium. % RDI: 12% calcium, 34% iron, 35% vit A,
35% vit C, 56% folate.

1	pkg (380 g) wontons (see tip, below)
6 cups	Stove-Top Chicken Broth (page 250), Slow Cooker Chicken Stock (page 248) or sodium-reduced chicken broth
dash	sesame oil
pinch	white or black pepper
4	heads baby bok choy (about 225 g total), chopped
1	green onion, thinly sliced

TIP FROM THE TEST KITCHEN
Frozen wontons are easy to find and super convenient.
Keep a few packages on hand (along with some frozen
homemade stock) so you can make this soup anytime
you need a comforting supper on a busy night.

COZY CHICKEN AND RICE SOUP

MAKES 4 SERVINGS

Nutty basmati rice, veggies and chicken make this a healthy, hearty dinner option.
For a fibre boost, swap in brown basmati rice and cook for a few minutes longer.

1 tbsp	olive oil
340 g	boneless skinless chicken thighs
1	leek, diced
2	ribs celery, diced
2	carrots, diced
1	yellow-fleshed potato, peeled and diced
half	sweet potato, peeled and diced
3	sprigs each fresh thyme and parsley
¼ tsp	each salt and pepper
4 cups	sodium-reduced chicken broth
½ cup	basmati rice, rinsed
1 cup	frozen peas

In large Dutch oven, heat oil over medium-high heat; brown chicken, 4 to 5 minutes. Transfer chicken to cutting board; cut into chunks. Set aside.

Add leek and celery to pan; cook over medium heat until softened, about 2 minutes. Add carrots, yellow-fleshed potato, sweet potato, thyme, parsley, salt and pepper; cook, stirring often, for 3 minutes.

Return chicken to pan along with any accumulated juices. Stir in broth and 4 cups water; bring to boil. Reduce heat and simmer for 5 minutes.

Stir in rice; cook until vegetables and rice are tender, about 13 minutes. Add peas. Discard thyme and parsley.

PER SERVING: about 345 cal, 25 g pro, 8 g total fat (2 g sat. fat), 43 g carb, 5 g fibre, 71 mg chol, 887 mg sodium, 625 mg potassium. % RDI: 7% calcium, 17% iron, 117% vit A, 27% vit C, 21% folate.

TIP FROM THE TEST KITCHEN
We often dilute commercial broth (even the sodium-reduced kind) with water when making soup to reduce the salt. If you substitute homemade stock, you can omit the water and use 8 cups stock instead. Just check the soup and season with salt at the end if necessary.

EGG AND ORZO CHICKEN SOUP

MAKES 4 TO 6 SERVINGS

Another take on Italian stracciatella, or egg drop soup, this light and simple recipe contains orzo pasta and bits of egg and cheese. Serve with more cheese to sprinkle over top if desired.

6 cups	Stove-Top Chicken Broth (page 250), Slow Cooker Chicken Stock (page 248) or sodium-reduced chicken broth
½ cup	orzo or other small pasta (see tip, below)
2	eggs
⅓ cup	grated Parmesan cheese
2 tbsp	chopped fresh parsley
pinch	nutmeg
pinch	white or black pepper

Set aside ¼ cup of the broth. In large saucepan, bring remaining broth to boil. Stir in pasta; cook until al dente, about 6 minutes.

Meanwhile, in bowl, whisk together eggs, Parmesan, parsley, nutmeg, pepper and reserved stock. Gradually pour into boiling broth mixture, stirring constantly, until eggs break into strands, about 2 minutes. Serve immediately.

PER EACH OF 6 SERVINGS: about 139 cal, 11 g pro, 5 g total fat (2 g sat. fat), 12 g carb, 1 g fibre, 68 mg chol, 281 mg sodium. % RDI: 8% calcium, 9% iron, 4% vit A, 2% vit C, 20% folate.

TIP FROM THE TEST KITCHEN
This soup works with any tiny pasta you like. Get creative and try ditalini, acini di pepe or even itty-bitty bow ties.

ASIAN CHICKEN NOODLE SOUP

MAKES 4 TO 6 SERVINGS

Make this meal-in-a-bowl even more satisfying by offering
a variety of fun garnishes to add at the table, such as bean sprouts,
watercress and pea shoots.

ASIAN CHICKEN BROTH: In stockpot or Dutch oven, combine chicken thighs
and breasts, carrots, celery, onions, ginger, garlic, parsley, salt, peppercorns
and bay leaf. Pour in cold water and bring to boil; reduce heat and simmer,
skimming off foam, until juices run clear when chicken is pierced, about
35 minutes.

Remove chicken; let cool enough to handle. Remove skin and bones;
return bones to broth. Discard skin. Shred chicken and refrigerate in airtight
container for another use. Cover and simmer broth over low heat for
30 more minutes.

Line fine-mesh sieve with damp cheesecloth; strain broth into large bowl,
pressing vegetables to extract liquid. Skim off fat. Stir in fish sauce. *(Make-
ahead: Let cool for 30 minutes; refrigerate in airtight container for up to 3 days.)*

SOUP: Mix together chicken, salt and pepper; set aside. Prepare noodles
according to package instructions. Drain and rinse under cold water; toss to
drain well. Divide among large soup bowls.

Ladle hot broth over noodles. Sprinkle with shredded chicken, tomatoes,
green onions, cilantro and hot pepper. Serve with lime wedges.

PER EACH OF 6 SERVINGS: about 189 cal, 17 g pro, 4 g total fat (1 g sat. fat),
19 g carb, 1 g fibre, 35 mg chol, 659 mg sodium. % RDI: 3% calcium, 9% iron,
4% vit A, 10% vit C, 8% folate.

ASIAN CHICKEN BROTH:

2	each bone-in skin-on chicken thighs and breasts
2	each small carrots, ribs celery, and small onions (unpeeled), coarsely chopped
4	slices fresh ginger
2	cloves garlic, smashed
8	sprigs fresh parsley
¾ tsp	salt
½ tsp	black peppercorns
1	bay leaf
9 cups	cold water
1 tbsp	fish sauce

SOUP:

2 cups	shredded cooked chicken
pinch	each salt and pepper
115 g	dried rice stick noodles (about ¼ inch/5 mm wide)
6	grape tomatoes, cut in wedges
3	green onions, chopped
¾ cup	fresh cilantro, basil or mint leaves
1	green hot pepper, thinly sliced
	lime wedges

QUICK CHICKEN CORN CHOWDER

MAKES 4 SERVINGS

This chowder welcomes you home with a delicious blend of sweet corn, potatoes and savoury broth. Partially puréeing the soup gives it a creamy texture so you don't have to add too much cream at the end.

In Dutch oven, heat oil over medium-high heat; cook onion, celery and garlic, stirring occasionally, until softened, about 5 minutes. Stir in corn, potatoes, red pepper, thyme, bay leaf, paprika, salt and pepper; cook, stirring, for 3 minutes.

Stir in broth and 3 cups water; bring to boil. Reduce heat and simmer until potatoes are tender, about 15 minutes. Discard bay leaf.

Using immersion blender, purée soup until almost smooth with a few chunks remaining. Stir in chicken and cream; cook until heated through, about 2 minutes.

PER SERVING: about 391 cal, 27 g pro, 17 g total fat (6 g sat. fat), 37 g carb, 4 g fibre, 88 mg chol, 688 mg sodium, 731 mg potassium. % RDI: 6% calcium, 14% iron, 20% vit A, 102% vit C, 25% folate.

1 tbsp	vegetable oil
1	onion, diced
2	ribs celery, diced
2	cloves garlic, minced
2 cups	fresh or frozen corn kernels
2	yellow-fleshed potatoes (about 340 g), peeled and diced
1	sweet red pepper, diced
1 tsp	chopped fresh thyme
1	bay leaf
½ tsp	sweet paprika
½ tsp	salt
¼ tsp	pepper
2 cups	sodium-reduced chicken broth, Stove-Top Chicken Broth (page 250) or Slow Cooker Chicken Stock (page 248)
2 cups	diced cooked chicken
⅓ cup	whipping cream (35%)

TIP FROM THE TEST KITCHEN
For a bit of Mexican flavour, top with fresh cilantro sprigs and serve with warm corn tortillas and lime wedges.

SPINACH AND CHICKEN SOUP
WITH PARMESAN
MAKES 6 TO 8 SERVINGS

A cooked supermarket chicken adds a pleasant rotisserie flavour to this soothing vegetable-and-noodle soup. It also cuts down on prep time dramatically.

2 tsp	olive oil
2	carrots, diced
3	cloves garlic, minced
1 tsp	chopped fresh thyme
pinch	each salt and pepper
1	pkg (900 mL) sodium-reduced chicken broth (see tip, below)
1¼ cups	small shell pasta (115 g)
4 cups	lightly packed baby spinach
3 cups	shredded rotisserie chicken (skin removed)
½ cup	finely shredded Parmesan cheese

In large saucepan, heat oil over medium heat; cook carrots, garlic, thyme, salt and pepper, stirring often, until slightly softened, about 5 minutes.

Pour in broth and 4 cups water; bring to boil. Add pasta; cook until al dente, about 8 minutes.

Stir in spinach and chicken; cook until chicken is warmed through, about 2 minutes. Sprinkle with Parmesan.

PER EACH OF 8 SERVINGS: about 196 cal, 20 g pro, 7 g total fat (2 g sat. fat), 14 g carb, 1 g fibre, 66 mg chol, 581 mg sodium, 287 mg potassium. % RDI: 10% calcium, 11% iron, 48% vit A, 3% vit C, 27% folate.

TIP FROM THE TEST KITCHEN
You can substitute 4 cups Stove-Top Chicken Broth (page 250) or Slow Cooker Chicken Stock (page 248) for the 900 mL package of store-bought broth.

CHICKEN MEATBALL SOUP
WITH PASTA
MAKES 4 SERVINGS

Here's a perfect soup for a blustery day. Each spoonful is full of tasty surprises: golden meatballs, bow tie pasta and tender veggies.

CHICKEN MEATBALLS: In large bowl, beat egg yolk; stir in bread crumbs, mustard, green onion, garlic, hot pepper sauce, salt and pepper. Mix in chicken. Roll by 1 tbsp into meatballs. Bake on foil-lined rimmed baking sheet in 375°F (190°C) oven until no longer pink inside, about 15 minutes.

SOUP: While meatballs are baking, in large saucepan, heat oil over medium heat; cook onion, garlic, oregano, salt and pepper, stirring occasionally, until onion is softened, about 5 minutes. Add tomatoes, broth, 1 cup water and tomato paste; bring to boil. Reduce heat, cover and simmer for 10 minutes.

Add meatballs and pasta; cover and simmer until pasta is al dente, about 10 minutes. *(Make-ahead: Let cool for 30 minutes; refrigerate in airtight container for up to 2 days.)* Add peas; heat through. Sprinkle with Parmesan.

PER SERVING: about 327 cal, 22 g pro, 14 g total fat (4 g sat. fat), 31 g carb, 5 g fibre, 101 mg chol, 1,160 mg sodium. % RDI: 18% calcium, 25% iron, 21% vit A, 62% vit C, 30% folate.

TIP FROM THE TEST KITCHEN
If you would like to pack this soup for lunch at school or work, pour boiling water into a vacuum bottle (such as a Thermos) and let warm for five minutes. Drain the water and fill the bottle with hot soup.

CHICKEN MEATBALLS:

1	egg yolk
2 tbsp	dried bread crumbs
1 tbsp	Dijon mustard
1	green onion, thinly sliced
1	clove garlic, minced
½ tsp	hot pepper sauce
pinch	each salt and pepper
225 g	lean ground chicken

SOUP:

1 tbsp	extra-virgin olive oil
1	onion, chopped
2	cloves garlic, minced
1 tsp	dried oregano
½ tsp	each salt and pepper
1	can (796 mL) diced tomatoes
2 cups	sodium-reduced chicken broth, Stove-Top Chicken Broth (page 250) or Slow Cooker Chicken Stock (page 248)
2 tbsp	tomato paste
½ cup	farfalline, tubetti or other tiny pasta (see tip, page 266)
1 cup	frozen peas
¼ cup	grated Parmesan cheese

POZOLE

MAKES 8 TO 10 SERVINGS

Pozole is a Mexican broth-based soup made with meat and hominy, a type of corn. This version tastes authentic but takes much less time than traditional recipes. Pozole is served with a garnish tray so everyone can add his or her own final touches.

TORTILLA STRIPS:

4	small flour tortillas
1 tbsp	vegetable oil

SOUP:

½ cup	pepitas (hulled green pumpkin seeds)
1	jar (430 mL) salsa verde (see tip, below)
4 tsp	dried Mexican or regular oregano
1	onion, chopped
4	cloves garlic, sliced
1	bay leaf
1.35 kg	bone-in skin-on chicken thighs or breasts
2 cups	sodium-reduced chicken broth, Stove-Top Chicken Broth (page 250) or Slow Cooker Chicken Stock (page 248)
2	cans (each 425 g) white hominy, drained and rinsed
4 tsp	chili powder
¼ tsp	each salt and pepper

GARNISHES:

	diced avocado tossed with lime juice
	shredded iceberg lettuce
	diced radishes
	thinly sliced green onions
	chopped fresh cilantro
	lime wedges

TORTILLA STRIPS: Brush tortillas all over with oil; stack and cut in half. Stack again and slice crosswise into thin strips. Separate strips; arrange on rimmed baking sheet. Bake in 350°F (180°C) oven until crisp and golden, 10 minutes. Let cool. *(Make-ahead: Store in airtight container for up to 2 days.)*

SOUP: In small skillet, toast pepitas over medium heat, stirring occasionally, until puffed and seeds pop, about 6 minutes. Let cool. In blender, purée together pepitas, salsa and oregano until smooth. Set aside.

In Dutch oven, bring 8 cups water, onion, garlic and bay leaf to boil; reduce heat and simmer for 10 minutes. Add chicken; cover and simmer, skimming off any foam, until juices run clear when chicken is pierced, about 25 minutes. Reserving cooking liquid, transfer chicken to plate; let cool enough to handle. Shred chicken into bowl, discarding skin and bones. Cover and refrigerate.

Strain cooking liquid into clean Dutch oven. Add salsa mixture, broth, hominy, chili powder, salt and pepper; bring to boil. Reduce heat and simmer, uncovered and skimming off any fat and foam, for 30 minutes. Stir in chicken. *(Make-ahead: Let cool for 30 minutes; refrigerate in airtight container for up to 2 days. Heat through to serve.)*

GARNISHES: Ladle soup into bowls. Serve with tortilla strips, avocado, lettuce, radishes, green onions, cilantro and lime wedges. Garnish as desired.

PER EACH OF 10 SERVINGS: about 316 cal, 29 g pro, 14 g total fat (3 g sat. fat), 19 g carb, 4 g fibre, 71 mg chol, 677 mg sodium. % RDI: 4% calcium, 31% iron, 6% vit A, 2% vit C, 53% folate.

TIP FROM THE TEST KITCHEN

Green salsa, or salsa verde, is made from tomatillos and has a thinner, smoother consistency than most tomato-based salsas. It's usually quite mild. There are a few brands widely available, and jar sizes vary slightly but not enough to make a difference to the recipe. Simply use one jar of whichever brand you like.

COQ AU VIN SOUP

MAKES 6 SERVINGS

We've tweaked the classic French recipe by turning it into a hearty soup that's faster and easier than the original braised dish. If you don't have red-skinned potatoes, substitute yellow-fleshed spuds. Serve with crunchy Salt and Pepper Croûtes (below).

2	strips sodium-reduced bacon, chopped
2 tsp	olive oil
450 g	boneless skinless chicken thighs, cut in ¾-inch (2 cm) chunks
500 g	red-skinned potatoes (about 4), cut in ½-inch (1 cm) cubes
1	pkg (227 g) cremini mushrooms, thinly sliced
1	leek (white and light green parts only), halved lengthwise and thinly sliced crosswise
2	cloves garlic, minced
2 tbsp	tomato paste
3 cups	sodium-reduced chicken broth, Stove-Top Chicken Broth (page 250) or Slow Cooker Chicken Stock (page 248)
⅔ cup	dry white wine
½ tsp	salt
¼ tsp	pepper
2 tbsp	chopped fresh parsley

In Dutch oven or large heavy pot, cook bacon over medium heat, stirring occasionally, until crisp, about 4 minutes. Using slotted spoon, transfer to paper towel–lined plate. Set aside.

Add oil to pan; heat over medium-high heat. Sauté chicken until golden, about 3 minutes. Using slotted spoon, transfer to plate. Set aside.

Reduce heat to medium. Add potatoes, mushrooms, leek and garlic to pan; cook, stirring, until mushrooms and leek are softened, about 3 minutes. Stir in tomato paste; cook for 1 minute. Stir in broth, 1 cup water, wine, salt and pepper; bring to boil. Reduce heat, cover and simmer gently just until potatoes are tender, about 10 minutes. Stir in bacon and chicken; cook, uncovered, until chicken is no longer pink inside, about 3 minutes.

Stir in parsley just before serving.

PER SERVING: about 238 cal, 20 g pro, 8 g total fat (2 g sat. fat), 19 g carb, 3 g fibre, 67 mg chol, 617 mg sodium, 800 mg potassium. % RDI: 4% calcium, 16% iron, 5% vit A, 32% vit C, 13% folate.

Salt and Pepper Croûtes

Cut half baguette lengthwise in half; cut crosswise into ¼-inch (5 mm) thick slices. Arrange on rimmed baking sheet. Brush with 2 tbsp extra-virgin olive oil; sprinkle with ¾ tsp each salt and pepper. Bake in 350°F (180°C) oven for 15 minutes. Turn and brush with 2 tbsp extra-virgin olive oil; sprinkle with ¾ tsp each salt and pepper. Bake until golden and crisp, about 10 minutes. Let cool.

MAKES 60 PIECES

THAI CHICKEN AND COCONUT MILK SOUP
MAKES 4 SERVINGS

This aromatic Thai-inspired soup is the perfect food to warm up a cold winter evening. Top with finely sliced red chilies for a little extra spice, if desired. You can also swap the rice for noodles, or serve the soup without a starch as a brothy starter.

1 cup	jasmine or white rice
1	pkg (900 mL) sodium-reduced chicken broth (see tip, page 270)
1	stalk lemongrass, halved crosswise and lengthwise
6	slices (½ inch/1 cm thick) fresh ginger
450 g	boneless skinless chicken breast, thinly sliced
1½ cups	thinly sliced button mushrooms
1 cup	frozen peas
2 tbsp	fish sauce
1 tbsp	packed brown sugar
1 tsp	Thai red curry paste
1	can (400 mL) coconut milk
⅓ cup	chopped fresh cilantro
2 tbsp	lime juice

Cook rice according to package instructions.

Meanwhile, in large pot, bring broth, lemongrass and ginger to boil over medium-high heat. Stir in chicken, mushrooms and peas; cook over medium-low heat until chicken is no longer pink, about 4 minutes.

In small bowl, whisk together fish sauce, brown sugar and curry paste. Stir into pot along with coconut milk; simmer until hot and fragrant, about 3 minutes. Discard lemongrass and ginger.

Stir in cilantro and lime juice. Serve over rice.

PER SERVING: about 551 cal, 37 g pro, 23 g total fat (19 g sat. fat), 50 g carb, 3 g fibre, 66 mg chol, 1,362 mg sodium, 753 mg potassium. % RDI: 6% calcium, 34% iron, 8% vit A, 12% vit C, 21% folate.

LEMON CHICKEN AND SPINACH NOODLE SOUP

MAKES 8 SERVINGS

Cooked spinach and pasta don't do well in the freezer. The solution: Omit them when you make the soup, and then freeze it for up to one month. Cook the pasta separately, and add the raw spinach to the soup as it reheats. Stir in the cooked pasta just before serving.

2 tbsp	extra-virgin olive oil
1	onion, diced
2	cloves garlic, minced
1	each carrot and rib celery, diced
1	sweet red pepper, diced
1 tsp	ground cumin
¼ tsp	pepper
8 cups	Stove-Top Chicken Broth (page 250) or Slow Cooker Chicken Stock (page 248), see tip, below
1 cup	small pasta (such as stars or small shells)
4 cups	packed fresh spinach, trimmed and chopped
2 cups	diced cooked chicken
2 tsp	grated lemon zest
⅓ cup	lemon juice

In large saucepan, heat oil over medium heat; cook onion, garlic, carrot, celery, red pepper, cumin and pepper, stirring often, until softened, about 8 minutes.

Pour in broth and bring to boil; reduce heat, cover and simmer for 10 minutes. Add pasta; simmer until vegetables and pasta are tender, about 5 minutes.

Stir in spinach, chicken, lemon zest and lemon juice; simmer for 5 minutes.

PER SERVING: about 236 cal, 19 g pro, 8 g total fat (2 g sat. fat), 21 g carb, 2 g fibre, 32 mg chol, 227 mg sodium, 474 mg potassium. % RDI: 5% calcium, 15% iron, 36% vit A, 53% vit C, 18% folate.

TIP FROM THE TEST KITCHEN
No homemade broth or stock on hand? Substitute 6 cups store-bought sodium-reduced chicken broth plus 2 cups water for the 8 cups of homemade we call for in the ingredient list.

CURRIED LENTIL AND CHICKEN SOUP

MAKES 4 SERVINGS

Chicken thighs are less expensive than breasts, and they give this robust soup added heartiness. If you prefer, top each bowl with sour cream instead of plain yogurt.

In Dutch oven or large heavy-bottomed saucepan, heat 1½ tsp of the oil over medium-high heat; sauté chicken until light golden, about 3 minutes. Using slotted spoon, transfer to plate; set aside.

Add remaining oil to pan; heat over medium heat. Cook onion and carrot, stirring occasionally, until beginning to soften, about 3 minutes. Add garlic, curry powder, coriander, cumin and salt; cook, stirring, until fragrant, about 30 seconds. Stir in broth and lentils; bring to boil. Reduce heat, cover and simmer until lentils are tender, about 10 minutes.

Stir in chicken and any accumulated juices. Cook, uncovered and stirring occasionally, until slightly thickened and chicken is no longer pink inside, about 5 minutes. Remove from heat; stir in lemon juice. Ladle into bowls; top with yogurt and parsley.

PER SERVING: about 385 cal, 36 g pro, 11 g total fat (3 g sat. fat), 37 g carb, 8 g fibre, 89 mg chol, 708 mg sodium, 949 mg potassium. % RDI: 11% calcium, 48% iron, 39% vit A, 20% vit C, 123% folate.

1 tbsp	olive oil
450 g	boneless skinless chicken thighs, chopped
1	each onion and carrot, diced
4	cloves garlic, minced
2 tsp	curry powder
1 tsp	ground coriander
½ tsp	ground cumin
¼ tsp	salt
3 cups	sodium-reduced chicken broth, Stove-Top Chicken Broth (page 250) or Slow Cooker Chicken Stock (page 248)
1 cup	dried red lentils, rinsed
1 tbsp	lemon juice
½ cup	Balkan-style plain yogurt
¼ cup	chopped fresh parsley or cilantro

ASIAN-STYLE CHICKEN AND CABBAGE NOODLE SOUP

MAKES 6 SERVINGS

Bold Asian flavours and thick, chewy udon noodles turn each bowl of this time-saving chicken soup into a meal. For a spicy note, add a few dashes of sriracha.

In Dutch oven or large heavy pot, heat vegetable oil over medium heat; cook garlic, stirring, until fragrant, about 1 minute. Add mushrooms; cook, stirring occasionally, until softened, about 2 minutes. Stir in broth and 3 cups water; bring to boil. Add chicken and cabbage; reduce heat and simmer, stirring occasionally, until chicken is heated through and cabbage is softened, about 5 minutes.

Add corn; cook until heated through, about 2 minutes. Stir in soy sauce, lime juice, fish sauce, sesame oil and green onions.

Meanwhile, in large pot of boiling water, cook noodles according to package directions; drain and stir into soup. Top with cilantro.

PER SERVING: about 358 cal, 23 g pro, 8 g total fat (2 g sat. fat), 48 g carb, 2 g fibre, 37 mg chol, 755 mg sodium, 363 mg potassium. % RDI: 5% calcium, 13% iron, 2% vit A, 12% vit C, 12% folate.

1 tbsp	vegetable oil
3	cloves garlic, minced
2 cups	shiitake mushrooms, stemmed and sliced
1	pkg (900 mL) sodium-reduced chicken broth (see tip, page 270)
2 cups	shredded cooked chicken
2 cups	finely shredded cabbage
1 cup	frozen corn kernels
1 tbsp	sodium-reduced soy sauce
1 tbsp	lime juice
2 tsp	fish sauce
2 tsp	sesame oil
4	green onions, sliced
2	pkg (each 200 g) fresh udon noodles
⅓ cup	fresh cilantro leaves, torn

LEMONY CHICKEN SOUP
WITH GNOCCHI
MAKES 6 SERVINGS

Gnocchi are really just little potato dumplings, which are the heart and soul of this warming soup. The fresh lemon zest and juice give it a pleasing, sunny flavour.

2 tbsp	butter or olive oil
2	ribs celery, diced
1	each onion and large carrot, diced
1	leek (white and light green parts only), thinly sliced
1½ tsp	grated fresh ginger
½ tsp	salt
1	pkg (900 mL) sodium-reduced chicken broth (see tip, page 270)
1 cup	fresh gnocchi (see tip, below)
2 tbsp	chopped fresh parsley
½ tsp	grated lemon zest
4 tsp	lemon juice

In large saucepan, melt butter over medium heat; cook celery, onion, carrot, leek, ginger and salt, stirring often, until softened, about 7 minutes.

Add broth and 2 cups water; bring to boil. Reduce heat and simmer for 6 minutes. Add gnocchi; simmer until gnocchi float to the top and are firm to the touch, about 5 minutes. Stir in parsley, lemon zest and lemon juice.

PER SERVING: about 132 cal, 4 g pro, 4 g total fat (3 g sat. fat), 21 g carb, 2 g fibre, 10 mg chol, 652 mg sodium, 330 mg potassium. % RDI: 3% calcium, 5% iron, 32% vit A, 30% vit C, 9% folate.

TIP FROM THE TEST KITCHEN
Look for packages of fresh gnocchi near the fresh pasta in the refrigerated section of the grocery store. There is also a dried pasta with the same name, which is similar in shape but hollow. It's great with tomato sauce, but it's not the right ingredient for this soup.

CASSOULET SOUP

MAKES 6 TO 8 SERVINGS

Here's another classic French dish that's been transformed into a hearty winter soup. It's also a delicious way to use up leftover cooked chicken.

SOUP: Rinse beans and soak overnight in three times their volume of water. (Or for quick-soak method, bring to boil and boil gently for 2 minutes. Remove from heat; cover and let stand for 1 hour.) Drain.

In saucepan, cover beans again with three times their volume of water; bring to boil. Reduce heat, cover and simmer until beans are tender, about 45 minutes. Drain and set aside.

In Dutch oven, heat schmaltz over medium-high heat; cook onions, kielbasa, thyme, salt and pepper until onions are softened, about 7 minutes.

Stir in wine; cook until reduced by half, about 1 minute. Stir in broth, beans and chicken; bring to boil. Reduce heat and simmer, uncovered, for 30 minutes, skimming off any foam. *(Make-ahead: Let cool for 30 minutes; refrigerate in airtight container for up to 2 days.)*

GARLIC BREAD CRUMBS: While soup is simmering uncovered, in food processor, process bread until fine with some coarse crumbs. In skillet, melt butter over medium heat; cook garlic and bread crumbs, stirring often, until crumbs are crisp, about 5 minutes. Stir in parsley; transfer to bowl. Let cool. *(Make-ahead: Let stand uncovered at room temperature for up to 6 hours.)*

Ladle soup into bowls; sprinkle with garlic bread crumbs.

PER EACH OF 8 SERVINGS: about 386 cal, 27 g pro, 16 g total fat (3 g sat. fat), 33 g carb, 8 g fibre, 66 mg chol, 939 mg sodium. % RDI: 8% calcium, 31% iron, 4% vit A, 5% vit C, 70% folate.

SOUP:

1¾ cups	dried cannellini or Great Northern beans
2 tbsp	Chicken Schmaltz (page 291) or vegetable oil
3	onions, diced
225 g	kielbasa or other smoked sausage, chopped
1 tbsp	chopped fresh thyme
½ tsp	each salt and pepper
1 cup	dry white wine
6 cups	sodium-reduced chicken broth, Stove-Top Chicken Broth (page 250) or Slow Cooker Chicken Stock (page 248)
3 cups	shredded cooked chicken thigh

GARLIC BREAD CRUMBS:

1½ cups	cubed crustless French or Italian bread
2 tbsp	butter
1	clove garlic, minced
1 tbsp	chopped fresh parsley

ROASTED RED PEPPER, FENNEL AND RICE STUFFING
MAKES ABOUT 10 CUPS

This stuffing is gluten- and dairy-free. It's fantastic with Barbecued Lemon Fennel Chicken (page 208), especially because it can bake away in the oven while the bird is on the grill.

3	sweet red peppers
2	small fennel bulbs
2	onions, chopped
4	cloves garlic, sliced
3 tbsp	extra-virgin olive oil
2 tsp	crumbled dried rosemary
1¼ tsp	salt
¾ tsp	pepper
2 cups	sodium-reduced chicken broth, Stove-Top Chicken Broth (page 250) or Slow Cooker Chicken Stock (page 248)
1 cup	wild rice
1¼ cups	basmati rice
½ cup	pine nuts, toasted
⅓ cup	chopped fresh parsley

Core and seed red peppers; cut into 1-inch (2.5 cm) pieces and place in large bowl. Trim tops off fennel; core and cut fennel into 1-inch (2.5 cm) chunks and add to bowl. Add onions, garlic, oil, rosemary, ¾ tsp of the salt and pepper; toss well. Spread on large rimmed baking sheet; roast in 425°F (220°C) oven until browned and tender, about 1 hour.

Meanwhile, in large saucepan, bring 2 cups water, broth, wild rice and remaining salt to boil; reduce heat, cover and simmer for 20 minutes.

Stir in basmati rice; cover and simmer until wild and basmati rice are tender, 15 to 20 minutes. Transfer to bowl. Add roasted vegetables, pine nuts and parsley; mix well. *(Make-ahead: Cover and refrigerate for up to 24 hours.)*

Spoon into greased 13- x 9-inch (3 L) baking dish; cover with foil. Bake in 400°F (200°C) oven for 20 minutes. Uncover and bake until hot and top is crisp, 10 to 15 minutes.

PER ½ CUP: about 129 cal, 3 g pro, 5 g total fat (1 g sat. fat), 20 g carb, 2 g fibre, 0 mg chol, 216 mg sodium. % RDI: 2% calcium, 6% iron, 8% vit A, 55% vit C, 9% folate.

ROASTED RED PEPPER, FENNEL AND RICE STUFFING (OPPOSITE)

JALAPEÑO CORNBREAD STUFFING WITH SMOKED SAUSAGE (PAGE 286)

JALAPEÑO CORNBREAD STUFFING
WITH SMOKED SAUSAGE
MAKES ABOUT 12 CUPS

Adding jalapeño to the cornbread carries the pepper's flavour throughout the whole stuffing. Make the cornbread a day ahead so it dries out a little—that will ensure the ideal texture in the finished stuffing.

CORNBREAD:

1¼ cups	cornmeal
¾ cup	all-purpose flour
1 tbsp	granulated sugar
1½ tsp	baking powder
¾ tsp	baking soda
½ tsp	salt
1½ cups	buttermilk
2	eggs
2 tbsp	butter, melted
1 cup	cooked corn kernels
2 tbsp	minced pickled jalapeño pepper

STUFFING:

1½ tsp	cumin seeds
2 tbsp	vegetable oil
225 g	kielbasa or other smoked sausage, cubed
2	onions, chopped
2	ribs celery, chopped
4	cloves garlic, minced
1 tsp	dried oregano
¼ tsp	pepper
½ cup	sodium-reduced chicken broth, Stove-Top Chicken Broth (page 250) or Slow Cooker Chicken Stock (page 248)

CORNBREAD: In bowl, whisk together cornmeal, flour, sugar, baking powder, baking soda and salt. Whisk together buttermilk, eggs and butter; pour over dry ingredients. Sprinkle with corn and jalapeño pepper; stir just until combined. Pour into parchment paper–lined or greased 8-inch (2 L) square cake pan, smoothing top.

Bake in 375°F (190°C) oven until cake tester inserted in centre comes out clean, about 30 minutes. Let cool in pan on rack for 5 minutes. Remove from pan; let cool completely. *(Make-ahead: Wrap and refrigerate for up to 2 days.)*

STUFFING: In large dry skillet, toast cumin seeds over medium heat until fragrant, about 2 minutes. Transfer to large bowl.

Add half of the oil to pan; heat over medium-high heat. Brown kielbasa, stirring occasionally, about 6 minutes. Add to cumin seeds.

Drain any fat from pan. Add remaining oil and heat over medium heat; cook onions, celery, garlic, oregano and pepper, stirring occasionally, until softened, about 8 minutes. Add to bowl.

Coarsely crumble cornbread into bowl. Drizzle with broth; mix well. *(Make-ahead: Cover and refrigerate for up to 24 hours.)*

Spoon into greased 13- x 9-inch (3 L) baking dish; cover with foil. Bake in 400°F (200°C) oven for 20 minutes. Uncover and bake until hot and top is crisp, 10 to 15 minutes.

PER ½ CUP: about 109 cal, 4 g pro, 5 g total fat (2 g sat. fat), 13 g carb, 1 g fibre, 26 mg chol, 229 mg sodium. % RDI: 4% calcium, 5% iron, 3% vit A, 3% vit C, 14% folate.

SAVOURY SLOW COOKER STUFFING

MAKES 8 SERVINGS

Classic flavours merge to make a deliciously moist stuffing that requires absolutely no oven space. Be sure to use day-old bread that is firm (but not as dry as croutons) instead of fresh bread—it makes all the difference between a moist and a soggy stuffing.

In large bowl, toss together bread, onion, celery, apple, sage, thyme, salt and pepper. Drizzle with broth and butter; toss to moisten. Scrape into slow cooker.

Cover and cook on low, stirring once, until apples and vegetables are tender, about 6 hours.

PER SERVING: about 174 cal, 5 g pro, 5 g total fat (2 g sat. fat), 29 g carb, 2 g fibre, 8 mg chol, 385 mg sodium, 124 mg potassium. % RDI: 6% calcium, 13% iron, 3% vit A, 3% vit C, 23% folate.

12 cups	cubed crustless day-old bread
1	onion, diced
2	ribs celery, diced
1	cooking apple (see tip, below), peeled, cored and diced
1½ tsp	crumbled dried sage
1 tsp	crumbled dried thyme
¼ tsp	each salt and pepper
½ cup	sodium-reduced chicken broth
2 tbsp	unsalted butter, melted

TIP FROM THE TEST KITCHEN
Choose an apple that holds its shape when cooked, such as Cortland, Braeburn or Crispin.

PANCETTA AND PRUNE STUFFING

MAKES ABOUT 12 CUPS

Salty pancetta and sweet prunes give this stuffing a lovely balance of flavours.
If you use bacon instead of pancetta, it will add a smoky note.

225 g	pancetta or thick-sliced bacon, diced
¼ cup	butter
4	ribs celery, chopped
2	onions, chopped
2	cloves garlic, minced
4 tsp	dried sage
1 tsp	each salt and pepper
1 tsp	crumbled dried rosemary
12 cups	cubed day-old sourdough bread
1 cup	chopped pitted prunes
½ cup	chopped fresh parsley
1 cup	sodium-reduced chicken broth, Stove-Top Chicken Broth (page 250) or Slow Cooker Chicken Stock (page 248)

In large skillet, fry pancetta over medium-high heat until crisp, about 5 minutes. Transfer to large bowl.

Drain fat from pan; melt butter over medium heat. Cook celery, onions, garlic, sage, salt, pepper and rosemary, stirring occasionally, until softened, about 10 minutes. Add to bowl. Add bread, prunes and parsley; mix well. *(Make-ahead: Cover and refrigerate for up to 24 hours.)*

Spoon into greased 13- x 9-inch (3 L) baking dish; drizzle with broth. Cover with foil. Bake in 400°F (200°C) oven for 20 minutes. Uncover and bake until hot and top is crisp, 10 to 15 minutes.

PER ½ CUP: about 103 cal, 3 g pro, 4 g total fat (2 g sat. fat), 15 g carb, 1 g fibre, 8 mg chol, 283 mg sodium. % RDI: 2% calcium, 5% iron, 4% vit A, 3% vit C, 8% folate.

TIP FROM THE TEST KITCHEN

The Test Kitchen no longer recommends stuffing a whole chicken. Stuffing should always be baked separately to ensure it's fully cooked and safe to eat.

CARAMELIZED ONION AND APPLE STUFFING

MAKES ABOUT 10 CUPS

Marble rye bread gives this stuffing a unique taste and a lovely look. It's great with chicken, and a terrific match with turkey or goose, too.

In large skillet, melt 2 tbsp of the butter over medium-low heat; cook onions and ¼ tsp each of the salt and pepper, stirring occasionally, until golden, about 30 minutes. Transfer to large bowl.

Add remaining butter to pan; melt over medium heat. Cook celery, apples, sage, caraway seeds and remaining salt and pepper, stirring occasionally, until softened, about 15 minutes. Add to bowl. Add bread, broth and parsley; mix well. *(Make-ahead: Cover and refrigerate for up to 24 hours.)*

Spoon into greased 13- x 9-inch (3 L) baking dish; cover with foil. Bake in 400°F (200°C) oven for 20 minutes. Uncover and bake until hot and top is crisp, 10 to 15 minutes.

PER ½ CUP: about 76 cal, 2 g pro, 3 g total fat (2 g sat. fat), 11 g carb, 2 g fibre, 6 mg chol, 177 mg sodium. % RDI: 2% calcium, 4% iron, 4% vit A, 5% vit C, 8% folate.

¼ cup	butter
3 cups	thinly sliced onions
½ tsp	each salt and pepper
2 cups	sliced celery
3	Golden Delicious apples, peeled, cored and chopped
2 tsp	dried sage
1 tsp	caraway seeds
8 cups	cubed day-old marble rye bread (or 4 cups each cubed day-old light rye and pumpernickel bread)
1 cup	sodium-reduced chicken broth, Stove-Top Chicken Broth (page 250) or Slow Cooker Chicken Stock (page 248)
½ cup	chopped fresh parsley

CHESTNUT AND MUSHROOM STUFFING

MAKES 12 TO 16 SERVINGS

Sweet chestnuts and meaty mushrooms add fall flavour to an otherwise classic stuffing.
Look for convenient ready-to-eat peeled whole chestnuts in the grocery store.

2 tbsp	olive oil
3	cloves garlic, minced
1	rib celery, diced
1	onion, diced
675 g	sliced mixed mushrooms (such as oyster and cremini)
¼ cup	dry white wine
12 cups	cubed day-old sourdough bread
1 cup	peeled roasted chestnuts (about two 100 g bags), coarsely chopped
¼ cup	sodium-reduced chicken broth, Stove-Top Chicken Broth (page 250) or Slow Cooker Chicken Stock (page 248)
¼ tsp	pepper
1 cup	grated Parmesan cheese
3 tbsp	chopped fresh parsley

In Dutch oven or large skillet, heat oil over medium heat; cook garlic, celery and onion, stirring often, until onion is softened, about 5 minutes.

Add mushrooms; cook, stirring often, until tender and almost no liquid remains, about 8 minutes.

Add wine; cook, stirring, until liquid is reduced by half, about 1 minute. Stir in bread, chestnuts, broth, ¼ cup water and pepper. Remove from heat.

Stir in ½ cup of the Parmesan. Scrape into lightly greased 13- x 9-inch (3 L) baking dish. Sprinkle with remaining Parmesan. *(Make-ahead: Cover and refrigerate for up to 24 hours. Bake, covered, in 425°F/220°C oven until warmed through, about 15 minutes. Uncover and continue with recipe.)*

Bake in 425°F (220°C) oven until top is crisp, about 5 minutes. Sprinkle with parsley.

PER EACH OF 16 SERVINGS: about 150 cal, 7 g pro, 4 g total fat (1 g sat. fat), 21 g carb, 2 g fibre, 6 mg chol, 263 mg sodium, 303 mg potassium. % RDI: 8% calcium, 10% iron, 2% vit A, 6% vit C, 32% folate.

CHICKEN SCHMALTZ

MAKES 3 CUPS

Schmaltz means "fat" in Yiddish and German. In cooking, it refers to chicken fat in the Jewish tradition, and pork, goose or duck fat in the German.

In heavy saucepan, combine fat, onions and ¾ cup water; bring to simmer over medium-low heat. Simmer, stirring occasionally, until fat is melted and onions are browned, 1 to 1¼ hours.

Line fine-mesh sieve with damp cheesecloth; strain schmaltz into heatproof bowl, pressing solids to extract liquid. Pour schmaltz into three 1-cup sterilized preserving jars; let cool before sealing. Refrigerate for up to 1 year.

900 g	chicken fat (see tip, below), chopped in small pieces
2	onions, chopped

PER 1 TBSP: about 119 cal, 1 g pro, 13 g total fat (4 g sat. fat), 0 g carb, 0 g fibre, 11 mg chol, 6 mg sodium, 12 mg potassium. % RDI: 1% iron, 3% vit A.

TIP FROM THE TEST KITCHEN
Trim the fat from chicken and save it in a resealable plastic bag in the freezer until you have enough to render and make schmaltz. If you don't have time to make this recipe, you can substitute vegetable oil, or chicken fat skimmed from soup, for schmaltz in recipes that call for it.

ACKNOWLEDGMENTS

NO ONE GETS TIRED OF CHICKEN, and I never get tired of thanking the incredible team that puts together Canadian Living's cookbooks. This is my dream job for good reason.

Thanks go first, as always, to the Canadian Living Test Kitchen: food director Annabelle Waugh; senior food specialist Irene Fong; food specialists Amanda Barnier, Jennifer Bartoli and Leah Kuhne; and food articles editor Gilean Watts. Without their deep knowledge and love of cooking, these recipes would never come into being. And without their tireless pursuit of perfection, these chicken dishes would never taste as wonderful as they do—or work so perfectly in kitchens from coast to coast to coast. These women are the best, most delightful collaborators.

Thanks next to our art director, Colin Elliott, for his creativity and ingenuity in designing this and many other books. He does everything with dedication and a keen eye, whether it's finding just the right typeface, discovering the perfect illustration of a hen (or is it a rooster?) or creating layouts that are reader-friendly as well as beautiful.

Next up, thanks to the excellent photographers and stylists who created the gorgeous images on these pages. Special thanks go to photographers Jeff Coulson and Maya Visnyei, food stylists Bernadette Ammar and Claire Stubbs and prop stylists Sasha Seymour and Catherine Doherty for the images they shot especially for this book. For a complete list of the talented photographers and stylists who contributed to these pages, see page 304.

Next up, a heaping spoonful of gratitude goes to our copy editor, Lisa Fielding, and our indexer, Beth Zabloski, for reading every single line of this book and making sure everything is in the right place, from the very first comma to the very last entry in the index. Without their eagle eyes, I would be lost. Thanks also to Sharyn Joliat of Info Access, who created the nutrient analysis for all of the recipes.

Thank you to our teams at Juniper Publishing and Simon & Schuster Canada for their work behind the scenes on this and many other books. I appreciate what they did to get this book to our readers all across the nation and beyond.

Finally, an extra-large helping of gratitude to Jacqueline Loch, Canadian Living's vice-president and group publisher; Sandra E. Martin, our multiplatform editorial director; and Jessica Ross, our content director, multiplatform editions, books and special issues, for their work on all of the book projects we undertake. Their support and hard work make the process smooth sailing.

TINA ANSON MINE
PROJECT EDITOR

INDEX